Art Therapy with Military Populations

For decades, art therapy has proved to be a practical treatment for veterans and other military populations suffering from trauma. *Art Therapy with Military Populations* provides an in-depth overview of both the theoretical and historical bases of art therapy with these groups while also chronicling the latest trends in treatment and the continued expansion of treatment settings. Edited by an art therapist with over 25 years' experience working with the military and including chapters by a variety of seasoned and innovative clinicians, this comprehensive new volume provides professionals with cutting-edge knowledge and interventions for working with military service members and their families. Available for download are employment resources for art therapists who would like to work in military settings, a bonus chapter, historical documents on establishing art therapy, a treatment objectives manual, and resources for art therapists.

Paula Howie, MA, ATR-BC, LPC, LCPAT, HLM, directed the Art Therapy Service at Walter Reed Army Medical Center from 1979 to 2002. She teaches at the graduate art therapy programs of the School of the Visual Arts in New York and Florida State University. Howie was president of the American Art Therapy Association (AATA) from 2005 to 2007 and remains an active member. She has a private practice in Washington, DC, where she focuses on the treatment of trauma, military members, and families.

"In this groundbreaking book focusing on art therapy with military populations, Paula Howie and selected authors address historical and contemporary treatment of service-related trauma. Various art therapy approaches—including art-based directives, open studio practices, and gallery exhibitions—are discussed. Ultimately, it is the fundamental nature of art therapy, core to which are individuals engaged in creative processes in protected environments and witnessed by art therapists, that is at the heart of this worthy addition to art therapy literature."

> **Linney Wix, PhD, ATR-BC**, Professor Emerita, Art Education, University of New Mexico; author, *Through a Narrow Window: Friedl Dicker-Brandeis and Her Terezín Students*

"Ms. Howie and colleagues offer an informative and moving book that reveals and deeply respects art therapy; the men, women and families who participated in these interventions; and the dedicated personnel who provided their care. The historical dimension of the development of art therapy, alongside the narratives about the conflicts in which the military personnel served, add substance to the case presentations. Having worked at Walter Reed Army Medical Center during that time, the manuscript is a strong reminder of the healing power of creativity."

> **Nancy B. Black, MD**, Colonel (retired), US Army; American Board of Psychiatry and Neurology, certified in Adult Psychiatry and Child and Adolescent Psychiatry; Distinguished Fellow, American Academy of Child and Adolescent Psychiatry and the American Psychiatric Association

Art Therapy with Military Populations

History, Innovation, and Applications

Edited by Paula Howie

NEW YORK AND LONDON

First published 2017
by Routledge
711 Third Avenue, New York, NY 10017

and by Routledge
2 Park Square, Milton Park, Abingdon, Oxon OX14 4RN

Routledge is an imprint of the Taylor & Francis Group, an informa business

© 2017 Taylor & Francis

The right of the editor to be identified as the author of the editorial material, and of the authors for their individual chapters, has been asserted by them in accordance with sections 77 and 78 of the Copyright, Designs and Patents Act 1988.

All rights reserved. No part of this book may be reprinted or reproduced or utilized in any form or by any electronic, mechanical, or other means, now known or hereafter invented, including photocopying and recording, or in any information storage or retrieval system, without permission in writing from the publishers.

Trademark notice: Product or corporate names may be trademarks or registered trademarks, and are used only for identification and explanation without intent to infringe.

Library of Congress Cataloging-in-Publication Data
Names: Howie, Paula, editor.
Title: Art therapy with military populations : history, innovation, and applications / edited by Paula Howie.
Description: New York : Routledge, 2017. | Includes bibliographical references and index.
Identifiers: LCCN 2016055899 | ISBN 9781138948631 (hardcover : alk. paper) | ISBN 9781138948662 (pbk. : alk. paper) | ISBN 9781315669526 (e-book)
Subjects: | MESH: Art Therapy | Stress Disorders, Post-Traumatic--therapy | Military Personnel--psychology | Veterans--psychology
Classification: LCC RC489.A7 | NLM WM 450.5.A8 | DDC 616.89/165608697--dc23
LC record available at https://lccn.loc.gov/2016055899

ISBN: 978-1-138-94863-1 (hbk)
ISBN: 978-1-138-94866-2 (pbk)
ISBN: 978-1-315-66952-6 (ebk)

Typeset in Minion
by Saxon Graphics Ltd, Derby

Visit eResources site: www.routledge.com/9781138948662

Contents

Figures	viii
Plates	x
Foreword Katherine Williams	xi
Preface Paula Howie	xiv
Acknowledgments	xxii
Notes on Contributors	xxv
Introduction Paula Howie	1
Part I. Theoretical Background: Understanding and Treating Soldiers and their Families—Formative Experiences	**15**

1 Art Therapy with Military and Veteran Populations:
   A Historical Context
   Martha Haeseler and Paula Howie
	17

2 Psychosis, Attachment, and Trauma Paula Howie	30
3 Inpatient Treatment Charlotte Boston and Jeanne Creekmore	41

4 Family Art Therapy Treatment at Walter Reed — 53
Paula Howie

5 Group Art Therapy: The Evolution of Treatment and the Power of Witness — 64
Paula Howie

6 Managing Suicide in the Military — 75
Paula Howie

Part II. Current Trends in Art Therapy Treatment in Military Settings and the Expansion of Treatment Settings — 85

7 Treating the Wounded Warrior: Cognitive and Neural Aspects of Post-Traumatic Stress Disorder — 87
Paul Newhouse and Kimberly Albert

8 Complicated Grief: Considerations for Treatment of Military Populations — 98
Jacqueline P. Jones

9 Integrative Approaches to Treating PTSD and TBI: Art Therapy Approaches within the National Intrepid Center of Excellence at Walter Reed National Military Medical Center — 111
Melissa S. Walker

10 The Giant Steps Program: Creating Fellowship and Meaning — 124
Martha Haeseler

11 Art Therapy with Substance Abuse and Co-occurring Disorders in Military Populations — 134
Eileen A. McKee

12 Using the Instinctual Trauma Response Model in a Military Setting — 147
Linda Gantt and Mary Ellen Vesprini

13 The Sketch Project: Volunteers Giving Veterans a New Perspective — 157
Doris Arrington and Nancy Parfitt Hondros

14 Group Therapy and PTSD: Acceptance and Commitment Art Therapy Groups with Vietnam Veterans with PTSD — 165
Amy Backos and Corrie Mazzeo

15 Art Therapy and the Treatment of Military Sexual Trauma — 177
Jeff Stadler

16	How the Studio and Gallery Experience Benefits Military Members and their Families Jennifer DeLucia	187
17	**Conclusion** Paula Howie	200
	Index	207

Figures

0.1	Students at work, *c.* 1944 to 1948	7
0.2	Students at work, 1944 to 1948	8
1.1	The garden created by veterans in the Giant Steps Program to welcome veterans and their families to the VA	19
1.2	Watercolor painting with pen and ink by the author, 22 × 30 inches	21
1.3	Aerial photo from 1931 showing the main campus of Walter Reed Georgia Avenue	23
2.1	Pastel drawing entitled "Angry Voices, Kill, Kill"	35
2.2	Pastel drawing entitled "Help! Rape!"	36
3.1	Pastel drawing entitled "Love Peace and Harmony," made in Themes Art Therapy group	47
3.2	Group mask project from Creative Arts Therapy (CAT) group	48
3.3	Art therapy studio	49
4.1	Tree as symbolic of self from group therapy	57
4.2	"Life's Baggage" drawn in family art therapy session	59
4.3	"Overwhelmed" drawn in family art therapy session	60
4.4	Drawn during group art therapy showing Kathy and her mother with a minefield between them	61
5.1	Debby's card for Alicia	68
5.2	Mary Lou being taken away by her demon	70
5.3a and 5.3b	Outside and inside of her mask	72
6.1	Sophie's earlier drawing (left) and later picture (right) prior to her suicide	79
6.2	John's depiction of the grim reaper	81

6.3	Lisa's destructive impulses	83
8.1a and 8.1b	Outside and inside of mask	106
8.2	Tree of life tattoo	108
9.1a, 9.1b, and 9.1c	Masks made in art therapy	116
9.2	Healthy change	120
10.1	Veterans' flags hanging in the new group space	131
10.2	Walking garden labyrinth	132
11.1	Twisted	141
11.2	Closet of choices	144
13.1	The artists	163
14.1	*Monsters on the Bus*—Brickhead	171
14.2	*Monsters on the Bus*—Dipshit	172
15.1	Transformation of a nightmare into a pleasant dream	182
15.2	Image of recovery from MST	185
16.1	*Simple Solution, Endless Execution,* mixed media on paper, 18 × 24 inches	193
16.2	Opening reception for a veterans' art exhibition in Our House Gallery	196

Plates

1. Pastel drawing entitled "God's Promises are True"
2. Group mask project from Creative Arts Therapy (CAT) group
3. Drawing entitled "Life"
4. Lisa's picture of the destroyer and the lover
5. Commemoration/memorial box
6. Drawing by individual experiencing nightmares following a blast injury
7. Service members accessing their strengths
8. Inner demons
9. A sketching artist
10. *Monsters on the Bus*—Tiny
11. Graphic expression of MST and the survivor's representation of the experience
12. Untitled, colored pencil on paper, 18 × 24 inches

Foreword
Katherine Williams

Driving into the Forest Glen Annex in 1977 felt like coming upon a foreign land. This impression was created partly by Greek-inspired statues, a pond, and a Japanese-style pagoda (remnants of its history as a wealthy landowner's mansion, a casino, and a finishing school). I felt out of place in my colorful civilian clothes as I drove past trim khaki-clothed people walking briskly to their destinations. My cousin's death while flying unarmed reconnaissance missions in Vietnam still haunted me and had occasioned my involvement in protesting the Vietnam War. And I knew that the military medical facility I was approaching was at best unfamiliar with and at worst dismissive of the art therapy I had been hired to provide.

But it was here that I met Paula Howie, with whom I was fortunate to work for four years at Walter Reed (both at this campus and in the new location to which we moved when the hospital complex was completed), and then for many years at the George Washington University where we were colleagues in the Art Therapy Program. Because of Paula and the people with whom I worked at Walter Reed, and because of the opportunity to participate in creative expression's capacity to unlock and assuage even a small bit of the pain of war, I eventually came to feel at home in what had seemed foreign territory.

As you will see when you read this fine book, Paula blossomed in her work at Walter Reed for 25 years, making her mark as a therapist and administrator of art and activities therapy. Paula recounts the history of the development of the multi-faceted art therapy program at Walter Reed, describes her understanding of the importance of attachment and trauma theories in designing treatment for active duty patients, and also includes chapters written by art therapists who have continued her work or who have developed specialized therapies with military populations, including veterans. Also helpful is a chapter on cognitive and neural aspects of PTSD, which describes ways in which art therapy may be particularly valuable in the treatment of some aspects of this condition.

The range of approaches to using art with the military is impressive. There are chapters on art therapy with military sexual trauma, substance abuse and co-occurring disorders, PTSD, complicated grief, and suicide. Diagnostic protocols, guided art therapy experiences and unstructured studio and gallery experiences are described. Modalities include individual, group, family, and child therapies as well as combinations thereof.

Reading the book took me back to the wards at Walter Reed as well as to a forgotten quotation from D.H. Lawrence. Although primarily a writer, Lawrence came to enjoy painting later in life when he overcame his childhood fear that he "couldn't draw." He wrote of his experience with art in this way:

> I never saw a picture that seemed to me ugly. The theme may be ugly, there may be a terrifying, distressing, almost repulsive quality. ... Yet, in some strange way, it is all swept up in the delight of a picture. No artist, even the gloomiest, ever painted a picture without the curious delight in image making.
>
> (in Ghiselin, 1952)

While many of the patients who made art might never endorse delight, their experience revealed a lightening, an opening into possibilities not accessible before they took up a brush or grabbed an unfamiliar hunk of clay. And in my experience, the darkness of some of the images depicted might be unspeakable, but they were human, and never ugly. The patients and practices described in *Art Therapy with Military Populations* bear out this observation.

Paula notes that in writing this book, she came to understand that she is a child of war. Reading the book has underscored my belief that as long as our country is fighting anywhere on earth, we are all in some way war's offspring. However, the men and women in the military who have risked their lives and affected their family's well-being are the ones who can least walk away from this experience.

A poem by David Keplinger written in the voice of a Civil War soldier brings this to mind:

The Dead on Culpeper Road

> It had become the natural thing.
> Dead animal smell. A long line
> Of parade watchers, faces
> Turned toward the light rain.

I will never go back to Culpeper Road.
The collapse of a pumpkin reminds me
Of a man's head stabbed into a fence post.
Twelve nights on Culpeper Road.
The world a pit of parades and disuse.

Culpeper Road, if you come for me,
I will not go along, sir. I left.
The morning rose like a curtain, sir.
I was the hero. This was my play.

Crows were quacking like ducks.
Ducks were taking easy flight.
Guns were being fired far off, no louder

Than a hoof beat.[1]

Even though this soldier leaves, we have the sense that the hoof beat does not ever go completely silent, and that to him, a pumpkin will never be simply a pumpkin.

Paula and her colleagues have worked to find ways to mitigate the powerful and lingering effects of the trauma of war. Learning about their experiences through reading this book has been inspiring to me. Whether or not you are working directly with the military, you, too, are a child of war, and I recommend this book to you.

Note

1 Reprinted with permission.

References

Ghiselin, B. (1952). *The Creative Process*. New York: New American Library.
Keplinger, D. (2015/2016). *War, Literature and the Arts, 27*, 10.

Preface
Paula Howie

> War is the mother of all poverty, a vast predator of lives and souls.
> Pope Francis (account, 2015)

I am a child of war. This realization came to me during the writing of this book, which has proved to be both a painful and an enlightening journey. I say this despite having lived my entire life in the contiguous United States, a country that has largely been spared invasion by another world power. After the American Revolution and during the War of 1812, my country was invaded by England, as it was by Mexico during the Mexican–American war. The American Civil War resulted in more US causalities than all other wars combined but there was no invasion from abroad. Perret (1989) points out that "since 1775, no nation has had as much experience of war as the United States—nine major wars in nine generations. At a thousand unnoticed points America's military past impinges on the average American's daily life," from taxes to electronics to the wristwatch she wears which was popularized in World War I (p. 563). In fact, much of what we take for granted, namely our computers, pesticides, telephonic communications, and airline flights to any lovely destination in the world, owe much of their beginnings and development to their usefulness during wartime.

Many in my baby-boomer generation were touched personally by World War II, a result of the substantial US death-toll of 350,000, and the nearly one million wounded (Perret, 1989). World War II was a staggeringly deadly war, the worst in the world's history with over 60 million dead or around 3 percent of the global population. The violence of the war, which began for the United States with the bombing of Pearl Harbor, Hawaii, has had resounding effects on my parents' and my generations.

My father was a First Lieutenant, part of the Tenth Army, and due to his combat wounds he became one of the war's one million-plus casualties. Consisting of five army divisions, the Tenth Army along with the Marines was a part of the invasion force of Okinawa, the last and the biggest of the Pacific Island battles of World War II. The battle of Okinawa was carried out at the beginning of April 1945 for 82 days and resulted in Japanese losses of more than 77,000 soldiers; the Allies suffered more than 65,000 casualties with 14,000 dead. "The net result made Okinawa a mass bloodletting both on land and at sea, among both the island's civilian population and the military" (history.com, 2009). My father received a Purple Heart, came home to his family, and hardly ever spoke to any of us about his military wartime experience. A few years after he died, I learned that he had mentioned to my sister that he had smoked opium before going into battle because he didn't know if he would survive. I can only imagine the fear and sense of doom he was experiencing, especially given the guerrilla type of combat common to that particular setting.

As a child, I was eager to learn about what had happened to him. Perhaps, or maybe because, my father never shared his wartime memories, it was a natural fit that I would work at Walter Reed Army Medical Center for much of my adult life and hear of others' experiences in wartime. In a vicarious way, I was surely trying to help my father. My implicit logic went thus: if I was able to bare the stories shared by our returning vets, I would be able to listen to my father should he ever deem to share his war memories. While teaching a family therapy class at the George Washington University (GWU) and completing a family mapping technique (Marr, personal communication, April 2011), I also discovered that working in Walter Reed not only satisfied a wish to help others who had been traumatized by war. Working in a hospital setting also symbolically meant helping my ailing mother who had suffered from torticollis following an automobile accident in 1948 from which she never fully recovered; consequently, my mother spent the last ten years of her life in a wheelchair.

A brief study of children (Rosenheck, 1986) whose fathers suffered from Post-Traumatic Stress Disorder as a result of combat experience in World War II demonstrated long-term, transgenerational effects from their father's combat trauma even though their children had no conscious knowledge of the veteran's combat experience. Although variable, the impact of the veteran on the affective life of his family and on his children showed that a continuing legacy of wartime trauma was apparent in the adult lives of many of these offspring. Studies of war-torn countries during World War II (Rand, 2014) show that those civilians who live through war had poorer health later in life, including a risk of diabetes and depression. Exposure to war (i.e., hunger, persecution by invaders, and loss of property such as a home) showed those who had dealt with these events of war as adults were less educated, less likely to marry, and were less satisfied with their lives. Epigeneticist Nessa Carey (2013) studied the effects on the Dutch population of starvation they suffered from November 1944 to spring 1945 due to German occupation. Much of the population was able to consume only 30 percent of the required daily calories. She found that children conceived during this period demonstrated lasting health effects into their adulthood depending on the timing and prevalence of the starvation of their mothers.

The personal memoir of a colleague whose Marine husband was involved in fighting in Okinawa was shared from his private journal:

> People don't realize what a front line infantryman is faced with … the infantry man goes forward till the enemy opens fire on him … his life is in danger 24 hours a day regardless of weather conditions … for the American infantryman it is kill or be killed.
>
> (Fritz, 2000)

Several things become clear when reading this detailed chronicle. On the surface, the soldier cannot think on his own even when he knows something is wrong. He must follow orders whether he believes in them or not. In this journal, the enemy became less human as the account ensued. And yet, Sergeant Fritz's dignity and humanity show through the entire version of his harrowing experience in Okinawa. It is easy to criticize when we were not the ones in the line of fire or to refute history by hindsight reaching back almost 70 years. How could any of my generation possibly know what their parents faced where the difference between life or death hinges upon being lucky enough to be in a different foxhole from the one the grenade was tossed into or when the timing of going to the bathroom coincides with a sniper's opportunistic bullet? Reading this journal, one becomes acutely aware of the whimsicality and capriciousness of war.

Having been born into a generation of survivors of World War II is only one part of my indirect but meaningful relationship to war. As stated earlier, my country has been at war for much of my lifetime (Perret, 1989). Following World War II, the USA was involved in the Korean War from 1950 to 1953. The Vietnam War from 1965 to 1973 was by far the most devastating for my generation. I remember friends and acquaintances who had low draft numbers, the last war in which a draft was used, trying to decide whether to sign up or become conscientious objectors. Vietnam took over 58,000 American lives with around 160,000 wounded. It was through the lobbying efforts of Vietnam service veterans that the diagnostic category of Post-Traumatic Stress Disorder (PTSD) was adopted by the American Psychiatric Association (APA) and became the measure of traumatic injury (Morris, 2016). In more recent times, my country has been involved in the first Gulf war in 1990 and 1991, the Iraq war from 2003 to 2011 including Operation Enduring Freedom (OEF) and Operation Iraqi Freedom (OIF), and finally the war on ISIL from 2014 to the present. This list does not include such conflicts as the Cold War, Grenada, and the Invasion of Panama, to mention a few other conflicts in which we had "boots on the ground."

Walter Reed

According to John Pierce, a retired Army colonel and Walter Reed historian, President Dwight D. Eisenhower signed the bill that established the Interstate highway system in 1956 while a patient at Walter Reed (Tavernise, 2011). Eisenhower later spent the last 11 months of his life in the presidential suite as his health declined, along with his wife, Mamie, who lived in a small room nearby. On occasion, I had meetings in the "Eisenhower suite," so I have sampled its history firsthand. I must say, the whole experience was quite impressive. Eisenhower reached the coveted rank of a five-star general. He warned us about the power of the military machinery.

> In the councils of government, we must guard against the acquisition of unwarranted influence, whether sought or unsought, by the military industrial complex. The potential for the disastrous rise of misplaced power exists and will persist. We must never let the weight of this combination endanger our liberties or democratic processes. We should take nothing for granted. Only an alert and knowledgeable citizenry can compel the proper meshing of the huge industrial and military machinery of defense with our peaceful methods and goals, so that security and liberty may prosper together.
> (Military-Industrial Complex Speech, Dwight D. Eisenhower, 1961)

What follows is a spectacular account of how we, as a country, have failed to follow Eisenhower's advice and that those who pay most for our lack of mindfulness to this warning are those who fight our wars, who are killed or injured, and return home suffering physical and mental trauma.

In addition to my country's propensity to wage war, the number of those on active duty, which is now over 2.2 million, including reserve forces with about 550,000 minorities, and over 200,000 women (Office of the Deputy Assistant Secretary of Defense, 2013), the United States continues to have the second-largest standing army in the world, next to the China. Given that there are also 19.3 million surviving military veterans in the United States (U.S. Census Bureau, 2015), I submit to you that many art therapists, those in private practice and in non-military facilities, will be called upon to treat ex-military or their family members during their career. Because of the unique culture of the military, therapists would be wise to familiarize themselves with military customs and with treating PTSD. It is estimated that a quarter of service members returning from combat zones have diagnosable PTSD with a higher rate for veterans of the war in Iraq because of greater combat exposure (Hoge, Auchterlonie, & Milliken, 2006). The plight of these newly returning service members and those of wars past has been the focus of much national sorrow and regret. Our returning service members often show resilience and strength by being able to resume their lives and relationships. My sincere hope is that all will be able to get help with healing and that this book will be a guide in doing so.

In 2013, Ray Suarez on *PBS NewsHour* reported that more US troops died by suicide in 2012 than in the Afghanistan combat. "The statistics are stunning. According to the Associated Press, suicides among active-duty troops reached a new high last year ... 349 service members took their lives, more than the 295 killed in combat in Afghanistan" (*PBS NewsHour*, 2013). Many soldiers returning home from prolonged wars in Iraq and Afghanistan have been plagued by their experiences in the military and have been unable to cope well enough to function effectively when they were released from military service. Hence, the alarming number of suicides reported above. Along with PTSD, service members have had to cope with Traumatic Brain Injury (TBI), and major physical impairment.

I have spent many of my adult years working with military personnel and their families to help them deal with the consequences of deployment and reintegration into home and, ultimately, into civilian life. In many ways, working for Walter Reed was like being part of a very large family with a unique culture, set of mores, and code of conduct. I have written about some aspects of this unique culture of the military elsewhere (Howie, Prasad, & Kristel, 2013) and have continued to see military service members in my private practice.

I worked part-time for two years at Walter Reed, Georgia Avenue before being hired in a full-time position, which I occupied for 25 years. For those of us working at this facility, life was complicated. We were civilians in a military setting, non-physicians in a hospital setting, and mostly women in the military world largely dominated by men. Despite these differences, or maybe partly because of them, we found a place that valued us for our differences (most of the time) and we were sought out for our unique observations and contributions. We also trained hundreds of art and recreation therapy students from programs across the country. It was a big undertaking and much of the success of the program was due to the hard work and dedication of the art therapy and activities therapy staff.

In the 1980s and 1990s, the Walter Reed campus employed around 4,000 staff, making the campus as populated as some small towns. There were politics and internal struggles as one might expect and, in typical military fashion, when we were not fighting external enemies we were embroiled in struggles over space, time with clients, and personnel levels. The sustaining part of the work for me was having meetings with clients where life stories were shared, witnessed, and honored in a way that provided closure. When successful, the power of art therapy intervention was palpable, as art therapy occupies a unique place in working with trauma. In addition to there being no words to cover what they wished to express, there is the added lethality of military life. Many clients had carried out missions which were "unspeakable" and found art as a way to release some of these thoughts and feelings in a metaphorical and indirect way. Adding the story later is possible, as the art remains after the session and as a segue into follow-up sessions. "Writers, especially writers of war, do not create; they re-create, and reading is both a recreation and the re-creation of what has slipped away from present grasp and into the soul's recesses, avoided, forgotten" (Hillman, 2005, p. 29).

Preface xix

When I left Walter Reed in 2002, I thought about writing about my experiences many times, but I wondered whether I would be able to do justice to the service members whom I met and worked with there. In 2007, *Washington Post* reporters Dana Priest and Ann Hull uncovered that the facility was housing patients off post in rat-infested, dilapidated buildings (Priest & Hull, 2007). Each received a Pulitzer Prize for her work. I watched as "heads rolled." After the story broke in 2007, the Secretary of Defense announced he had relieved the Post Commander, and, in short order, the Secretary of the Army (Abramowitz & Vogel, 2007). The most famous military hospital in the world (I remember watching a segment of *MASH* where Frank was saying to Margaret something to the effect of "I'm going to play Walter Reed, the big one") was reduced to being described as a disgusting, rodent-infested place. This was too much cognitive dissonance for me and I could no longer leave the story of the people that I had touched and who had so inspired and motivated me to that historical narration.

In writing this book, I wish to give the reader a glimpse of not only the external condition of those treated but also the "internal" living conditions that each soldier and family member confronts daily. My hope is that the reader will glean a deeper understanding of the lives of those who sacrificed so much for this country, who have paid such a high price for their military service, and who have survived horrifying trauma. I have a need to bring the reader to appreciate the hundreds of thousands of people seen there by many thousands of staff and the difficult work carried out there every day. I wish I could count the many times I witnessed staff members, recreation and horticultural therapists, nurses, physicians, techs, social workers, psychologists, occupational therapists, the cleaning staff, and fellow patients helping to give alternatives to the suffering and angst encountered there. The facility on Georgia Avenue closed in September 2011 with a ceremony on the hospital lawn. This had been the home of Walter Reed for 102 years. The retirement of this army facility signified the end of something I couldn't quite fathom, an anticlimactic closure to something so significant, weighty, and visceral that I was at a loss to think about or describe it. Walter Reed was merged into the National Naval Medical Center in Bethesda and is now called the Walter Reed National Military Medical Center. The new Walter Reed is an amalgamation of different military branches, which have their own ways of operating and unique histories. I am happy to say that the work begun at Walter Reed Georgia Avenue continues under the capable hands of art therapists at the facility in Bethesda, at Fort Belvoir, and across the country. Much of their work is covered in the second part of this book. Art therapists as well as a plethora of staff continue to work daily with grace and dedication to provide the best services possible to the military members who are seen. Those with whom we work have taught us so much about resilience, grief, and the importance of family, brotherhood, and dedication.

Having evolved in different roles over the course of 27 years, starting as a part-time employee and moving into several leadership positions, I have been able to impart a unique perspective into the working of this intricate and multi-leveled system. The military has provided the prototype and has been at the forefront of trauma treatment due to its members' exposure to harmful situations. And I am certain we can use some of what we have learned to be effective with this population to treat other traumatized people.

Yes, war, the predator of lives and souls, can do horrible things to people. It can lead to re-experiencing the trauma, avoiding memories of it, dissociation and disruptions in one's time perspective and life narrative. As a gaping wound it can bubble up, leaving people frozen and out of sync with the world around them, when what was once part of one's survival strategy becomes a hindrance and gets in the way of one's healing. All the contributors to this book have studied and worked with service members and their families. It is my fervent hope that the contributors' expertise will help therapists working with this population and other traumatized populations understand their needs and culture in a more humane and nonjudgmental way.

Paula Howie, Silver Spring, MD, 2016

References

Abramowitz, M., & Vogel, S. (2007, March 3). Army secretary ousted. *The Washington Post*. Retrieved April 5, 2017, from http://www.washingtonpost.com/wp-dyn/content/article/2007/03/02/AR2007030200438.html.

account, P.F.V. (2015, September 4). War is the mother of all poverty, a vast predator of lives and souls [microblog]. Retrieved April 5, 2017, from https://twitter.com/pontifex/status/639739685326065664.

Carey, N. (2013). *The Epigenetics Revolution: How Modern Biology Is Rewriting Our Understanding of Genetics, Disease, and Inheritance* (Reprint edition). New York: Columbia University Press.

Fritz, R.G. (2000). *World War II Experiences of Russel G. Fritz*. Unpublished manuscript.

Hillman, J. (2005). *A Terrible Love of War* (Reprint edition). New York: Penguin Books.

history.com. (2009). Battle of Okinawa – World War II. Retrieved April 21, 2016, from http://www.history.com/topics/world-war-ii/battle-of-okinawa.

Hoge, C., Auchterlonie, J., & Milliken, C. (2006). Mental health problems, use of mental health services, and attrition from military service after returning from deployment to Iraq or Afghanistan. *JAMA*, 295(9), 1023–1032. http://doi.org/10.1001/jama.295.9.1023.

Howie, P., Prasad, S., & Kristel, J. (Eds.). (2013). *Using Art Therapy With Diverse Populations: Crossing Cultures and Abilities* (1st edition). London: Jessica Kingsley.

Military-Industrial Complex Speech, Dwight D. Eisenhower, 1961. (n.d.). Retrieved April 22, 2016, from http://coursesa.matrix.msu.edu/~hst306/documents/indust.html.

Morris, D.J. (2016). *The Evil Hours: A Biography of Post-Traumatic Stress Disorder* (1st edition). Boston, MA: Eamon Dolan/Mariner Books.

Office of the Deputy Assistant Secretary of Defense. (2013). *2013-Demographics-Report. pdf*. Retrieved April 22, 2016, from http://download.militaryonesource.mil/12038/MOS/Reports/2013-Demographics-Report.pdf.

PBS NewsHour: KQED: January 15, 2013 3:00pm–4:00pm PST. (2013). Retrieved April 5, 2017, from http://archive.org/details/KQED_20130115_230000_PBS_NewsHour?q=Suicides+by+active+duty+U.S.+troops#start/2100/end/2160.

Perret, G. (1989). *A Country Made by War: From the Revolution to Vietnam—The Story of America's Rise to Power* (1st edition). New York: Random House.

Priest, D., & Hull, A. (2007, February 18). Soldiers face neglect, frustration at Army's top medical facility. *The Washington Post*. Retrieved April 5, 2017, from http://www.washingtonpost.com/wp-dyn/content/article/2007/02/17/AR2007021701172.html.

Rand. (2014). Lasting consequences of World War II means more illness, lower education and fewer chances to marry for survivors. Retrieved December 31, 2015, from http://www.rand.org/news/press/2014/01/21/index1.html.

Rosenheck, R. (1986). Impact of posttraumatic stress disorder of World War II on the next generation. *The Journal of Nervous and Mental Disease, 174*(6), 319–327.

Tavernise, S. (2011, July 28). An emotional ceremony as Walter Reed Army Medical Center prepares to close. *New York Times*. Retrieved April 5, 2017, from http://search.proquest.com.proxygw.wrlc.org/docview/1620491235/abstract/F45A281A53F244E5PQ/1?accountid=11243.

U.S. Census Bureau. (2015). FFF: Veteran's Day 2015: November 11, 2015. Retrieved April 22, 2016, from https://www.census.gov/newsroom/facts-for-features/2015/cb15-ff23.html.

Acknowledgments

Several years ago I contacted a client I had worked with at Walter Reed to ask her permission to include her for a chapter in another book. I ended up writing about someone else, so I included her story in Chapter 2 of this book. When we met, she encouraged me to undertake my own book about Walter Reed, telling me, it's been years, and I think it's time that you were able to write about it. Indeed, it had been almost a decade since I left although I continued to see service members in my private practice. No doubt I had been mulling over the enormous effort this task would be, dreading the wellspring of my conflicted feelings and procrastination. After all, some of the stories included here have dark endings. Some, like June, still deal with the aftermath of their illness. Yet, she had the faith that I could accomplish this difficult undertaking. My fondest thanks to her and to all the soldiers who go to work in dangerous places to support others as part of their job; to their family members; and to all the clients I have seen over the past 30-plus years, who have inspired and encouraged me. I owe them a profound debt; without them and what they have taught me, this book could not exist.

    I wish to thank my family, Chris and Laura, Lauren and Aaron, Tom and Rachael (who was my "go to" graphic designer and explained everything about photos, pixels, and spoke geek for me) for their undying support and for listening to my endless machinations. A special thanks to my husband Hugh, who eagerly read each chapter, helping me to edit and shape the book into its present form. I could not have done this without their help and without the help of friends who believed in me, such as Shirley Spory and Mildred Kadin, two pals from my Walter Reed days. William Stockton, MD, helped me grow in my professional life, guiding me through missteps at this challenging and sometimes stressful worksite. Also, without the direction of Julie Bondanza who saw me through times when I was feeling overwhelmed and stuck while writing this book, I might have been forever caught in the quagmire of obsession and may never have completed it.

A book such as this would not be possible without standing on the shoulders of many talented people who went before me. Each day, art therapists, recreation therapists, horticultural therapists, nurses, physicians, psychologists, and other healthcare workers bring healing into the lives of others. They have inspired and encouraged me throughout the years. To all those who worked at Walter Reed, too numerous to recount here, I will be forever grateful for their guidance and patience. To my dear friend Katherine Williams, who has written the Foreword for this book, my special thanks for many years of collegiality and friendship. To Patricia Ravenscroft, who began the Walter Reed program in the early 1970s and whose vision of art therapy included a special place for the artistic process in the recovery and healing of our service members, I owe all of what follows. She established a program that is still flourishing today. To many of those who worked at Walter Reed over the years, including Charlotte Boston and Jeanne Creekmore (who wrote Chapter 3), Kristy Jensch, Mari Fleming, Drew Conger, Vanita Tarpley, Gail Edwards, Elaine Parks, Judy Bridenbaugh, Ronnie Kaufman, Karen Bladengroen, Nancyann Turner, Carol Cox, and numerous others as well as horticultural and recreation therapists who added so much to our work and professional presence, my profoundest thanks. And a special recognition for Kerry Datel, who died much too soon, and upon whose work prototypes all of our subsequent program descriptions were based. And finally to the hundreds of students who trained there who added so much energy and so many new ideas to our interventions. They made the art therapy training program at Walter Reed a nationally known training site as many of them went on to do great things, head training programs, research, and become fine clinicians in their own rights.

My heartiest thanks go to the 16 authors who contributed their time and effort to this book, who were willing to share their experiences, thoughts, and visions of art therapy from their own unique perspective. Through each lens, we can see different aspects of what working with the military means to them.

Others gave their time and energy along the way. Linney Wix was willing to answer any questions and to send archival information about Mary Huntoon, our earliest art therapy pioneer working with returning vets after World War II. Many thanks to Eric Boyle, who arranged a whole afternoon in which Alan Hawk and I dug through archives at the Medical Museum at Forest Glen. The archivists at the Museum of Modern Art (MOMA), where I would encourage anyone interested in the earliest roots of art therapy and the military to seek out answers, were most helpful.

And last but not least, my special thanks to the staff at Routledge Publishers. To Nina Guttapalle who stepped in to fill the shoes of another editor and who answered my questions with patience and clarity, always finding the time to email (early in the morning until the wee hours). She was always there helping and trying to find a way to support my ideas. And finally, to Chris Teja, who had faith in this undertaking and provided me with this chance to follow my passion and to write the first book on art therapy in the United States to address working with service members and their families.

Notes on Contributors

Kimberly Albert, PhD, works at the Center for Cognitive Medicine, Department of Psychiatry and Behavioral Sciences at the Vanderbilt University School of Medicine.

Doris Arrington, Ed.D., ATR-BC, HLM, is an Adjunct Professor, Notre Dame de Namur Graduate Art Therapy Program. Since 2009, she has been collaborating with the Recreational Department at the VA hospital in Menlo Park, CA and PTSD Veterans using the Instinctual Trauma Response.

Amy Backos, PhD, ATR-BC, is a licensed psychologist and art therapist and Chair of the Graduate Art Therapy Psychology Department at Notre Dame de Namur University, located in the San Francisco Bay area.

Charlotte Boston, ATR-BC, LCPAT, has been an art therapist for 25 years and has worked with clients from ages 5 to 97, inpatient, military, and residential, with a broad range of psychiatric diagnosis. She is currently an art therapist at an inpatient psychiatric facility.

Jeanne Creekmore, PhD, ATR-BC, is an art therapist and psychologist who practices Jungian-oriented psychotherapy in Washington, DC. After leaving the Walter Reed Army Medical Center, she became a military wife and traveled around the United States for ten years. She incorporates art, music, and dreams into her work with adults, and she enjoys using paint, fabric, and collage to make her own artistic creations.

Contributors

Jennifer DeLucia, DAT, ATR-BC, LCAT, worked for more than six years in the veteran space addressing the psychosocial needs of service members, veterans, and their family members at the Veterans Outreach Center in Rochester, NY.

Linda Gantt, PhD, ATR-BC, HLM, has been in art therapy for 40 years. She and her late husband, Louis Tinnin, MD, developed a trauma treatment approach with art therapy at its core (the Instinctual Trauma Response model).

Martha Haeseler, ATR-BC, is a painter and fiber artist, student of Edith Kramer, and an art therapist since 1972. She directed the Giant Steps Psychiatry Program, VA, Connecticut Healthcare System, and she recently headed a team to provide art therapy trainings on US Army installations.

Nancy Parfitt Hondros, MA, completed her training at Drexel University, receiving the Future Promise Award. She had a 20-year career in the private sector and 23 years at the National Institutes of Health.

Jacqueline P. Jones, MEd, MA, ATR, works with active duty service members as the Creative Arts Therapist at Intrepid Spirit One, the National Intrepid Center of Excellence satellite at Fort Belvoir Community Hospital.

Corrie A. Mazzeo, Psy.D., is a clinical psychologist practicing at the Louis Stokes Cleveland Department of Veterans Affairs since 2007 in outpatient mental health and primary care mental health integration.

Eileen A. McKee, ATR-BC, LCPAT, has built her career developing practical and accessible introductions to art therapy within multidisciplinary treatment teams and was previously a contract art therapist with the Department of Defense.

Paul Newhouse, MD, holds the Jim Turner Chair of Cognitive Disorders at Vanderbilt University School of Medicine and is Professor of Psychiatry, Pharmacology, and Medicine. He is also Director of the Center for Cognitive Medicine and the Division of Geriatric Psychiatry in the Department of Psychiatry and Behavioral Sciences at Vanderbilt University Medical Center.

Jeff Stadler, MA, LPC, graduated from Notre Dame de Namur University in 2001 and has worked for 15 years on art therapy in programs ranging from community-based to highly secure inpatient treatment settings. He worked for five years at the VA in a PTSD specialty program, using art therapy in the treatment of combat and sexual traumas.

Mary Ellen Vesprini, MEd, LICSW, is currently working with the homeless veterans' population in Worcester, MA through the Western Central Massachusetts

Veterans Health Care System. She has worked with victims of sexual assault, childhood neglect, mass casualties, and combat exposure.

Melissa S. Walker, ATR, served as an art therapist on Walter Reed's inpatient psychiatric unit before transferring to the National Intrepid Center of Excellence (NICoE) where she developed and implemented the NICoE Healing Arts Program.

Introduction
Paula Howie

[R]ather the youth of our country who were never trained for war, and who almost never believed in war, but who have … brought forth gallantry. … If our country takes these sacrifices with indifference, it will be the cruelest ingratitude the world has ever known.

Ensign William R. Evans, Jr. (missing in the Battle of Midway, 1942)

When I began working at Walter Reed in 1976, I would be questioned by friends who wanted to know how I could work with the military, did I believe in the (Vietnam) war, and weren't all the returning soldiers baby killers? I knew that few of those returning had committed what they considered atrocities but I also knew they were fighting a guerrilla war in villages and among civilians. The people they had killed still haunted some of them, as did the decisions they had made to stay alive. When I first began working, I, too, would silently ask myself questions such as "what are you doing working here? You are a pacifist; you attended candlelight vigils and regularly went to anti-war protests. You think war is a last resort."

Vietnam has been something of a conundrum that entailed a loss of compassion and soul for my generation. What I came to understand was that I absolutely could not condone war and yet I could work with the soldiers coming back from our wars. The individual soldier does not decide to go to war and, since Vietnam, has not been blamed for doing so. He or she is not responsible for the war any more than I or those asking questions were to blame. Or perhaps, the culpability belongs equally to us all. War becomes a stain on our national conscience and can be overlooked or ignored at times as many of us did not have to give up our legs, arms, or our psyche to fight in Southeast Asia. An alarming fact is that our country behaves, on the world stage, as if it might not exist without being ensconced in a war (Perret, 1989).

I began to see friends' queries as political. His or her questions did not take into account the average soldier, someone who is performing a job and who may not believe in war either. Each must obey orders, whether they agree with them or not. Some had little say in the matter when there was a draft. The last "recent" war in which there was a draft was in the Vietnam War. Today, although we have a "volunteer" army fighting in Desert Storm and Operation Iraqi Freedom, these soldiers may not have known that they would be sent to such theaters of war in Iraq or Afghanistan and may have joined to learn a skill or escape a depressed economy (Thorpe, 2015). However, some soldiers signed up after 9/11 specifically to protect the USA from future terrorist attacks. The important thing to remember when working with the military is that there are as many reasons for serving as there are service members.

This is the first art therapy book to address working exclusively with those in the active duty military, veteran service members, and their families. We aspire to give you practical information for how to think about and approach treatment with this population and by extension to work with others who have been traumatized. Due to the lethality of their jobs and their experiences prior to military service, members of the military returning from combat and service abroad have been very difficult to treat with traditional psychotherapy approaches. The following pages offer an expanded vision of care, giving both a historical account of art therapy provided for military personnel as well as addressing current trends in their care. The reader will see that the practice of art therapy has been informed by treating this population and that the profession further owes much early success to its effective and practical treatment to being able to address those with traumatic injuries.

Beginnings: A Profession Facilitated by War

An old English idiom goes, "hindsight is 20/20." Although art has been used for millennia in healing the human psyche, spirit, and body (Gussak & Rosal, 2016; Malchiodi, 2011; Junge, 2015), I believe no history of our profession would be complete without considering the major contribution of the military experience and particularly of the trauma of World War II to our profession's beginnings. There are compelling reasons for reaching this conclusion, not the least of which is that art therapy, from its very creation, has shown great application to and effectiveness for treating those who have suffered from psychological and physical trauma. Our current interest in neurobiology and brain research (Hass-Cohen, Findlay, Cozolino, & Kaplan, 2015, Chapman, 2014) has led to irrefutable information about why and how art therapy can elucidate and process trauma due to its visual and storytelling properties without re-traumatizing the individual (Gantt & Tinnin, 2009). Hass-Cohen et al. (2015) do a spectacular job of taking aspects of brain development including the importance of relationships and elucidating how the directives we use in art therapy approaches engage "sensory, relational, affective, verbal and non-verbal cognitive transitional processes" (p. 310) and contribute to optimism and resilience. Art can assist in turning implicit body memories into explicit conscious narratives leading to a transformed sense of self. "The manipulation of art media and the weekly generation of new creations in a supportive interpersonal context target sensory-emotive-cognitive processing area of the brain that are needed for psychological transformation" (Hass-Cohen et al., 2015, p. 440).

Since its formal inception in the 1940s, art therapy has been acknowledged as a way in which individuals can bring order from their confused thoughts and make struggles more manageable by expressing them in tangible form (Ulman & Dachinger, 1987). The literature points to art therapy helping in the management of stress, physical symptoms, intrusive or avoidant symptoms, problematic behaviors and affect, as well as ultimately promoting the integration of a traumatic event into the patient's life history (Collie, Backos, Malchiodi, & Spiegel, 2006). Further, as a treatment for those returning from prolonged service and several tours of duty in war zones, art therapy operates on multiple levels, simultaneously addressing trauma symptoms and their underlying structures. With trauma treatment in general, the goal of narrative trauma processing is to eliminate intrusive and arousal symptoms and diminish numbing symptoms. This is accomplished by processing traumatic memories in order to achieve narrative closure. The objective is to integrate all of the dissociated images into a graphic form that depicts the entire traumatic experience as an historical event. The artist reviews the pictured event, puts it into words, and avows it as personal history. Importantly, this transforms the images from unfinished (seemingly present) experience to past history. Once narrative closure and verbal coding is achieved, the images are no longer dissociated (Tinnin & Gantt, 2013). In this way, military personnel are able to process and narrate the traumatic events that contributed to combat stress symptomology.

There is much to be said for the therapeutic power of visual depiction of disassociated thoughts and memories. Since memories can be kinesthetic and verbal as well as visual, sometimes access to them is most efficient through the visual or kinesthetic; in other words, the hand remembers what the mind has forgotten. In the mid-nineteenth century, French psychiatrist Pierre Janet wrote about the connection between disassociation and traumatic memory as past events that intrude into the present (van der Hart, Brown, & van der Kolk, 1989). Contemporary German psychiatrist Hans Prinzhorn, who served as an army surgeon in World War I, in his collection of the 1922 Artistry of the Mentally Ill, attempted to analyze the artistic work of the mentally ill through scientific and artistic analysis. Not only was it helpful to observe; it became clear to him (Prinzhorn, 2011) that using creative and non-verbal therapies helped the person relate their experience to others.

As you might expect, trauma-informed treatment owes much of its advancement in recent years to the military, which has been forced to deal with this subject since the beginning of military conflicts. In our Western culture, the first mention of psychological battlefield injuries occurs in the chronicles of the Battle of Marathon by the Greek historian Herodotus, written in 440 BCE. Hippocrates, a Greek physician who is sometimes referred to as the Father of Western medicine (467–377 BCE), discusses frightening battle dreams in his work with soldiers. Physicist Lucretius, in *De Rerum Natura*, which was written in 50 BCE, describes a rather compelling case of hysterical blindness (Crocq & Crocq, 2000).

Art therapy as a profession predates the designation of PTSD by several decades. The history of trauma follows military interventions very closely. In the Civil War, Joseph DeCosta termed it "soldier's heart" because he noticed that due to the stress of war, some soldiers appeared to have heart disease, which manifested as increased heart rate, disorientation, and fatigue. In 1890, Pierre Janet, whom I have already mentioned, called trauma a fixed idea that included intrusion. He also noticed that trauma memories do not have a linear narrative (van der Hart et al., 1989). In 1917 during World War I, trauma responses to battle were called "shell-shock." This was descriptive of the intensity of the bombardment and fighting, particularly with bombing in the trenches that produced a helplessness appearing variously as panic and being scared, or flight, an inability to reason, sleep, walk, or talk. Unfortunately, this reaction was also thought to display a lack of moral fiber (Crocq & Crocq, 2000). In 1945 during World War II, combat stress reaction (CSR) was a term used within the military to describe acute behavioral disorganization seen by medical personnel as a direct result of the trauma of war. Also known as "combat fatigue" or "battle neurosis," it has some overlap with the diagnosis of acute stress reaction used in civilian psychiatry. It included symptoms like fatigue, slower reaction times, indecision, disconnection from one's surroundings, and an inability to prioritize. Combat stress reaction was a precursor to acute stress disorder, post-traumatic stress disorder (PTSD), or other long-term disorders attributable to combat stress. Our current designation of PTSD from 1975 was due to the lobbying efforts of Vietnam service members to the American Psychiatric Association who believed they needed a diagnosis (Morris, 2016).

In World War I, occupational therapists, artists, Red Cross workers, and volunteers provided therapeutic art interventions for military service members who suffered physical and psychological trauma. Included in this artistic tradition were sculptors Francis Wood and Anna Watts. They assisted plastic surgeons and patients during World War I by creating wearable masks for disfigured soldiers (Alexander, 2007). Due to their diverse backgrounds, some of the providers were more therapy oriented and some were more art focused. Quiroga (1995) reports that in 1917, the first occupational therapist (OT) was hired at Walter Reed and "demonstrated its value in treating both the mind and the body of the wounded service member using occupation in the form of treatment: physically, to improve upper extremity function; and psychologically, to help prevent depression, control attention, and calm the wounded" (pp. 159–160). OTs, other professionals, and volunteers continued to work with trauma survivors throughout both World Wars.

When I visited the National Museum of Health and Medicine in Forest Glen, Maryland, I found samples of OT from the 1930s when it became a military specialty and remains so to the present day (Newton, 2007). The most expressive work contained there was done in ceramics. There was a focus on rehabilitation and providing craft projects and examples of the kits, and art activities that were scripted. However, the archives contained no materials from art therapy sessions.

Looking through our military lens, it is more than a coincidence that British artist Adrian Hill first used the term "art therapy" in 1942 in a wartime environment. Although never in the military, Hill, recovering from tuberculosis in a sanatorium, discovered the therapeutic benefits of drawing and painting while convalescing. One could certainly argue that the experience of being in a sanatorium was a traumatic one. In addition, he was acutely aware the huge toll World War II was having on the human psyche. He said,

> [I]t is natural that the soldier as much as the artist should turn to seek mental refuge in the creative arts and thence hope. When the world is seething with death and despair the man in the street and his brother in arms crave for such antonyms as expressed by life and faith; art provides nourishment for such longings.
>
> (Hogan, 2001, pp. 135–136)

He also spoke about the art therapies' applicability for treating wounded soldiers returning from the war. Hill suggested artistic interventions to his fellow patients, which was documented in 1945 in his book *Art Versus Illness*. Artist Edward Adamson joined Adrian Hill to extend Hill's work into British rehabilitation mental hospitals after serving in the Royal Army Medical Corps (Hogan, 2001). During his career, Adamson collected over 100,000 pieces of art made by patients and displayed them. It was his hope to foster greater understanding of the creativity and contributions of the mentally ill by sharing the fruits of their labor with the public at large.

During World War II, Dr. Karl Menninger, who had been an important supporter of the career of Mary Huntoon, was Director of the Psychiatry Consultants' Division in the office of the Surgeon General of the United States Army. After the war, he founded the Menninger Clinic in Topeka, Kansas with his father. He was also instrumental in founding the Winter Veterans' Administration Hospital, which, in its day, became the largest psychiatric training center in the world. He chaired the committee which produced the document Medical 203, a major revision of existing US military classification of mental disorders. It was adopted by all the armed services and was later used as a basis for the first Diagnostic and Statistical Manual (DSM) (Houts, 2000).

The Homecoming

As stated earlier, while researching this book it became clear that no history of art therapy would be complete without taking into account the profound influence of World War II (1939–1945) on the inception and growth of our profession. World War II was a catastrophic human tragedy, which took the lives of between 30 and 50 million people and touched almost every nation on the globe (Miller, 2010), producing profound cultural, societal, familial, and individual impacts. The confusion, horror, and long-lasting effects of the psychological injury are part of our dialectic, cultural, and personal accounts of

6 *Introduction*

battlefield trauma. However, despite the carnage inflicted over its time period, World War II ushered in massive innovations and transformations of social, political, gender, and racial roles. It transformed almost every field of endeavor, including medicine, electronics, computers, and the aerospace industry. Computers had begun as code breakers, an investment in radar laid the foundation for the postwar electronics industry, and airplanes would allow civilians to move in vast numbers around the world. The GI bill allowed service members to remake their postwar lives, giving the returning veteran more flexibility and hope (Miller, 2010).

As millions of service members returned home, our historical review confirms that art therapy's ability to address trauma and the changing societal context in which it emerged gave it special access to and meaning in post-World War II society. One art program offered to service members post-World War II was held at the Museum of Modern Art (MOMA) in New York City and was called the War Veteran's Art Center. This program ran from 1944 to 1948; therapists were trained in the visual arts as a means of rehabilitation of service members and goals included "to discover the best and most effective ways to bringing about, through the arts, the readjustment of returning to civilian life" (D'Amico, 1944). Veterans were offered classes in a variety of artistic media, including drawing, painting, and the fundamentals of design, jewelry, metalwork, sculpture, and ceramics, to name a few. While looking through the MOMA archives, it became clear that this facility had an expressive component, which was extremely therapeutic for its participants. The picture shown in Figures 0.1 and 0.2 is reminiscent of the 2,000-yard stare by World War II artist and correspondent Tom Lea. This stare became the epitome of PTSD. The picture is a graphic expression of the disassociated gaze of a battle-weary soldier but the symptom it describes may also be found among victims of other types of trauma. There were many examples in the archives which demonstrated the therapeutic aspect of this program that existed in conjunction with artistic instruction aspects of the program (D'Amico, 1944). Unfortunately, there does not exist any information about who the artists were who attended this program.

Of note to current practitioners of art therapy is the vivid description of a controversy, which may have been one of several factors ultimately responsible for the program morphing into the People's Art Center in 1948, when it became open to civilians. Apparently there was a special committee set up to identify whether the War Service Members' Art Center was providing what they could to improve the program. The committee carried out volumes of interviews and culminated their work in a report describing a conflict of:

> [A]ntipathy and professional jealousy between the therapist on the one hand and those the field of creative art… Their approach, however—therapeutic on one hand and artistic on the other—is very different. There must be a common ground established between the two approaches, before the two organizations can work closely together.
>
> (D'Amico, 1944, p. 5)

Figure 0.1 Students at work, *c.* 1944 to 1948. War Veterans' Art Center, The Museum of Modern Art, New York. Victor D'Amico Papers, III.A.4. The Museum of Modern Art Archives, New York.
Source: Digital Image © The Museum of Modern Art/Licensed by SCALA/Art Resource, NY, printed with permission.

8 *Introduction*

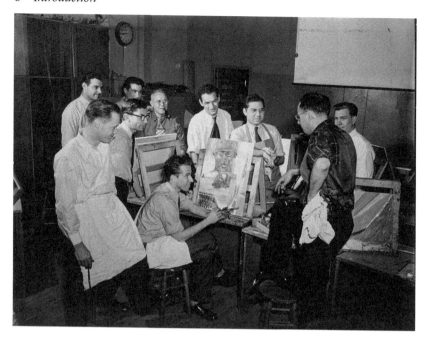

Figure 0.2 Students at work, 1944 to 1948. War Veterans' Art Center, The Museum of Modern Art, New York. Victor D'Amico Papers, III.A.4. The Museum of Modern Art Archives, New York.
Source: Digital Image © The Museum of Modern Art/Licensed by SCALA/Art Resource, NY, printed with permission.

And further, "the service members art center, as it has done in the past, should continue to steer a course in the middle of the road in the therapist-creative art controversy.... In the last analysis it is the veteran who suffers from controversies of this kind" (D'Amico, 1944, p. 11). This conflict was primarily played out between those trained therapists (OTs) who were concerned about the more artistic "volunteers" who did not have the training in therapy. One could see this being extended today in the arts offered in certain settings. Further, we could see this as a part of our art therapy roots, as there has been such concern about the level of art and therapy in our hybrid profession. It is reminiscent of Bob Ault asking if someone woke you at night, and asked whether you are an artist or a therapist: how would you answer? Many of us have answered that we are both, but it is edifying to note that the antagonism of these discussions has been going on for many years and in other contexts. As Randy Vick said, "Art therapy is a hybrid discipline based primarily on the fields of art and psychology, drawing characteristics from each parent to evolve a unique new entity" (in Malchiodi, 2011, p. 5).

In the mid-1940s, psychologist Margaret Naumburg, widely regarded as the founder of art therapy in the United States, began her work (Junge, 2015). Unlike Hill, Naumburg's work was based on the idea of using art to release the unconscious by encouraging free association (Naumburg, 1987). The resulting artwork was considered symbolic speech that the therapist encouraged the patient to interpret and analyze. I am not aware of any military members with whom she worked.

Mary Huntoon: Art Therapy at the Winter Veterans' Hospital

The first mention of an art therapist service for returning soldiers from World War II was the groundbreaking work of Mary Huntoon at the Winter Veterans' Administration (VA) in Topeka, Kansas from 1946 until her retirement in 1958 (Wix, 2000) where she was Director of Fine and Manual Arts. Mary was first hired by the Menninger Clinic in 1934. A dedicated artist, she wanted to spend one year at the VA but after being told by the curator of prints and drawings at the Philadelphia Art Museum that she was too old to pursue her artistic goals, she remained at the VA for 12 years. In her lifetime, Mary personally produced 126 oil paintings, 958 sketches, 206 watercolors, 131 original prints, six pastels, six sculptures, 116 poems, and 22 stories (Wix, 2000, p. 175), "Her deep faith in arts ability to heal is inspirational."

Mary wrote a paper about her experience at the Winter VA in which she does not discuss the unique qualities of working in the military or trauma. Indeed, as she was beginning a new profession, she focused on how to work with different types of patients, referring to them as students. She describes a process of *painting out* which means that the subject matter emerges from deeper levels of consciousness, and that the person does this intuitively, not consciously, as he reveals the thoughts behind his bizarre ideas (Huntoon, 1953). She talks about working with psychotic and suicidal patients from whom she amassed over 3,900 paintings from the VA in the museum collection, which were loaned to hospital staff and patients for display in their rooms. This artwork also decorated the halls of the hospital. Being first an artist, Mary provided studio experiences for World War II vets and believed deeply in the artistic process as therapeutic. "I am as much one of them (indicates patients) except that I make adjustment to reality. I firmly believe all artists are practicing self-therapy. They always have been aware of the self-therapeutic power of their trade" (Wix, 2000, p. 174). Don Jones, a conscientious objector in World War II, and Bob Ault followed Huntoon at Menninger and continued her work there.

Hanna Kwiatkowska, a teacher in the GWU program who also helped establish the American Art Therapy Association, supervised interns working at Bethesda Naval Hospital. I was a practicum student there in 1974. This was my first foray into working with those in the military and was an invaluable experience for working in a structured and regulated environment.

About this Book

In describing her eclectic approach, Harriett Wadeson (in Gussak & Rosal, 2016) reminds us that each therapist must make sense of and integrate treatment approaches tailored to each individual with whom they work. As she notes, one size does not fit all. She implores us to merge myriad ideas together in order to develop our way of approaching the hybrid profession of art therapy. As Wadeson (in Gussak & Rosal, 2016) so aptly states, we must "continue to enlarge our canvas," including working with trauma and working in certain settings and client populations such as the prison system and, by extrapolation, the military. Each client and therapist is unique and there is surely no one way to accomplish the meeting of two separate minds and worldviews. I agree that one must be open, creative, and integrative when providing therapy. Dan Siegel promulgates that openness and integration are necessary for any therapeutic endeavor in order to achieve neural integration, and therefore for therapy to be successful (Siegel, 2010).

Art therapy students, teachers, and related mental health professionals will find this book applicable to their classes where students and professionals are working with military personnel and trauma. Professionals working with a military population who are focusing on re-entry into country and community will also find important information and interventions. Using easily accessible visual art materials provides non-verbal access to traumatic memories. Art therapists who see traumatized clients and counselors who use art with their clients will be better able to respond to their needs and to provide effective treatment interventions. The reader will be introduced to many approaches, which they can apply to working with members of the military, service members, their families, and those who have experienced trauma. A variety of outcomes have also been presented. At times, our clients make great strides and move forward to accomplish huge changes in their lives. There are times when they hope to survive a major mental illness, and holding onto reality day by day becomes their objective. The therapist must take all of this into deliberation when working toward a co-created intervention that allows hope, goodwill, and love to emerge. Cathy Malchiodi states "I can say from experience that this challenge is the 'coolest' part of my work with clients – to invent a creative strategy to promote change, insight, and well-being" (Malchiodi, 2010). Yes, it is the coolest and possibly the most difficult part of our work. The experience provided by those writing chapters in this book will assist the novice or experienced therapist to be successful in their approach to this population and to those who have experienced trauma and PTSD.

The book is divided into two parts. Part I encompasses the foundation of art therapy in the military, including sections on what differentiates the military from other settings and the theoretical underpinnings of this groundbreaking treatment. It includes work from the Walter Reed Army Medical Center (WRAMC) and the Veterans' Administration (VA). This includes a great deal of our formative experiences and original work done at the VA and at WRAMC with service members and their families. Fontana and Rosenheck (1994) studied service members from World War II, the Korean War, and the Vietnam War and discerned that there are similarities in the quality of PTSD experienced across wars, and therefore conclude that the information gleaned from the traumatic injuries of earlier wars can be built upon to treat those suffering PTSD from later wars. Chapter 1 covers the history of art therapy with military and veteran populations. Martha Haeseler describes her early work with at the Veterans' Administration Hospital in Connecticut and I describe the beginnings of art therapy at Walter Reed. Chapter 2 covers the early clinical recognition of the overlap between psychosis and trauma, which is demonstrated by a case study. Chapter 3, written by Charlotte Boston and Jeanne Creekmore, elucidates the structure and development of early inpatient group therapy. Chapter 4 discusses the early interventions with individuals and their families, the effect of individual illness on the family system, and recent advances in treatment. Chapter 5 points out the evolution of art therapy interventions in outpatient groups in the military and includes several cases from a long-term group experience held twice weekly at Walter Reed. Chapter 6 discusses the difficult topic of suicide; a malady that we face relatively often because our clientele may be both depressed and have the means to be lethal. It is illustrated by several case studies.

Part II of the book encompasses those working in military hospital or outpatient military settings, in trauma clinics, or in private practice. Most are working with returnees from the Iraq and Afghanistan wars who have been diagnosed with PTSD. Beginning with Chapter 7, art therapy and the brain encompasses treating the wounded warrior by Paul Newhouse and Kimberly Albert. Dr. Newhouse is a retired colonel and a neuropsychiatrist who worked with me for many years at Walter Reed and has been an advocate for art therapy treatment. They give us a comprehensive overview of how art therapy works with traumatized people from a neuropsychological point of view. Building on this chapter, the authors share their unique and overlapping perspectives on the neurobiology of the brain and why they believe their interventions have been so effective. In Chapter 8, Jacqueline Jones gives the reader a comprehensive view of working with complicated grief in a military setting. Chapter 9 includes integrative approaches to treating PTSD and TBI by Melissa Walker who continues her work at Walter Reed in Bethesda. She has documented several approaches which she has found to be effective with recent combat service members. In Chapter 10, Martha Haeseler describes in detail the Giant Steps Program she designed and the approaches she found helpful with the population she saw at the Connecticut VA. Chapter 11 by Eileen McKee tells us about treating substance abuse and co-occurring disorders. Eileen gives us insight into how to deal with and make progress with this difficult population. In Chapter 12, Linda Gantt and Mary Ellen Vesprini give us an overview of the ITT approach and how they tailor this approach when working with military personnel in an outpatient setting. In Chapter 13, Doris Arrington and Nancy Parfitt Hondras discuss the service members' sketch project elucidating an intervention by those artists and art therapists who do not work routinely with service members. They have found portraits to be a helpful way to reach the injured and traumatized veteran, and do so without a great deal of experience working with this population. In Chapter 14, Amy Backos and Corrie Mazzio expound upon their groundbreaking work with Vietnam War veterans who

12 Introduction

find that their lives are still impaired by their experiences and trauma from that war. In Chapter 15, Jeff Stadler tackles the important and timely topic of sexual trauma and assault. This is a problem that has been ignored and denied, making it less likely that those who have experienced it will report it. In Chapter 16, Jennifer DeLucia addresses the studio setting as a treatment approach for returning veterans to assist in their reintegration into civilian life. Chapter 17 includes the conclusion which applies what has been learned over the years through treating the military, and highlights future directions for this work. We hope the reader will glean from these pages how honored we have been to work with the military and their families, and how much we strive daily to improve their lives and the great burden they bear for us all.

References

Alexander, C. (2007, February). Faces of war. *Smithsonian Magazine*. Retrieved April 5, 2017, from http://www.smithsonianmag.com/history/faces-of-war-145799854/.

Chapman, L. (2014). *Neurobiologically Informed Trauma Therapy with Children and Adolescents*. New York: W.W. Norton & Company. Retrieved March 29, 2016, from http://books.wwnorton.com/books/Neurobiologically-Informed-Trauma-Therapy-with-Children-and-Adolescents/.

Collie, K., Backos, A., Malchiodi, C., & Spiegel, D. (2006). Art therapy for combat-related PTSD: Recommendations for research and practice. *Art Therapy*, 23(4), 157–164. https://doi.org/10.1080/07421656.2006.10129335.

Crocq, M.-A., & Crocq, L. (2000). From shell shock and war neurosis to posttraumatic stress disorder: A history of psychotraumatology. *Dialogues in Clinical Neuroscience*, 2(1), 47–55.

D'Amico, V. (1944, 1948). *Victor D'Amico Papers*. New York: The Museum of Modern Art Archives.

Fontana, A., & Rosenheck, R. (1994). Traumatic war stressors and psychiatric symptoms and World War II, Korean, and Vietnam War veterans. *Psychology and the Aging*, 9(1), 27–33.

Gantt, L., & Tinnin, L.W. (2009). Support for a neurobiological view of trauma with implications for art therapy. *The Arts in Psychotherapy*, 36(3), 148–153. https://doi.org/10.1016/j.aip.2008.12.005.

Gussak, D.E., & Rosal, M.L. (2016). *The Wiley Handbook of Art Therapy*. West Sussex, UK: Wiley-Blackwell. Retrieved April 5, 2017, from http://www.amazon.com/Handbook-Therapy-Clinical-Psychology-Handbooks/dp/1118306597/ref=sr_1_1?s=books&ie=UTF8&qid=1464197284&sr=1-1&keywords=rosal+and+gussak.

Hass-Cohen, N., Findlay, J.C., Cozolino, L., & Kaplan, F. (2015). *Art Therapy and the Neuroscience of Relationships, Creativity, and Resiliency: Skills and Practices* (1st edition). New York: W.W. Norton & Company.

Hogan, S. (2001). *Healing Arts: The History of Art Therapy*. London: Jessica Kingsley.

Houts, A.C. (2000). Fifty years of psychiatric nomenclature: Reflections on the 1943 War Department Technical Bulletin, Medical 203. *Journal of Clinical Psychology*, 56(7), 935–967.

Huntoon, M. (1953). Art therapy for patients in the acute section of Winter VA Hospital, Topeka, Kansas. *Department of Medicine and Surgery Information Bulletin*, 10, 29–32.

Junge, M.B. (2015). History of art therapy. In D.E. Gussak & M.L. Rosal (Eds.), *The Wiley Handbook of Art Therapy* (pp. 7–16). New York: John Wiley & Sons. Retrieved April 5, 2017, from http://onlinelibrary.wiley.com/doi/10.1002/9781118306543.ch1/summary.

Malchiodi, C.A. (2010, February 11). The ten coolest art therapy interventions. Retrieved May 25, 2016, from http://www.psychologytoday.com/blog/arts-and-health/201002/the-ten-coolest-art-therapy-interventions.

Malchiodi, C.A. (2011). *Handbook of Art Therapy, Second Edition*. New York: The Guilford Press.

Miller, D.L. (2010). *The Story of World War II: Revised, Expanded, and Updated from the Original Text by Henry Steele Commager* (Rev. exp. edition). New York: Simon & Schuster.

Morris, D.J. (2016). *The Evil Hours: A Biography of Post-Traumatic Stress Disorder* (1st edition). Boston, MA: Eamon Dolan/Mariner Books.

Naumburg, M. (1987). *Dynamically Oriented Art Therapy: Its Principles and Practice*. Chicago, IL: Magnolia Street Publishers.

Newton, S. (2007). The growth of the profession of occupational therapy. *US Army Medical Department Journal*, Jan–Mar, 51–58.

Perret, G. (1989). *A Country Made by War: From the Revolution to Vietnam—The Story of America's Rise to Power* (1st edition). New York: Random House.

Prinzhorn, H. (2011). *The Art of Insanity: An Analysis of Ten Schizophrenic Artists*. Place of publication not identified: Solar Books.

Quiroga, V.A.M. (1995). *Occupational Therapy: The First 30 Years, 1900 to 1930*. Bethesda, MD: Amer Occupational Therapy Association.

Siegel, D.J. (2010). *The Mindful Therapist: A Clinician's Guide to Mindsight and Neural Integration* (1st edition). New York: W.W. Norton & Company.

Thorpe, H. (2015). *Soldier Girls: The Battles of Three Women at Home and at War* (Reprint edition). New York: Scribner.

Tinnin, L., & Gantt, L. (2013). *The Instinctual Trauma Response And Dual-brain Dynamics: A Guide for Trauma Therapy*. Linda Gantt.

Ulman, E., & Dachinger, P. (1987). *Art Therapy in Theory and Practice* (1st edition). New York: Schocken.

van der Hart, O., Brown, P., & van der Kolk, B. (1989). Pierre Janet's treatment of post traumatic stress. *Journal of Traumatic Stress*, *2*(4). Retrieved April 5, 2017, from http://www.onnovdhart.nl/articles/treatmentptsd.pdf.

Wix, L. (2000). Looking for what's lost: The artistic roots of art therapy: Mary Huntoon. *Art Therapy*, *17*(3), 168–176. https://doi.org/10.1080/07421656.2000.10129699.

PART I

Theoretical Background: Understanding and Treating Soldiers and their Families—Formative Experiences

CHAPTER 1

Art Therapy with Military and Veteran Populations: A Historical Context

Martha Haeseler and Paula Howie

Art Therapy at Veterans' Administration, West Haven, Connecticut: Martha Haeseler

When I was in high school in the late 1950s, I took painting classes given by a local artist. I recall that she told us that she was holding art sessions, as a volunteer, for the "shell-shocked" veterans at the VA Medical Center in West Haven, CT. She said she enjoyed the work and found veterans very responsive and expressive in their artwork.

While I worked for many years as an art therapist on an inpatient psychiatric unit in a corporate hospital, I went to VA Connecticut Healthcare System (VACT) a few times for consultations and presentations. In 1994 I received a call from David Read Johnson, PhD, offering me a job there. My job had developed many frustrations, and I gladly accepted. I recall that my unit director at the time, who had been a unit chief at VACT, told me that I would be going from a greenhouse to a desert. I told him that I was very fond of desert plants.

David Read Johnson was a drama therapist who was widely recognized in his field. When he became unit chief on an inpatient psychiatric unit, his innovative programming, including drama, video, art, and poetry therapies, drew the attention of a new Medical Center Director, who asked him what improvements he would suggest for psychiatry. Dr. Johnson said the VA needed a Recreation and Creative Arts Therapy Section (RCATS). He was given two positions to fill, and hired a drama and an art therapist. In 1989, he became director of a newly created National Center for PTSD program, for which he hired a music therapist, pioneering the use of creative therapies for the treatment of PTSD. Currently, the National Center for PTSD includes five creative arts therapists' positions.

In 1995, I replaced an art therapist on the inpatient neuropsychiatry unit. Within a year, I was established in an outpatient psychiatry group program called Giant Steps, and eventually became its director. Giant Steps offers art therapy and other services to between 65 and 70 veterans. After an exhibition of veterans' art, the Honorable Rosa L. DeLauro, U.S. House of Representatives (2005), wrote to me: "It is so exciting to see that the Giant Steps Program is continuing with such great success. Beginning as only a small program at the Veteran's Hospital, it has grown to become a model for long-term outpatient programs" (DeLauro, personal communication).

At VACT, art therapy was so valued that three of my former art therapy interns were hired for the Inpatient Psychiatry Unit, the PTSD Residential Treatment Program, and the Substance Abuse Day Program. In addition, art therapy interns do groups in the Blind Center and in the Hospice and Rehabilitation Units. We still have a drama therapist and a music therapist, and there is currently a job opening in the Cancer Care Center for a second music therapist for the VA; art therapy interns will offer groups there as well.

Although there had been no official account of art therapists employed nationally in the VA system, in 2007, when I was member of the VA National Recreation Therapy Service Advisory Board, we estimated the count to be about 18. When I left VA in January 2015, there were at least 40 accredited art therapists at VA working in positions throughout the country. VA Connecticut Healthcare System, with its large group of creative arts therapists, serves as a model for VA nationwide. My experience at VACT has shown that when an institution sees what art therapy can do, every service wants one.

The Veterans' Administration has recently shown an interest in Complementary Alternative Therapies (CAM). Although most VA research has been directed toward the use of yoga and meditative practices, art therapy is considered a CAM. The director of one of the medical clinics at VACT hosted presentations on CAM for several years, and we creative arts therapists presented our work. This resulted in referrals beyond our capacity, and proposals to create at least one new creative therapist job. According to the US Department of Veterans Affairs Office of Research and Development, "In 2011 a VA survey determines that about 9 in 10 facilities provide CAM therapies or refer patients to licensed practitioners. VA expands funding for studying complementary and alternative medicine to treat PTSD and other conditions" (US Department of Veterans Affairs Office of Research and Development, n.d.). In a 2012 survey of CAM being used in the VA National Centers for PTSD, 79 percent of residential programs and 25 percent of inpatient programs had art therapy (Libby, Pilver, & Desai, 2012, p. 1135). In a 2014 presentation, Heidi Tournoux-Hanshaw said the VA Center for Innovation wanted to see if art therapy works, and she received a grant to develop an art therapy program at the VA, Ft. Worth, TX, and at another local clinic.

A few years ago a National Initiative for Arts and Health in the Military was created. "The initiative is a collaborative effort across the military, government, private and nonprofit sectors to advance the arts and creativity for the benefit of military health" (O'Donnell, n.d). There have been three summit conferences on Advancing Research in the Arts for Health and Well-being Across the Military Continuum, which some creative therapists from VACT attended, and some funding has been made available for research (Edwards, n.d., par. 2).

So the momentum for the establishment of research networks is building and the potential for public–private partnerships is great. It is comforting to know, however, that some exciting and promising creative arts-based programs are already providing much-needed relief to our military populations and their families (Edwards, n.d. par. 8).

Although my job description as a creative arts therapist was different from that of recreation therapists, at the VA the creative arts therapists usually work within the recreation therapy service and share a federal job description. When I was on the VA Advisory Board, I suggested adding Creative Arts Therapy to the name of the National Recreation Therapy Service, but at the time this idea was not supported. At VACT, the creative arts therapists work well together with the recreation therapists; the current RCATS Chief is a recreation therapist supportive of creative arts therapy. However, at many VA Medical Centers, creative therapists are working toward having a stand-alone service or an art therapist in charge, which is a very positive move. Creative therapists at VA have their own email group, monthly calls which usually feature a clinical presentation, and have recently formed a research committee.

The VA's commitment to the creative arts is shown in the National Veterans' Creative Arts Festival, a yearly competition for veterans practicing in all branches of the creative arts. At first, I did not like the idea of competition. Then I realized that it gave all veterans a chance to have their art exhibited, seen, and taken seriously, and from that point I worked hard to help veterans who wished to enter. RCATS staff worked together to hold an annual arts expo and award

Figure 1.1 The garden created by veterans in the Giant Steps Program to welcome veterans and their families to the VA.

ceremony at VACT. On a national level, the competition culminates in a festival to which winning veterans are invited, and every year veterans from VACT have been invited; I escorted veterans to three festivals. There are arts activities throughout the festival and a stage performance, and veterans are greatly honored for their works.

My experience at VACT was very positive. In general, I found veterans to be open to treatment and grateful for their care. I had a lot of autonomy and my ideas were welcomed, and there were means to implement them. In 1998 I wrote: "Despite the diversity in race, ethnicity and education, there is a specific VA culture, grounded in the spirit of service … and comradeship, a culture that transcends difference and provides a deep sense of identity and belonging" (Haeseler, 1998, p. 334).

In this day of the institutional revolving door and brief treatment for mental health, VA is dedicated to the lifetime treatment of the veterans in its care. VA puts veterans first, and its mission is "to fulfill President Lincoln's promise 'To care for him who shall have borne the battle, and for his widow, and his orphan' by serving and honoring the men and women who are America's Veterans" (US Department of Veterans Affairs, n.d., para 1).

Art Therapy at Walter Reed Army Medical Center, Washington, DC: Paula Howie

For 102 years, from 1909 until 2011, Walter Reed Army Medical Center was the US Army's flagship hospital, operating on over 113 acres in Northwest Washington, DC. The staff of the facility served more than 150,000 active and retired personnel from all branches of the military (Institute, 2009). Major Walter Reed's (1851–1902) family donated the land on which the hospital was erected, which was then named after him. As an army physician, he led the team which confirmed that yellow fever is transmitted by mosquitoes rather than by direct contact with an infected person. In the ceremony which marked the building's closing and move to Bethesda, General Hawley-Bowland described its medical care as being among the best in the country, particularly in the area of prosthesis (I would add in the treating of trauma) which specialties have improved significantly since the Persian Gulf War in 1991 (Tavernise, 2011).

Since the facility was legendary, its halls resounded with many famous patients. There was a room named for World War I General John J. Pershing, the only American to be promoted in his own lifetime to General of the Armies, the highest possible rank in the service (Inskeep, 2011). He lived his last years on the campus, close to his doctors. Several presidents also received medical treatment at Walter Reed, including Harry Truman and Richard Nixon (Inskeep, 2011). Eisenhower lived there for the last years of his life until his death in 1969.

The campus included the old and new hospitals, an outpatient psychiatry building, military medical museum, civilian personnel building, restaurants

Art Therapy: A Historical Context 21

and small Post Exchange (PX), and the Walter Reed Army Institute of Research (WRAIR), among other buildings. It appears that not much thought was given to tying in the old, quaint brick façade of the original hospital built before World War I to the monolith that was the new hospital. At first glance, the exterior of the new hospital is impressive, yet overwhelmingly cold. The concrete pillars were amazing to look at, and I could imagine that when extra-terrestrials come across the ruins of our civilization eons after an apocalypse on earth, they would wonder about the civilization that could move such massive pieces of pre-stressed concrete and stone, much as we marvel at the Egyptians and the Pyramids. From the front, the building was so huge and forbidding that it was easy to fantasize adding a colorful mural to it, a rainbow, or some abstract shape to make it appear more human. In 2011, I painted a picture of the front entrance at Walter Reed, giving myself permission to add the color of my visions through a montage of angles.

In 1977, I began work as a part-time art therapist in an annexed building in the grounds of Forest Glen, Maryland. This was the temporary home of

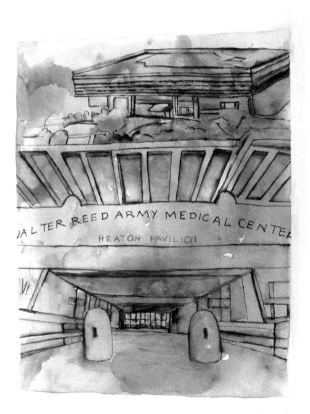

Figure 1.2 Watercolor painting with pen and ink by the author, 22 × 30 inches.

Psychiatry, Neurology, and Research. It was a charming set of buildings, which according to legend had been a hotel, a girls' school, and a hunting lodge. It had a round building, a pagoda, a castle, a fantastic art nouveau ballroom, and many old sculptures (it has since been renovated and sold as condominiums preserving some of the original buildings). The patient areas were cloistered in the basement of some of the buildings, which had a drab, worn look to them. The art therapy offices in this annex were spacious, since old patient rooms were converted into studios. Patti Ravenscroft, ATR, MSW, a mentor and friend, began the creative arts and activities programs in 1974. She pulled together a staff of professional, dedicated, and stimulating people. When Patty left there were two full-time positions. Katherine Williams, PhD, ATR-BC, a dear colleague and later Director of the GW Graduate Art Therapy Program, was also employed in the "dungeons" of wards 106 and 110.

After a year in the annex, we moved to the main hospital in the grounds in Northwest DC. For much of the 25 years the author worked there, the hospital maintained a 1,000-bed capacity expanding to 1,200 beds during the First Gulf War, finally downsizing to fewer than 500 beds in 2002. Every evening there was a ceremony at the retiring of the colors complete with taps and firing of 21 blank rounds. There was a small orange flag on the rooftop used by helicopter pilots to ascertain wind directions when landing on the helipad beside the hospital. The move to the main campus was definitely a boon to the patients who got rooms with window views. At one point, the art therapy staff had eight full-time positions. For patients who had privileges to leave the ward, we also ran groups in our own art studio on another ward.

Art therapy, being a relatively young profession (the George Washington University program began in 1971 and was one of a handful of graduate-level training programs in the country) and not being a military specialty, was not planned for in this monolithic new building. We moved from floor to floor and office to office until, in the 1990s, a studio was built for us using part of the dayroom on ward 52. The studio had a large space for meeting with groups or individuals, storage, a two-way mirror for training purposes (there were at least four students assigned to the program in a given semester), and a kiln room for firing clay pieces (See photo of the studio in Figure 3.3). The hospital underwent many modifications as the beginnings of base realignment and downsizing took its toll on clinical staff and patient census. The closure of Walter Reed and the move to Bethesda was intended to reduce the number of facilities in the area in order to better fit the military's needs. At its closing in 2011, Walter Reed had retained only 150 inpatient beds.

Walter Reed was a longer term facility for those who were stabilized at the front but who needed further treatment (it was called a tertiary care facility because we saw people who were cared for at the site of their injuries and in a hospital theater before coming to WR). There were five such medical centers in the country but none of the others employed art therapists when the program began at Walter Reed. Although housing many medical specialties, Psychiatry was the largest service in the hospital and included outpatient, child and

Art Therapy: A Historical Context 23

Figure 1.3 Aerial photo from 1931 showing the main campus of Walter Reed Georgia Avenue. The "old" hospital is shown in the foreground before the "new" hospital was built behind it.
Source: National Archives, photo no. 18-AA-158-10, printed with permission.

adolescent, partial hospital, consultation/liaison, and inpatient services. The latter had a capacity of 120 inpatient beds or three 40-bed wards. The Psychiatry service offered comprehensive mental health services that included art, recreation, and horticultural therapy programs. The hospital also had a large training component. During it zenith in late 1980 to the early 1990s, the facility had over 4,000 employees on its grounds, making it larger than some small towns. The rooms were spacious, with plastic tiles on the floor in different colors, polished weekly within an inch of their lives and cleaned daily by a brigade of housekeeping personnel.

There was a large lobby at the first-floor entrance, which had an information desk, a small flower shop, snack bar, and scads of people milling around and waiting for appointments. The second floor held the offices and administration, the post commander, conference rooms, and the audiovisual department. The third floor had the cafeteria, called the "mess hall" and a small PX, like a small store. A bigger PX is still housed in the annex at Forest Glen. The fourth floor and above were the wards, which housed the inpatients, staff offices, and nursing stations. Each ward had areas that were patient rooms, which could be closed off for privacy. On the fifth floor there were courtyards in the center of the hallways outside the dayrooms. It was a spectacular sight to see large trees and bushes growing there; it was a nod to humanity in an otherwise rather stark-looking facility. The courtyards proved to be a challenge for psychiatric nursing staff who constantly had to dig up sharp items (razors, knives) that patients hid from them as well as other confiscated items. Many of us tried to have meetings outside as often as possible, and when life became tough it was always reassuring to be able to access the trees right outside the studio door.

The "average" individual seen on the ward was young, male, and had only been in the military for a short time. Since leaving the military required a great deal of paperwork and documentation, including what benefits the person would receive, this process could take as long as two to three months and, on odd occasions, up to a year. Therefore, it was possible to see inpatients for several months even if they were transitioning to civilian life, often to discuss what this would be like for them, as so many were crestfallen at having their military service turn out badly. For some, it was the last hope to make a life outside poverty, neglectful, or abusive families, or in a depressed job market with no marketable training. Many had come into the military expecting to use the GI bill, as had those before them, to gain job training to access better opportunities and a middle-class lifestyle.

The doors in the hallways were painted bright orange and purple. Although happy it was not institutional green, the staff was never told why the halls and doors were painted these colors. To my way of thinking, anyone who tried to think outside the box in order to negate the effect of the outside façade should be appreciated. The true warmth or lack thereof was always to be found in the people who worked there inside its somewhat sterile walls.

In the 1990s, art therapy morphed into the activities therapy service. The service included art, recreation, and horticultural therapy, and had 22 full- and two part-time staff members. Due to the training mission and our large staff, hundreds of art therapy students were trained in this facility. Personnel visited us from the other medical centers and the Ft Belvoir campus, curious about how to set up art therapy programs in other Department of Defense facilities. However, by 2002, the activity therapy staff consisted of eight full-time art and recreational therapy members. Although this type of attrition was happening throughout the hospital, we found ourselves competing with others for staff. The expansiveness of the late 1980s and 1990s had turned into the managed care of the 2000s.

Art therapy and activity therapy spaces on the ward varied, from using the dayrooms for large groups (sometimes as many as 20-plus people for inpatient groups which were held on the ward), to individual offices for one-to-one or family work, which were small and located in the center of the hallway without windows. At one time there was a greenhouse and during the summer months some of the recreation therapy staff would provide picnics off-site.

I would be remiss if there was no mention of *The Washington Post* articles exposing poor living conditions and excessive bureaucracy for soldiers at the hospital. However, there was never anyone who made it sound like the staff was neglectful or incompetent while soldiers were being cared for on the ward, with the exception of one article about ward 53 (Priest & Hull, 2007). "It had nothing to do with patient care," Dr. Pierce (Walter Reed historian) said. "It was housing of the soldiers, and it had to do with the administrative processes of either assessing their disability or releasing them from active duty" (Inskeep, 2011). Although no patient care was called into question, in essence the reputation of the whole center was at risk.

When Walter Reed closed in August 2011, all patients and staff were transitioned either to an expanded Bethesda, Maryland location which was renamed the Walter Reed National Military Medical Center, or to Fort Belvoir hospital in Northern Virginia, which transitioned to 120 beds. With managed care initiatives and the amalgamation of military personnel, the new facilities are being maintained and run by all branches of the Military, not just by the Army. Melissa Walker, Jacqueline Jones, and others who have written chapters for this book continue to expand the boundaries of art therapy interventions with the military and to carry on the fine tradition of clinicians serving the Military and the Department of Defense (DOD) in the national capital area.

As indicated by treatment interventions, art therapy services were integrated into the daily schedule of most of those on the inpatient psychiatry service as well as those on the partial hospital program and outpatients who could benefit from further treatment post inpatient or partial hospital treatment. Art therapy provided assessment and therapy services with a focus on fostering change and independence through the process of creation. Jeanne Creekmore and Charlotte Boston have expounded upon the programs offered on the inpatient service in Chapter 3. Outpatient programs and transitional programs are also covered in several of the historical chapters.

For those involved in art therapy services, treatment consisted of making their struggles more manageable by expressing feelings in tangible form. A means of communication, artwork conveys a person's functional and developmental levels and their unique strengths and conflicts. Thus, the art therapist assisted the treatment team in setting up individualized treatment goals and objectives for each person seen on the ward. Part of this early work effort culminated in the treatment planning guide and the guidelines for beginning art therapy programs in other military facilities (see e-resource materials).

Part of our early work was also dedicated to researching the effectiveness of our interventions and ascertaining the best treatment approach for the individual. We worked on efficacy studies and research protocols, which were often interdisciplinary. Some examples include a study looking at military inpatient psychiatry and forensic psychiatry to see an overlap in the use of art therapy within these populations (Lande, Howie, & Chang, 1997); looking at themes related to wartime experiences (Lande, Tarpley, Francis, & Boucher, 2010); and a study to determine the efficacy of prolonged exposure therapy (Roy, Francis, Friedlander, Banks-Williams, Lande, Taylor, Blair, McLellan, Law, Tarpley, Patt, Yu, Mallinger, Difede, Rizzo, Rothbaum, 2010).

Lessons learned from Vietnam and the First Gulf War

We saw many soldiers who had served in Vietnam and who were having trouble leaving the Military and transitioning into civilian life. Some of them were plagued both by memories of what they had done in theater and by the public's antipathy toward them upon their return. Fortunately, more recently, the public has been able to differentiate more clearly between the soldiers and the policies that sent them into war—we no longer blame the soldiers. After all, they are doing a job and have to follow orders whether they believe in them or not. Seeing people from this era gave me grounding in psychotherapy with trauma, which enabled me to continue to see those who were traumatized in other wars or in peacetime and to be able to help them come to terms with their distress and to successfully aid their return to civilian life. Art therapists also met with many returnees from the First Gulf War (for case studies and detailed information about this work see the e-resource). Of course, one of the most significant events to befall the Military before I left was 9/11. Several of us have written about this work (Howie, Burch, Conrad, & Shambaugh, 2002), and it is fair to say that the facility became more and more aware of threats and doubled its focus on controlling access and increasing safety.

After working with many combat veterans suffering from traumatic memories and PTSD and with their family members, it became clear that graphic media and its associated dialogue could assist in consolidating new memories. Providing a fresh narrative without having to relive the trauma is part of the transformative function of symbols. Exploring one's emotional reaction to the traumatic memory within a therapeutic framework can help manage affect by allowing the individual distance and, to some degree, objectivity. Art therapy, because of its active, kinesthetic nature, can assist the exploration of basic emotion and affect without causing further stress to the individual (Tinnin & Gantt, 2013). Through fine motor activity such as drawing and painting with brush, and gross motor activity such as clay pounding, scribbling, and painting without brush, art therapy can help lessen fight-and-flight or freeze responses.

We found that we were able to process the trauma as soon as the person was physically and psychologically able. This can be initiated at the beginning of therapy rather than waiting. In the beginning I believe we held back, fearing that working on the trauma would open up the person, exposing them to more traumatic symptoms and pain. However, we found that those who had recently been transported from war zones were able to process these memories and to reconsolidate traumatic material more quickly. Much of the time, we found that the person had spent a great deal of their psychic energy dealing with their thoughts and memories before seeking treatment, and many received relief from having the complete story told. Having a beginning, middle, and end is important in putting the traumatic event into the past (Gantt & Tinnin, 2009).

We also found that the trauma has a couple of aspects, one which interferes with the person's daily life (trauma symptoms such as flashbacks, nightmares, and avoidance) and one which may radically alter the cognitive maps of how the self articulates in the world, making the world a frightening place (see Herman's (1997) description of a damaged person in a dangerous world). After trauma processing which addresses the trauma itself, the second part of the work includes the exploration of the effects of the trauma on the individual's sense of self and may require long-term intervention. When we discuss PTSD and trauma, we are deliberating the interaction of complex body and brain systems (see Chapter 7). Interventions such as art therapy that target a dynamic interplay of these systems, specifically supporting the stress system, show promise in addressing trauma symptoms (Hass-Cohen, Findlay, Cozolino, & Kaplan, 2015).

Conclusion

According to CNN, the care of service members in the United States has been lacking since the revolutionary war. At that time, Congress promised disabled veterans compensation; yet many veterans never received anything. In 2003, a commission reported that around 236,000 veterans had been waiting six months or more for initial or follow-up visits, "a clear indication," the commission said, "of lack of sufficient capacity or, at a minimum, a lack of adequate resources to provide the required care" (Pearson, 2014). In 2016, there were descriptions of altering wait-time data to comply with a VA mandate for primary care members to see service members within 14 days or fewer (Fisher, 2016). The report also mentions the need for more specialists, including those in mental health fields. Despite our successes, there is much we must continue to do to see that our service members are given the care they require and that it is done so in a timely manner.

As two of the major employers of military art therapists, the strides in providing the creative arts therapies that have been made at the DOD and the VA have been impressive. However, military personnel continue to be an underserved population. In the DOD during the late 1990s, there was a precipitous drop in art therapy staffing levels. As a profession, we need to advocate for making art therapy services available at all VA and DOD facilities, all medical centers and their satellite clinics, and anywhere there are vets suffering the effects of trauma. In addition, the American Art Therapy Association can continue to support the recognition, influence, and dedication of those to serve the Military and prioritize bringing those who would like to work with this population into the profession. This may entail art therapists working toward their own civil service or creative arts GS series and continuing to raise consciousness of this need with Office of Personnel Management (OPM) staff. The beginning research and research networks delineated above and the potential for public–private partnerships is much needed and required for us to proceed further in the quest of having sufficient art therapy and healthcare services for our military members.

References

Edwards, E. (n.d.). Closing the gap: Research on the impact of creative arts in military. NCCIH Research Blog. National Center for Complementary and Integrative Health. Retrieved April 5, 2017, from Populations. https://nccih.nih.gov/research/blog/creative-arts-in-military-populations.

Fisher, J. (2016, April 7). VA managers manipulated wait times in Del., other states [web newspaper]. Retrieved September 25, 2016, from http://www.delawareonline.com/story/news/local/2016/04/07/va-managers-urged-schedule-tricks-del-other-states/82755274/.

Gantt, L., & Tinnin, L.W. (2009). Support for a neurobiological view of trauma with implications for art therapy. *The Arts in Psychotherapy, 36*(3), 148–153. https://doi.org/10.1016/j.aip.2008.12.005.

Haeseler, M. (1998). Different minds, different voices. *Art Therapy: Journal of the American Art Therapy Association, 15*(2), 128–129. Retrieved April 5, 2017, from http://dx.doi.org/10.1080/07421656.1989.10758725.

Hass-Cohen, N., Findlay, J.C., Cozolino, L., & Kaplan, F. (2015). *Art Therapy and the Neuroscience of Relationships, Creativity, and Resiliency*. New York: W.W. Norton & Company. Retrieved April 5, 2017, from http://books.wwnorton.com/books/Art-Therapy-and-the-Neuroscience-of-Relationships-Creativity-and-Resiliency/.

Herman, J. (1997). Trauma and Recovery: The Aftermath of Violence – from Domestic Abuse to Political Terror. New York: Basic Books.

Howie, P., Burch, B., Conrad, S., & Shambaugh, S. (2002). Releasing trapped images: Children grapple with the reality of the September 11 attacks. *Art Therapy, 19*(3), 100–105. https://doi.org/10.1080/07421656.2002.10129401.

Inskeep, S. (2011, August 29). Where generations of soldiers healed and moved on. Retrieved April 24, 2016, from http://www.npr.org/2011/08/29/139641794/where-generations-of-soldiers-healed-and-moved-on.

Institute, WRAMCB. (2009). *Walter Reed Army Medical Center Centennial: A Pictorial History, 1909–2009*. (J.R. Pierce, M.G. Rhode, M. Gjernes, K. Stocker, C.F. Sorge, & D. Wise, Eds.) (1st edition). Washington, DC: Department of the Army.

Lande, R., Howie, P., & Chang, A. (1997). The art of crime. *American Journal of Art Therapy, 36*(1), 2–5.

Lande, R.G., Tarpley, V., Francis, J.L., & Boucher, R. (2010). Combat trauma art therapy scale. *The Arts in Psychotherapy, 37*(1), 42–45. https://doi.org/10.1016/j.aip.2009.09.007.

Libby, D., Pilver, C., & Desai, R. (2012). Complementary and alternative medicine in VA specialized PTSD programs. *Psychiatry Services, 63*(11), 1134–1136.

O'Donnell, E. (n.d.). Summit explores creative arts as healing aids in military. *NIH Record*. Retrieved April 5, 2017, from https://nihrecord.nih.gov/newsletters/2015/06_05_2015/story5.htm.

Pearson, M. (2014, May 30). The VA's troubled history [News]. Retrieved July 15, 2016, from http://www.cnn.com/2014/05/23/politics/va-scandals-timeline/index.html.

Priest, D., & Hull, A. (2007, February 18). Soldiers face neglect, frustration at Army's top medical facility. *The Washington Post*. Retrieved April 5, 2017, from http://www.washingtonpost.com/wp-dyn/content/article/2007/02/17/AR2007021701172.html.

Roy, M.J., Francis, J., Friedlander, J., Banks-Williams, L., Lande, R.G., Taylor, P., Blair, J., McLellan, J., Law, W., Tarpley, V., Patt, I., Yu, H., Mallinger, A., Difede, J., Rizzo, A., & Rothbaum, B. (2010). Improvement in cerebral function with treatment of posttraumatic stress disorder. *Annals of the New York Academy of Sciences, 1208*(1), 142–149. https://doi.org/10.1111/j.1749-6632.2010.05689.x.

Tavernise, S. (2011, July 28). An emotional ceremony as Walter Reed Army Medical Center prepares to close. *The New York Times*. Retrieved April 5, 2017, from http://search.proquest.com.proxygw.wrlc.org/docview/1620491235/abstract/F45A281A53F244E5PQ/1?accountid=11243.

Tinnin, L., & Gantt, L. (2013). The Instinctual Trauma Response And Dual-Brain Dynamics: A Guide for Trauma Therapy. Linda Gantt.

US Department of Veterans Affairs. (n.d.). About VA, mission, vision, core values & goals. (para.1). Retrieved April 5, 2017, from http://www.va.gov/about_va/mission.asp para. 1.

US Department of Veterans Affairs, Office of Research and Development. (n.d.). VA research on complementary and alternative medicine. Retrieved April 24, 2016, from http://www.research.va.gov/topics/cam.cfm.

CHAPTER 2

Psychosis, Attachment, and Trauma
Paula Howie

> All sorrows can be borne if you put them in a story or tell a story about them.
> Isak Dinesen (Karen Blixen)

Giving narrative expression to our most frightening experiences is not a unique idea. From antiquity, people have been writing about their unforgettable experiences, putting these memories into pictures and adding stories so they can be translated into a complete narrative and shared with others. There is relief in doing so, in getting personal trauma out into the world and into the light of day rather than leaving memories to be triggered by visions, sounds, smells, or having them haunt our dreams. Morgan and Johnson (Morgan & Johnson, 1995) in researching PTSD nightmares found that clients who used art versus just writing to express their nightmares reported fewer and less intense nightmares and had an improved ability to return to sleep and a reduction in startle response upon awakening. Many clinicians have found that the non-verbal brain encodes traumatic material in pictures giving rise to nightmares and that because the encoding of traumatic memories is a visual process, an arts-based approach offers a unique means by which these may come to consciousness (Byers, 1996; Howie, Burch, Conrad, & Shambaugh, 2002; Lloyd & Kalmanowitz, 1999; Roje, 1995).

Given the ubiquity of trauma, it has been apparent for much of my art therapy career that psychosis and PTSD are similar entities, part of a spectrum of responses to a traumatic event (Morrison, Frame, & Larkin, 2003). Further, "child abuse is a causal factor for psychosis and 'schizophrenia'... understanding the mechanisms by which child abuse leads to psychosis requires a genuine integration of biological and psychosocial paradigms which acknowledges that adverse events can alter brain function" (Read, van Os, Morrison, & Ross, 2005, p. 330).

Those with whom we worked in the 1980s and 1990s were often diagnosed with psychosis as well as early and recurring trauma, which affected the expression of their illness, the symptoms they experienced, and the disembodied voices they heard. These observations have been supported by subsequent studies, including one in 2002, which found that 52.3 percent of inpatients in their study met criteria for post-psychotic PTSD (Shaw,

McFarlane, Bookless, & Air, 2002). In fact, they found that the more frequent and earlier the trauma, the more difficult and intractable the illness. Others report that psychiatric populations show a higher incidence of traumatic experiences than non-psychiatric samples (Morrison et al., 2003).

It wasn't until the post-Vietnam War era that veterans lobbied the American Psychiatric Association in the 1980s leading to the diagnosis of Post Traumatic Stress Disorder (PTSD) being added to the *Diagnostic and Statistical Manual* (DSM III) (Morris, 2016). When I began working on the Inpatient Psychiatry ward at Walter Reed in 1977, trauma, not yet considered under the rubric of PTSD, was rarely mentioned in context of the many people diagnosed with schizophrenia or other psychotic illnesses. Neurophysiological research on trauma and the unique way in which traumatic memories are stored in the brain have afforded us a more basic understanding of the connection of the symptoms of trauma and psychosis. These theories have converged to focus our attention on the pervasive aspects of trauma; the effect of timing of the trauma; and whether it was experienced multiply, over time, or was a one-time occurrence. Finally, we have come to recognize the effects of attachment on the experience of trauma. Today, there is intense interest in the effect of trauma and attachment on brain functioning and development. These considerations have led to the contemplation of the overlap of symptoms between psychosis, attachment, and PTSD.

In parallel with PTSD studies, those looking at the impact of attachment have highlighted the effects of child abuse and neglect on the developing brain. If a parent is abusive and unpredictable, the child is unable to develop a strategy for getting his or her attention, reassurance, and nurturance. This leads to a view of the world as frightening and unreliable, what Herman refers to as a damaged person in a dangerous world (1997). These children are more vulnerable to psychosis and to the effects of trauma. They may be socially ostracized and their observation of the world as a frightening place makes it harder for them to experience or seek support. Herman's statement also relates to what attachment theorists call internal working models.

In order to develop a healthy identity and a coherent personality, the child must have a secure attachment (Bowlby, 1988), one that is adequate to provide a safe base to allow the child to explore and learn. Unhealthy relationships with a caregiver who is not a secure base may result in less resilient and vulnerable children. Cortina and Marrone state:

> [W]e are defining transference as the implicit and unconscious (occasionally explicit and conscious) expectations, attributions, beliefs, and attitudes that are embodied in internal working models (IWM's) of self or others (e.g. self as unworthy of love, others untrustworthy or rejecting) carried forward in development.
>
> (Cortina & Marrone, 2003, p. 27)

In order to experience the world as a safe place, one must have secure attachment and a responsive caregiver. Bowlby described developmental pathways, some of which are optimal and promote resilience, and some of which create vulnerability to life stressors (Bowlby, 1988). "The greatest deviance from an optimal pathway takes place when a child has been severely traumatized within attachment relationships that is when sexual, emotional or physical abuse occurs" (Bowlby, 1988, pp. 3, 4). Schacter described dissociated and fragmented information as part of the implicit memory system (Schacter, 1987). This material lacks temporal, causal, or logical connections and therefore intrusive traumatic memories are experienced as occurring in the present. Linear (declarative) memories of an event may become disconnected during the trauma, making it hard to describe the events in words and to integrate it as part of one's life history (van der Kolk & Fisler, 1995).

Resilience, namely the ability to recover from adverse experiences and to seek and utilize support, allows the child to develop a coherent narrative and to integrate past experiences into one's identity. However, if the child is unable to transform his or her past memories, a survival mechanism can be pre-empted to become a liability. The trauma is relived in the body and is not available to resolution. Thus children turn brain processes from learning into survival (Krystal & Neumeister, 2009).

Read, Agar, Argyle, and Aderhold found that hallucinations were significantly tied to sexual and child physical abuse (Read et al., 2003). They acknowledge that it is common for victims of sexual abuse to experience flashbacks, intrusive images, and bodily flashbacks associated with abuse years after the event. There is a wealth of research pointing to the role of traumatic life experiences in the development of psychosis (Morrison et al., 2003, p. 338). Dissociation, a hallmark of PTSD, may also be seen in psychosis through the individual's behavior and affect, from a spacy demeanor to being out of touch with reality, the latter being a classic definition of psychosis. Van der Kolk and Fisler highlight the role of disassociation as an important predictor of trauma (van der Kolk & Fisler, 1995). Ross, Anderson, and Clark suggest that there are at least two pathways to schizophrenia: an endogenously driven pathway characterized by negative symptoms (avoidance and emotional numbing) and a pathway determined by childhood trauma (Ross et al., 1994). Read concludes that it is reasonable to assume there is a relationship between childhood abuse and trauma (Read, 1997). Research, in combination with our clinical observations, highlights the strong probability that psychosis and PTSD may be similar entities, and part of a spectrum of responses to a traumatic event (Morrison et al., 2003).

Marr (personal communication, July 2012) refined the categories of universal trauma treatment to include safety, stabilization, assessment, and therapy. Safety includes a holding environment; stabilization includes helping the person regulate affect and disassociation; trauma assessment includes considering the degree of disassociation and utilizing a trauma list. Trauma therapy includes re-narration and ameliorating any disruption in the life story.

Positive emotions are important for feeling a part of and thriving in society and for resilience. Therefore, any treatment for PTSD needs to include increasing pleasant activities in order to rekindle responsiveness to rewards and to re-establish adaptive social functioning (Kashdan, Elhai, & Frueh, 2006).

As a treatment for PTSD, art therapy operates on multiple levels simultaneously, addressing immediate symptoms as well as underlying conditions that cause symptoms to persist. In the overlap between psychosis and trauma, art therapy is especially beneficial with disassociation, which occurs in both disorders. It brings grounding to individuals, compelling the client to live more fully into the present. Art therapy is successful in addressing avoidance and emotional numbing, both of which are predictors of PTSD and psychosis (Solomon, Mukulincer, & Avitzur, 1988). The American Art Therapy Association has identified four major contributions of art therapy to the treatment of PTSD which include reducing anxiety and mood disorder common to military personnel with PTSD; reducing behaviors that interfere with emotional and cognitive functioning; externalizing, verbalizing, and resolving memories of traumatic events; and reactivating positive emotions, self-worth, and self-esteem (American Art Therapy Association, n.d.).

Programs offered at Walter Reed for treating psychosis and acute psychiatric illnesses included art therapy, recreational, and horticultural therapy. These services were integrated into the daily schedule of most of those on the inpatient psychiatry service as well as those on the partial hospital program. Outpatients, such as the individual described below, who could benefit from further treatment post inpatient or partial hospital treatment, also received ongoing, long-term art therapy. The art therapist provided assessment and treatment services with a focus on fostering change and independence through the process of creation, and making struggles more manageable by expressing feelings in tangible form. Self-understanding and self-esteem were also goals of interventions provided. Artwork conveys a person's functional and developmental levels and their unique strengths and conflicts, serving as an aid in assessment and assisting the treatment team in setting up treatment goals and objectives.

Case Study

When the author first met June (pseudonym), a 35-year-old enlistee, she had been sent to the inpatient service at Walter Reed due to unusual behavior and psychotic thoughts. Although she did not experience the trauma of combat, June had found the Military to be difficult partly due to her pre-existing traumas, which made her extremely vulnerable to the stresses of military life. Her traumas include her father's physical abuse of her, her siblings, and her mother; and sexual abuse by extended family members. She was admitted to the inpatient ward, given medications, and after assessment entered into programs on the therapeutic milieu. Post release from the hospital, June received an honorable discharge with medical benefits. These benefits included being able to receive continued treatment at Walter Reed. In that capacity, the author worked with her from 1997 to 2002 in an outpatient art therapy group.

During infrequent hospitalizations, an art therapist on the acute care ward would see her. June had been given diagnoses, which included chronic schizophrenia, schizoaffective disorder, and borderline personality. With our current knowledge, she most certainly suffered from type II trauma due to her childhood physical and sexual abuse. In considering her attachment styles, it was believed she may have had different attachments to her mother and father. The attachment to her mother, who was more predictable, was probably an insecure one given her mother's own limitations and abuse. Berry, Barrowclough, & Wearden (2007) assert that attachment styles are usually stable from one generation to another. They believe attachment theory could illuminate the relative importance of childhood compared to adulthood trauma, and of trauma or negative relationship experiences involving significant others or trauma perpetuated by acquaintances or strangers. There is evidence to support a relationship between dismissing attachment and failure to report distress, and insecure attachment and less resilient or less integrative recovery styles. Many of the studies found that understanding one's attachment is vital in understanding one's relationship with the world. June's attachment to her father was most likely of a disorganized nature, as he was described as "flying off the handle" for no reason and physically abusing June and other family members.

June presents an example of how survival strategies and her internal working models, which were important when she was younger, no longer make sense to her now. Her internal world was dangerous, although her external world was not. She was happily married and had three children. Two of her children have remained functional with minimal involvement in mental health services. It is not surprising that one of her children, a daughter, has been diagnosed with schizophrenia. However, this child was able to finish high school and was thinking of attending college. When I last spoke with June, her daughter was volunteering as an aide at a nearby clinic as a receptionist.

One of the unique aspects of June was her strong belief and faith, which was a characteristic of her resilience. She felt that with faith she would endure difficult times to include hearing voices telling her to hurt herself and her family. In the end, she believed she would be protected and prevail over these voices. She produced many pictures of her voices (such as the one shown in Figure 2.1) during the time I saw her. These voices are encouraging her to stop her struggle and attain the peace of heaven and also to kill herself and her family. Voices or disassociated parts need to be engaged by the client and are treated by acknowledging them as June has done in these pictures. This begins a dialogue allowing the voice (part) to be externalized and acknowledged. June often used the relationship with the author and with group members to express her deep emotions, to acknowledge her voices, and to begin a dialogue for self-understanding. June was able to express these parts, although her pictures would sometimes show her with her family, protected by a rainbow of religion withstanding these voices. June's suicidal ideation could be monitored through her pictures, she could be asked about

Figure 2.1 Pastel drawing entitled "Angry Voices, Kill, Kill."

suicidal plans, and alternatives to these voices could be discussed. The physician could increase her medications if that was helpful. Because she accessed these voices while in a supportive environment, June was clearly helped to deal with them and she was able to continue to choose to live. In art therapy, we might see dissociation as cut off, encapsulated, unexplained, dead, or frozen parts in a picture. Indeed, there was a static quality to June's pictures as if they were stuck in time. June's pictures highlight the tendency of the verbal mind to reject the memories of the non-verbal mind as if they were something alien and had no connection to rational thinking. It is clear that art therapy can work as an integrator of verbal and non-verbal cognition, which alleviates avoidance, dissociation, and aversion to what the non-verbal mind "knows." The art therapy group served her by engendering self-reflection and self-understanding.

Pace (2009) notes creation in therapy that a "reciprocal and attuned relationship, an exchange of energy and information between minds, co-construction of an autobiographical narrative, and the establishment of an internal map of self across space and time, encourages neural integration in adult clients" (p. 17) as essential characteristics of neural integration. Hass-Cohen, Findlay, Cozolino, and Kaplan (2015) state that manipulating art media in a supportive, interpersonal context "targets sensory-emotive-cognitive processing areas of the brain that are needed for psychological transformation" (p. 5).

36 P. Howie

Figure 2.2 Pastel drawing entitled "Help! Rape!"

The picture shown in Figure 2.2 was completed when June had been in treatment for several years when she felt ready to deal with one of her most difficult traumas. Her trust in the group was paramount, enabling her to express this gruesome event and not have to relive the trauma or require hospitalization. The picture shows her "baggage" when she was raped by her uncle at 12 years old. In this depiction, June calls for help, which is a modification of the story. In actuality, her uncle took her far away from the family home and raped her in the woods. No one was around to hear her cries and she was too afraid to tell anyone about what he had done. In this picture, she brings her parents in to help her, implying that this incident is a memory and that she is able to insert protective parents who would not let this happen to her again.

Drawing makes it possible for the artist to bypass her own conscious resistance and gain access to traumatic images that are not verbally coded. Narrative drawing collects the image fragments and integrates them into the story. The therapist helps the artist identify and fill in gaps in the narrative and bring it to closure. This picture is a good example of self-regulation in therapy, and it involves creating a "good enough" narrative. Objective study of the traumatic memory, which is depicted in the art product without reliving the trauma, is essential in constructing a good enough narrative. Rankin and Taucher (2003) state that trauma-focused art therapy involves emotional, physical, and mental states, and culminates in constructing a narrative of trauma that ties together feelings, thoughts, and behaviors which can then be explored. As with other trauma therapies, they emphasized that art therapy helps to ultimately promote an integration of the trauma event into the person's life history.

When the individual tries to remember past events, she taps into those that were verbally encoded and stored in the "explicit" or "declarative" system. She may be quite unaware of the non-verbal "implicit" memory system that also holds a record of traumatic events except when they trigger a fear response or reach consciousness as dreams (Scaer, 2005). The unique ability of art to access implicit memories in the non-verbal brain relies on the visual nature of its intervention to assist in addressing avoidance or hyper-arousal (Malchiodi, 2014; Gantt & Tinnin, 2007). However, in art therapy, these memory systems may merge when the individual completes the trauma story.

Please refer to Plate 1 in the color plate section.

In this slide, titled "Gods Promises Are True", her narrative includes times when June's life was less traumatic and, once again, shows her hope and faith. She often drew fish, which she avowed as symbols of her Christian faith, and rainbows, symbols of hope. Here she is seen with a small child, perhaps the 12-year-old child inside her, protected and happy. Befriending internal states and personalizing the experience (van der Kolk, McFarlane, & Weisaeth, 1996), has increased June's self-observation, and self-reflection, allowing her adult self to acknowledge and support the ways the child tried to manage the trauma. Art therapy practitioners such as Margaret Naumburg have described having special comprehension about the minds of children and having access to primary process thinking or implicit memory (Naumburg, 1987), which becomes accessible through the window of art.

Conclusion

Art therapy gives visual substance to the "memory shrapnel" (Gantt, personal communication, July 2011) contained in those fragmented bits of recollection encoded the non-verbal brain. Both Elinor Ulman (Ulman & Dachinger, 1987) and Edith Kramer (Kramer, 1993) describe art's ability to "bypass the defenses." It allows self-regulation and can engender self-reflection and self-understanding. It is also possible to see a part of the person, which is not otherwise observable. The verbal mind is more easily defended against or hides memories it does not wish to address. These memories may be held in a Part, or may be an ego state, which can be hidden or obscured from the conscious mind. Art therapy increases the flow of information from the non-verbal brain to the verbal brain. By using images and partial images from the non-verbal brain that are given word and form and through a graphic story "telling," the verbal brain understands what has transpired. According to Gantt and Tinnin (2007), drawing is used to eliminate intrusive and arousal symptoms and to diminish numbing symptoms which is accomplished by processing traumatic memories in order to achieve narrative closure. After picturing the event in graphic form, the artist transforms the images from unfinished (seemingly present) experience to past history and disassociation is eliminated. Dissociation, which is an unconscious form of forgetting, demonstrates the disconnect between our verbal and non-verbal minds. After picturing her abuse, June's story is sufficiently complete for the verbal mind to make sense of it and to put the event in the past. Many authors have found that art therapy is a valuable treatment in the area of sexual abuse trauma and in the treatment of trauma and disassociation (Backos & Pagan, 1999; Pifalo, 2006; Powell & Faherty, 1990; Yates & Pawley, 1987).

In addition, art interventions offer many benefits to those suffering from the symptoms of psychosis and trauma. Research points to the reduction of depression, an increase of emotional expression, reduction of emotional numbing, and facilitation of a coherent trauma narrative. Art therapy introduces the verbal to the non-verbal mind by combining non-verbal images and the verbal narrative in the art product, which can then be studied and understood within a safe therapeutic environment. While in the group, June was able to tolerate her emotions and fears so that she was not overwhelmed by anxiety. Panic, a result of overwhelming emotion, implies a narrow window of tolerance. In order to withstand panic, people must have coherent stories they tell themselves or others about who they are and how they came to be. For instance, one may have been bullied in school but, instead of leaving permanent damage, the victim may have enough support and a good enough environment that she can see this as not occurring because she is a bad person but because others are behaving in a mean manner. On the other hand, this same abuse can become quickly intolerable and lead to panic when faced with similar situations without support. This can lead the person into thinking that the world is full of abusers and this is happening because she is a bad person.

Although mental illness has continued to be a part of her life much as her medical diagnosis of diabetes was, June continues to maintain her health, to work toward integration, and to resist her outmoded ways of interacting with the world. Through her resilient attitude, I am happy to report, she continues to nurture herself, and to work in therapy to come to terms with her voices, emotions, and impulses. She reports a better quality of life and that she is able to live more fully, despite some limitations. It would be great if all of her ills could be ameliorated; yet, it is testament to her faith, resilience, and optimism that she has resisted suicide and continues to have a reasonably good life that she can appreciate more day by day, and year to year.

References

American Art Therapy Association. (n.d.). Art therapy, posttraumatic stress disorder, and veterans. Retrieved from www.arttherapy.org.

Backos, A., & Pagan, B.E. (1999). Finding a voice: Art therapy with female adolescent sexual abuse survivors. *Art Therapy: Journal of the American Art Therapy Association*, 16(3), 126–132.

Berry, K., Barrowclough, C., & Wearden, A. (2007). A review of the role of adult attachment style in psychosis: Unexplored issues and questions for further research. *Clinical Psychology Review*, 27(4), 458–475. https://doi.org/10.1016/j.cpr.2006.09.006.

Bowlby, J. (1988). *A Secure Base: Parent–Child Attachment and Healthy Human Development* (Reprint edition). New York: Basic Books.

Byers, J. (1996). Children of the stone: Art therapy interventions in the West Bank. *Art Therapy: Journal of the American Art Therapy Association, 13*(4), 238–243.

Cortina, M., & Marrone, M. (2003). *Attachment Theory and the Psychoanalytic Process* (1st edition). London; Philadelphia: John Wiley.

Gantt, L., & Tinnin, L.W. (2007). Intensive trauma therapy of PTSD and dissociation: An outcome study. *The Arts in Psychotherapy, 34*(1), 69–80. https://doi.org/10.1016/j.aip.2006.09.007.

Hass-Cohen, N., Findlay, J.C., Cozolino, L., & Kaplan, F. (2015). *Art Therapy and the Neuroscience of Relationships, Creativity, and Resiliency: Skills and Practices* (1st edition). New York: W.W. Norton & Company.

Herman, J. (1997). *Trauma and Recovery: The Aftermath of Violence—from Domestic Abuse to Political Terror*. New York: Basic Books.

Howie, P., Burch, B., Conrad, S., & Shambaugh, S. (2002). Releasing trapped images: Children grapple with the reality of the September 11 attacks. *Art Therapy, 19*(3), 100–105. https://doi.org/10.1080/07421656.2002.10129401.

Kashdan, T., Elhai, J., & Frueh, B. (2006). Anhedonia and emotional numbing in combat veterans with PTSD. *Behavior Research and Therapy Journal, 44*(3), 457–467.

Kramer, E. (1993). *Art As Therapy With Children* (2nd edition). Chicago, IL: Magnolia Street Publishers.

Krystal, J. H., & Neumeister, A. (2009). Noradrenergic and serotonergic mechanisms in the neurobiology of posttraumatic stress disorder and resilience. *Brain Research, 1293*, 13–23. https://doi.org/10.1016/j.brainres.2009.03.044.

Lloyd, B., & Kalmanowitz, D. (1999). Fragments of art at work: Art therapy in the former Yugoslavia. *The Arts in Psychotherapy Special Issue: Healing Troubled Communities through the Arts, 26*(1), 15–25.

Malchiodi, C. (Ed.). (2014). *Creative Interventions with Traumatized Children (2nd edition)*. New York: The Guilford Press.

Morgan, C., & Johnson, D.R. (1995). Use of a drawing task in the treatment of nightmares in combat-related post-traumatic stress disorder. *American Journal of Art Therapy, 12*, 244–247.

Morris, D.J. (2016). *The Evil Hours: A Biography of Post-Traumatic Stress Disorder* (1st edition). Boston, MA: Eamon Dolan/Mariner Books.

Morrison, A.P., Frame, L., & Larkin, W. (2003). Relationships between trauma and psychosis: A review and integration – 7.pdf. Retrieved April 8, 2016, from http://sygdoms.com/pdf/trauma/7.pdf.

Naumburg, M. (1987). *Dynamically Oriented Art Therapy: Its Principles and Practice*. Chicago, IL: Magnolia Street Publishers.

Pace, P. (2009). *Lifespan Integration: Connecting Ego States through Time*. Eirene Imprint.

Pifalo, T. (2006). Art therapy with sexually abused children and adolescents: Extended research study. *Art Therapy: Journal of the Americn Art Therapy Association, 23*(4), 181–185.

Powell, L., & Faherty, S.L. (1990). Treating sexually abused latency age girls. *The Arts in Psychotherapy, 17*, 35–47.

Rankin, A.B., & Taucher, L.C. (2003). A task-oriented approach to art therapy in trauma treatment. *Art Therapy: Journal of the American Art Therapy Association, 20*(3), 138–147.

Read, J. (1997). Child abuse and psychosis: A literature review and implications for professional practice. *Professional Psychology: Research and Practice, 28*(5), 448–456. https://doi.org/10.1037/0735-7028.28.5.448.

Read, J., Agar, K., Argyle, N., & Aderhold, V. (2003). Sexual and physical abuse during childhood and adulthood as predictors of hallucinations, delusions and thought disorder. *Psychological Psychotherapy, 76*(Pt. 1), 1–22. https://doi.org/10.1348/14760830260569210.

Read, J., van Os, J., Morrison, A.P., & Ross, C.A. (2005). Childhood trauma, psychosis and schizophrenia: A literature review with theoretical and clinical implications. *Acta Psychiatrica Scandinavica, 112*(5), 330–350. https://doi.org/10.1111/j.1600-0447.2005.00634.x.

Roje, J. (1995). LA '94 earthquake in the eyes of children: Art therapy with elementary school children who were victims of disaster. *Art Therapy: Journal of the American Art Therapy Association, 12*(3), 237–243.

Ross, C.A., Anderson, G., & Clark, P. (1994). Childhood abuse and the positive symptoms of schizophrenia. *Hospital & Community Psychiatry, 45*(5), 489–491.

Scaer, R. (2005). *The Trauma Spectrum: Hidden Wounds and Human Resiliency*. New York: W.W. Norton & Company.

Schacter, D. (1987). Implicit memory: History and current status. *Journal of Experimental Psychology: Learning, Memory, and Cognition, 13*(3), 501–518.

Shaw, K., McFarlane, A.C., Bookless, C., & Air, T. (2002). The aetiology of postpsychotic posttraumatic stress disorder following a psychotic episode. *Journal of Traumatic Stress, 15*(1), 39–47. https://doi.org/10.1023/A:1014331211311.

Solomon, Z., Mukulincer, M., & Avitzur, E. (1988). Coping, locus of control, social support, and combat-related posttraumatic stress disorder: A prospective study. *Journal of Personality and Social Psychology, 55*(2), 279–285.

Ulman, E., & Dachinger, P. (1987). *Art Therapy in Theory and Practice* (1st edition). New York: Schocken.

van der Kolk, B., & Fisler, R. (1995). Dissociation & the fragmentary nature of traumatic memories: Overview and explatory study. *Journal of Traumatic Stress, 8*(4), 505–525.

van der Kolk, B., McFarlane, A., & Weisaeth, L. (Eds.). (1996). *Traumatic Stress: The Effects of Overwhelming Experience on Mind, Body, and Society*. New York: Guilford Press.

Yates, M., & Pawley, K. (1987). Utilizing imagery and the unconscious to explore and resolve the trauma of sexual abuse. *Art Therapy: Journal of the American Art Therapy Association, 4*(1), 36–41.

CHAPTER 3

Inpatient Treatment

Charlotte Boston and Jeanne Creekmore

Soldiers can't feel because there's no time. ... When you're in the situation, you have a job to do. The only way you can identify is if you've been there.

These were the words of a Vietnam vet who was trying to explain the difficulty he was having with the assigned art therapy group exercise of using colors and shapes to draw reactions to different feeling words. During the discussion of the artwork, he and other vets attempted to describe how identifying feelings was contrary to their training and experience as soldiers: they were taught to act, not feel, and the work in art therapy required that they do just the opposite.

The authors worked on an inpatient psychiatric ward at Walter Reed Army Medical Center on Georgia Avenue for 12 and 10 years respectively in the 1980s and 1990s. This facility closed and in 2011 all patients and staff moved to Bethesda. Prior to this move, art therapy was an integral part of the treatment milieu in the Inpatient Psychiatry Service. First, we will describe the unique culture of an inpatient ward in a military hospital and then we will explain the role of art therapy in assessing and treating patients.

Organizational Structure of Military Inpatient Setting

Working in a military hospital is a lesson in cross-cultural awareness: not just because many of its members are from different ethnic groups, but because the military itself has its own unique beliefs, customs, and language. A visitor to the inpatient ward where we worked would notice right away that some of its staff members were dressed in military uniforms that differed according to their branch of service, rank, and position. They would also most likely hear patients and staff referring to each other by rank or title; the only time first names were used was when patients addressed each other or the civilian therapists. Patients on the ward would be in hospital gowns or in street clothes; only when getting ready for discharge or transfers would they be allowed back into uniform. If the visitor had permission to observe a treatment planning conference, they would hear acronyms used in nearly every sentence that would make most communications inscrutable. For example, a patient arriving on our unit might be seeking CVL or wanting a PCS and not an MEB. (They wanted convalescence leave or a permanent change of station but not a medical board.) This guest may be wondering why this particular patient who had been laughing and joking with a peer a minute ago was now answering in two word sentences, "Yes, Sir" and "Yes, Ma'am." There is no way our visitor could have known that the patient's peer had worked with him years ago at the same duty station or that in our meeting he was reacting to the authority of the doctors and nurses, all medical officers higher in rank.

The staff itself was a mix of military and civilians with some military residents being supervised by civilian attending doctors and active duty and civilian nurses. Everyone used military time, and morning report (where staff heard the news from the night shift) started at 0730 hours every day. Military patients and staff were expected to maintain their appearance according to code; translated, this meant a certain length of hair for the men and only approved hairstyles for the women. Since the hospital was now their assigned duty station, patients were also expected to keep their rooms neat and beds made according to regular military standards. Staff was also subject to many transitions as the military members were constantly being reassigned. The biggest changes came on July 1 when a new group of residents would arrive on the ward and the process of building a working team would have to begin anew every year. These times of transition were difficult because alliances with the departing doctors were lost and new working relationships had to be rebuilt. This rupture in the ward's process was particularly noticeable if a new department chief arrived; usually that person would institute changes which would require adaptation by everyone. Outer events also had a great impact on our military staff and patients. During Desert Storm or after 9/11, it was our co-workers who left to take up new duties overseas, sometimes with temporary reservists taking their place or with the remaining staff having to cover. Collectively, these events led to a high degree of staff turnover with the result that it was usually the civilian staff members who maintained the history of the ward since they had been there the longest.

There were two inpatient wards at Walter Reed with 40 beds each and a transitional ward (for patients awaiting medical boards) that was also a part of Psychiatry for a total of 120 beds. Each inpatient ward was divided into two treatments teams that consisted of two residents, an attending doctor, nurses, a social worker, occupational therapist, art therapist, recreation therapist, and horticultural therapist. There were also psychiatric technicians, a psychologist, chaplain, drug and alcohol abuse counselors, and medical students and interns. Each team met daily for morning report and then three times a week for "Treatment Planning Conferences" (TPCs) where a patient's goals and progress would be discussed. The average length of stay was two weeks with a range of several days to several months. If a patient was awaiting a medical board they might be discharged from the unit and sent to Medical Holding Company, a housing unit on the nearby grounds. Sometimes, if their symptoms were severe, patients remained on the ward awaiting discharge and became long-term members of the therapy groups.

Both inpatient psychiatric units were locked and patients required an escort to other appointments unless they had earned the privilege of unaccompanied travel. The ward was set up with a status system that followed certain guidelines.

The ward followed a "milieu therapy" approach that focused on the importance of interpersonal relationships. Basic tenets of milieu therapy include safety, consistency, structure, and process (Young, 1992). Community meetings were held twice a week and run by patients. All patients and staff were required to attend. The purpose of the community meeting was to discuss business related to the entire community such as shared space and planned activities. Occasionally it was used to address patient-related events such as an attempted suicide or an elopement from the ward. Sometimes it included a general "check-in" that required everyone to state a goal or a feeling. For the staff it was a helpful way to gauge patients' feelings or concerns and to discern the hot topics of the moment. After the meeting, the staff would crowd into a nearby room to "rehash" the meeting and determine what concerns needed to be addressed during the day either individually or in groups.

The art therapists were required to attend staff and community meetings. Morning report was a chance to share patient artwork from recent groups or the assessment drawings from a new patient. A series of patients' work could be shown in Treatment Planning Conferences with the art therapist reporting on changes in the art, recurring themes, and concerns. There was an art therapist on each team who was responsible for leading four different types of groups (described below). Once the doctor indicated that their patient was to go to art therapy, an assessment was completed and a note put in the chart. Based on the information gathered during the assessment, the art therapist would then schedule the patient for art therapy groups. Attendance in groups was required but could be excused for other medical appointments. If a client missed too many groups, this could negatively impact their request for a status increase.

As an active member of the team, the art therapist was required to chart their observations about the patient's participation and behavior. Like other members on the team, art therapists were to pick a goal from the treatment plan and write notes addressing the patient's progress on that goal. For example, if the treatment plan identified the goal of decreasing depression, then the note might talk about the number of colors the patient used or how they covered the space on the page as indicators of their depression. In addition, the way the patient responded to certain themes could be useful, such as identifying three strengths or three sources of support. Since the treatment plans often used common goals, these authors and their colleagues created a manual that outlined art therapy objectives for problems that we often encountered with the most commonly used DSM-IV diagnoses (Major Depression, Psychosis not otherwise specified, Post Traumatic Stress Disorder, Traumatic Brain Disorder, Bipolar Disorder, Anorexia, Bulimia, Schizophrenia, Borderline Personality Disorder, Antisocial Personality Disorder, Dissociative Identity Disorder, Obsessive Compulsive Disorder). This manual helped us streamline our charting and provide ideas for treatment-related themes we could use in our art therapy groups (see e-resource).

44   C. Boston and J. Creekmore

Assessment

One of the advantages of working in a military hospital is the focus on training new residents and staff. At least twice a year, residents, staff, and chiefs would change and the process of educating the new staff would begin again. In this atmosphere, art therapists contributed to this teaching effort. The treating psychiatrists would consult art therapy to administer an art therapy assessment; these assessments were unique to our field and different from the tests given by psychologists. Every patient was subject to being assessed within 24 and 72 hours of admission by the treatment team if he or she were capable. Conducting an art therapy assessment session was our way to confirm or refute questions, a diagnosis, identify areas of strengths and weaknesses, personality traits, reality orientation, and coping strategies.

> Art therapy assessments are used by art therapists to: determine a client's level of functioning; formulate treatment objectives; assess a client's strengths; gain a deeper understanding of a client's presenting problems; and evaluate client progress. To ensure the appropriate use of drawing tests, evaluation of instrument validity and reliability is imperative.
> (Betts, 2006, p. 423)

Our assessment not only supported the treatment team's efforts to understand the soldier; it also helped us plan a course of action relevant to the problems identified in the treatment plan. We were required to match our art therapy intervention with the problem[s] identified in the treatment plan.

The art therapy assessments used in this setting had been well established in the field. During the late 1970s to early 1980s they were: the Ulman Personality Assessment Procedure (UPAP) (Ulman, 1975); the House, Tree, Person (HTP) (Buck, 1948); the Diagnostic Drawing Series (DDS) (Cohen et al. 1988, 1994); the Person Picking an Apple from an Apple Tree (PPAT) (Gantt, 2001); and the Kinetic Family Drawing (KFD) (Burns & Kaufman, 1987). The PPAT now has a rating system that was developed further following the time of our use (Gantt & Tabone, 1998). In the past we had used the House Tree Person but we as art therapists ran into conflicts with psychologists, since they used it as part of their testing protocol, so it began to be used less frequently.

It was helpful to have a variety of assessments to choose from, since our rationale for using one versus another varied based on patient, time, and available art materials. The DDS was efficient, usually shorter than Ulman, and was comprehensive in yielding information. It included three sheets of 18 × 24-inch white paper and 12 chalk pastels. In our setting, this assessment provided a mixture of concrete and abstract directives, could be administered either individually or in groups, and we always had these materials on hand. This assessment was used with patients who were depressed, psychotic, or dissociative. The UPAP included four sheets of 18 × 24-inch gray paper with Nupastels. This assessment took at least an hour and provided a very comprehensive perspective of the patient. The UPAP was often used for a broad spectrum of diagnoses and if the patient's reality orientation was relatively stable. The PPAT was used when our time was very limited, i.e., less than an hour. This assessment used one sheet of paper 8½ × 12 inches and markers, pencils, or crayons and included universally familiar subjects. The patient was asked to "Use the materials to draw a person picking an apple from an apple tree." This assessment was often used for patients who were psychotic.

Treatment

One of the earliest art therapy programs with the military population in an inpatient setting was in the 1960s at the Menninger Clinic in Topeka, Kansas, and at Bethesda Hospital in Boston, Massachusetts. WRAMC's art therapy services began around 1974 and services continue to be provided today in Walter Reed National Military Medical Center in Bethesda. At WRAMC, four main groups were offered to military psychiatric inpatients. Table 3.1 outlines these groups and related details which distinguish the groups from each other.

The Themes group focused on assessment, stabilization, and containment. Themes were very concrete to support reality orientation. This group was usually the first group which patients attended. The duration of their

Table 3.1

Group	Purpose	Population	Art Materials (and/or modality)	Structure
Assessment Group	Provides diagnostic information for treatment	Most patients or by doctor's order	Varied pending type of assessment	Small group of 4-6 or individual sessions
Themes Group	Improve safety and/or reality orientation	Patients were suicidal, psychotic or depressed, (withdrawn)	Controlled materials: pencils, markers, chalk	Most controlled art materials, structured group size 4–6
Creative Art Therapy	Explore feelings and interactions, improve self-esteem, insight oriented	Patients were stable, reality oriented, patients have the privilege of leaving the unit	Drawing materials, clay, acrylic paints or watercolors, pastels, group projects, music, movement	Loosely structured discussion encouraged, group size 6–10
Expressive Art Therapy	Encourages self-expression, self-understanding	Patients were able to leave the unit; long-term projects	Broad range	Least structured, self-directed, size: N/A

involvement varied based on their level of psychiatric stability or acuity. Patients who were psychotic or actively suicidal would attend this group until they were therapeutically stable. Often the organization of their artwork, ability to draw according to the theme, and broad use of space and color was a reliable gauge for their stabilization and readiness to move on to another group.

A sample of the themes used in these groups is as follows:

- *Assessment:* A safe place, a problem you want help with, draw yourself in the past, present, and future, draw your mood using a type of weather or landscape.
- *Stabilization and containment themes*: Create a picture of a goal and three steps toward it, create a container and place in it what you need to discard.
- *Group themes*: Self symbol, volcano, barriers, doors, create the cover for your autobiography.

Often we related the themes to holidays or to special events occurring at that time as a way of providing reality orientation. For example, the theme of "Three Wishes for Christmas" was given just a few days before that holiday with the option of using three pre-drawn squares on white paper.

An example of the use of this theme follows. This was the second group for a 28-year-old patient who had been sent to our hospital because he was having hallucinations and delusions. He decided not to use the squares and instead he drew a multicolored heart with a red outline and a bird above it; at the top is a star (Figure 3.1).

The patient explained that these symbols stood for "love, peace, and harmony. Last year we were at war and all my friends were gone … this is the phoenix rising." His comments in the group became more tangential and further from the personal as he talked, suggesting that he needed to remain in the Themes group. Notice that this picture is literally "up in the air." The concrete themes provided a safe haven for expression, structure/control, and supported improved reality orientation.

The Creative Art Therapy group or CAT group was more insight oriented and involved themes that were more abstract and focused on self-perception, problem solving, coping skills. Here a broad range of art materials were available and an incorporation of music, guided imagery, and murals or group projects. Art therapy in this group provided a bridge to communication and emotional release. It was also a method for self-reflection, visual records of memories, enhanced motor skills, and improved self-esteem and mastery.

Please refer to Plate 2 in the color plate section.

One of the exercises offered in this group was to make a mask out of paper maché using a 3-D plastic mold and acrylic paints (Figure 3.2). For our active duty military patients who were sent home during Desert Storm, this exercise was introduced as a way to talk about which emotions they showed on the outside versus what they kept on the inside. The artist of this particular mask had served three tours in Vietnam and then had several family stressors while

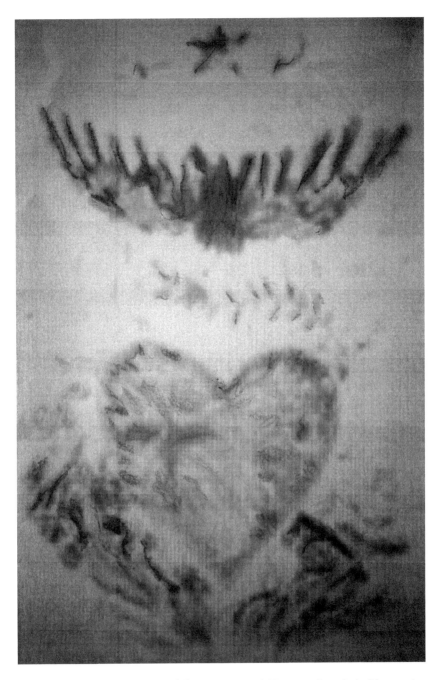

Figure 3.1 Pastel drawing entitled "Love Peace and Harmony," made in Themes Art Therapy group.

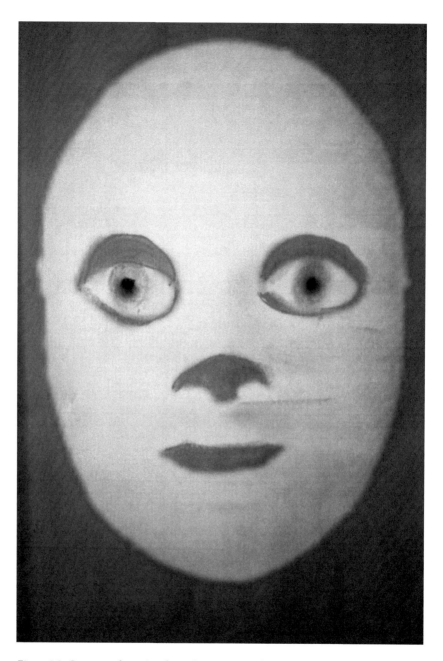

Figure 3.2 Group mask project from Creative Arts Therapy (CAT) group.

serving in the Gulf War that resulted in his threatening suicide. In CAT group he said,

> I just had my first board today—I'm still shook up ... it brought back a lot [of memories]. I haven't felt emotions for a while ... I saw the movie *Darkman* recently—that's what this mask is—in the movie, he gets his face burned ... that's all you can see—a little of his lips, nose and eyes. That's what it feels like; all these emotions coming up that I thought weren't there.

This image seems to suggest something ugly, burned, and wounded underneath the white exterior. In the group this patient talked about how, as in the movie, the character could change his face with new plastic skin, but it would only last for brief periods of time.

The Expressive Art Therapy group was more self-directed and held nearby in an art studio that used a variety of materials, including drawing supplies, acrylics and watercolors, clay, and collage. It also included a kiln where clay pieces could be fired and glazed (Figure 3.3). In the studio, group size was usually small and projects were often long term. Patients who attended usually had the opportunity to review and discuss their art folder with the art therapist before they were discharged.

Art therapy reduced anxiety and behaviors that interfered with emotional and cognitive functioning. In addition, the externalizing, verbalizing and resolving memories of traumatic events reactivated positive emotions, self-worth, and self-esteem (AATA.org, n.d. p. 2).

Figure 3.3 Art therapy studio.

Art therapists were agents for change and healing in this military setting and were able to witness change in the course of art therapy groups. Elinor Ulman (in Ulman and Dachinger, 1975) stated that the creative experience "is a way of bringing order out of chaos" and "a means to discover both the self and the world, and to establish a relation between the two" (p. 13). Howie (Howie, Prasad, and Kristel, 2013, p. 194) stated: "despite the constant changes in the environment, the art therapist provides a safe and welcoming environment which can allow change and independence to occur through the process of creation."

Summary

In retrospect, there were many lessons we learned as art therapists working on a military inpatient ward. Because we were civilians, we often found ourselves bearing witnesses to horrendous deeds that transpired in the course of our patients' duties but that were not always supported by the military structure. Some of these were listening to the experiences of war, the tragedy of "friendly fire" (when fellow soldiers are killed by mistake), and experiences of rape and suicide. We believed our function on the ward was a necessary and important one, since our use of a non-verbal modality was suited to address these traumatic experiences that were encoded in a non-verbal way. By offering choices of materials and encouraging creativity, we were also functioning in a compensatory way for what the Military lacked: a place where the individual mattered and creativity was valued over routine. It also meant that we had to be vigilant about our own self-care and consequently we set aside time for retreats where the activities therapies staff could interact together. We also attended weekly "Boundaries" meetings where all the staff on the ward were invited to participate and talk about our relationships with each other. Sometimes this involved clarifying the duties between two different groups or discussing how we felt about some event on the ward (the departure of a staff member, a suicide, a restraint of a patient). It offered space and time for staff to sort out our conflicts, give each other support, and express concerns in an honest and sometimes vulnerable way, all in hopes that it would create a better working environment on the ward.

There have been many changes in the military in the past 25 years. More recently, since 2002, more than 1.7 million US Service members have been deployed to Iraq and Afghanistan (Hosek & Martorell, 2011). In addition, many personnel, particularly soldiers and marines, face multiple deployments and have shorter times to recover between them. While the ratio of physical injury to death has improved, military members suffer long-term emotional and cognitive injuries from a variety of traumatic events, including roadside bombs, improvised explosive devices (IED), and suicide bombers. Some have had to kill enemy combatants and to handle human remains, and many have seen fellow soldiers and friends die or get injured (Hoge et al, 2004). Consequently, the "invisible wounds" of war are increasing. In a study by Tanielian and Jaycox (2008) 18.5 percent of all returning service members met the criteria for PTSD or depression and 19.5 percent reported experiencing a probable traumatic brain injury. In addition to needing more comprehensive services to treat these problems in the service member, additional support is needed for family members.

The inpatient unit is often the initial place where soldiers and family members in crisis receive mental health services. While the need for mental health services has increased, the numbers of creative arts therapists now working at military hospitals has been dramatically reduced with focused treatment being provided for veterans suffering from TBI and PTSD (Alexander, 2015). More often, one finds more community-based creative arts therapy services specifically geared to veterans and military families, such as Operation We Are Here, VetCATS Veterans Creative Arts Therapy Program on Facebook, and the 296 Project.

> In 2013, the National Endowment for the Arts expanded its arts partnership with the Department of Defense to bring art therapy to military patients at Fort Belvoir Community Hospital's satellite center of the National Intrepid Center of Excellence in Fairfax County, Virginia.
> (https://www.arts.gov/news/2013/national-endowment-arts-announces-expansion-creative-arts-therapy-program)

Based on our collective experience, inpatient practice no longer uses the milieu model and patients' lengths of stays have become shorter (CDC, 2001) due to the shift in reimbursement for mental health services. We support the continued work of our colleagues in military settings and encourage all who may be interested in working with this population to access the training and expertise to do so. It is work you will never forget and which will have a great impact on many lives.

References

Alexander, C. (2015). The invisible war on the brain. *National Geographic*, 227(2), 30–51.

American Art Therapy Association, Inc. (n.d.) Art therapy, posttraumatic stress disorder, and veterans. Retrieved April 5, 2017, from http://www.arttherapy.org/upload/file/RMveteransPTSD.pdf.

Betts, D. (2006). Art therapy assessments and rating instruments: Do they measure up? *The Arts in Psychotherapy*, 33(5), 422–434.

Buck, J. (1948). The H-T-P technique, a qualitative and quantitative scoring method. *Journal of Clinical Psychology Monograph Supplement No. 5*, 1–120.

Burns, R.C., & Kaufman, S.H. (1987). *Kinetic Family Drawings (K-F-D): An Introduction to Understanding Children Through Kinetic Drawings*. New York: Brunner/Mazel.

Centers for Disease Control (CDC). (2001, April 24). Hospital stays grow shorter. Retrieved April 5, 2017, from http://www.cdc.gov/nchs/pressroom/01news/99hospit.htm.

Cohen, B., Hammer, J., & Singer, S. (1988). The Diagnostic Drawing Series: A Systematic approach to art therapy evaluation and research. *The Arts in Psychotherapy*, 15, 11–21.

Cohen, B., Mills, A., & Kwapien, K. (1994). An introduction to the Diagnostic Drawing Series: A Standardized tool for diagnostic and clinical use. *Art Therapy: Journal of the American Art Therapy Association*, 11(2), 105–110.

Collie, K., Backos, A., Malchiodi, C., & Spiegel, D. (2006). Art Therapy for combat-related PTSD: Recommendations for research and practice. *American Journal of Art Therapy*, 23(4), 157–164.

Gantt, L. (1997). *PPAT Rating Manual: The Formal Elements Art Therapy Scale (FEATS)*. © 1997 by Linda Gantt & Carmello Tabone.

Gantt, L. (2001) The formal elements art therapy scale: A measurement system for global variables in art. *Art therapy: Journal of the American Art Therapy Association*, *18*(1), pp. 50–55.

Gantt, L., & Tabone, C. (1998). *The Formal Elements Art Therapy Scale: The Rating Manual*. Morgantown, WV: Gargoyle Press.

Hoge, C.W., Castro, C.A., Messer, S.C., McGurk, D., Cotting, D.I., & Koffman, R.L. (2004). Combat duty in Iraq and Afghanistan mental health problems, and barriers to care. *New England Journal of Medicine*, 351(1), 13–22.

Hosek, J., & Martorell, F. (2009). *How Have Deployments during the War on Terrorism Affected Reenlistment?* Arlington, VA: Rand Corporation.

Howie, P., Prasad, S., & Kristel, J. (2013). *Using Art Therapy with Diverse Populations: Crossing Cultures and Abilities*. London: Jessica Kingsley.

Tanielian, T., & Jaycox, L. (eds). (2008). *Invisible Wounds of War: Psychological and Cognitive Injuries, Their Consequences, and Services to Assist Recovery*. Arlington, VA: Rand Corporation.

Ulman, E. (1975). Art therapy: Problems of definition. In E. Ulman & P. Dachinger (Eds.), *Art Therapy: In Theory and Practice* (pp. 3–13). New York: Schocken Books.

Young, S. (1992, May). *Milieu theory: A model of inpatient psychiatric treatment*. Unpublished paper presented at Psychiatry In-service, Walter Reed Army Medical Center, Washington, DC.

CHAPTER **4**

Family Art Therapy Treatment at Walter Reed

Paula Howie

> Home is where the military sends us.
>
> (Old service member adage)

Military Family Life

Two distinctive aspects of life for the average soldier's family are being told where they must live and when they must move. Military families relocate ten times more often than civilian families, which can necessitate a move as often as every two to three years (dosomething.org, n.d.). Due to this disruption and their need to find "home" wherever they are, military families must provide their own stability and rely on the structure of the Military for support. Families provide food, shelter, and other basic needs as well as assist in their members' continued emotional growth and development from childhood through adulthood. The military family must deal with normal family development and life cycle changes (Carter & McGoldrick, 1989) as well as accommodate the unique requirements of their military culture.

Mary Wertsch (2011) describes the Military as a warrior culture. The military family often has an authoritarian organization that extends to the rules that govern the home; the necessity of mobility results in isolation and alienation from both civilian communities and, most importantly, extended family; and placement out of country, in compounds usually walled off from the outside culture, lead to "an oddly isolated life, one in which it is possible to delude oneself that one is still on American soil" (Wertsch, 2011, p. 330). Also unique to this culture are the two subcultures of the officer and enlisted ranks, each with very different lifestyles. In addition, each service branch brings its own culture and pride to the workplace. Each specializes in different contexts of battle (land, sea, sky) and each operates different lengths of deployment, ranging on average from 6 to 15 months (Huebner, n.d.).

Angela Huebner (n.d.) also discusses the "warrior ethos." The military ethos relies on strength, cunning, and the ability to successfully confront challenge. Service members do not want to appear weak by asking for help. This prohibition applies to those in charge as well as lower ranking soldiers. No one wants to be considered the "weakest link" and many believe their families to be a direct reflection on them (Huebner, n.d.). This puts one in an untenable position, especially if mental healthcare is sought. Therapists must be aware of these viewpoints in order to address them if they emerge during the course of treatment.

Knowledge of the military must include an understanding of the importance of the military mission, which has "historically been perceived as requiring a total commitment to the military. ... This is the very essence of the concept of military unit cohesion" (Martin & McClure, 2000, p. 15). This includes a felt sense of mission to make the world a safer place and constant preparation for disaster, i.e., war. Martin and McClure state that the conditions of military family life, "including long and often unpredictable duty hours, relatively low pay and limited benefits, frequent separations, and periodic relocations ... remain the major stressors of military family life" (2000, p. 3).

In this setting, the family art therapy program endeavors to foster change and independence in each participant through the process of working together to identify common issues and to help resolve them. The therapist must be aware of the unique tasks of the Military and understand that parental absence makes adults unavailable for the big moments in their children's lives; thus such important events as entering school, the prom, the big football game, the dance recital, the drama production, the gymnastics meet, or high school graduation, which are ordinarily seen as positive events, can become stressors, putting undue strain on the family unit. They must also have a grasp of normal family developmental milestones such as becoming a couple, and making space for children, family with latency-aged children, etc. (Carter & McGoldrick, 1989). Because the family is seen together in family art therapy, much of what is unique to the military family can be normalized. Sometimes the family will be stuck in a developmental shift and not be able to move forward. At other times, when there is a premature loss of a family member, among the most difficult of all family issues, the art therapist is obliged to witness the remaining member's pain, to help stabilize the family structure, and to allow the family to plan the next steps to move forward (Howie, Burch, Conrad, & Shambaugh, 2002).

Beginnings: Family Therapy and Family Art Therapy

Following World War II, there was an increased interest in treating families. This is not surprising, as the end of the war coincided with the changing roles of women. Women had served as heads of their households and had maintained vital jobs outside the family home. The desegregation of the Military in 1948 culminated in altering concepts such as race and gender. Most importantly, there was a great need to assist with the re-entry into the civilian life of a generation of traumatized soldiers as they tried to accommodate and fit into peace time society . Even with conservative estimates of 20 percent of returnees having PTSD, this is a staggering number of returning vets. As well as individual and family system dynamics, various forces still affect families, including multi-generational, cultural, and societal influences.

In a unique family context, one must integrate systematic factors into effective clinical intervention skills and culturally sensitive treatment plans. As the links between secure attachment and the impact of stress upon evolving brain development have become more apparent, we have come to view individual growth as functioning within the context of relationships. Individuals are part of a larger, complicated system of early familial connections, which influence brain development and functioning in later life. "The individual patient is being viewed from a relational perspective, in terms of the early contacts with important others in his or her life and the emotional roles the patient has assumed within the family" (Singer, Klein, & Bernard, 1992, p. 16).

Family therapy has its roots in social work, anthropology, systems theory, and psychoanalytic psychotherapy, and developed around the same time as art therapy. In my first year at Walter Reed, I joined a multidisciplinary family therapy seminar held by the Social Work Department. This was a large training seminar with military and civilian participants from across the region, which met monthly from September to June. The seminar covered all aspects of thinking about family interventions and what were at that time current schools of thought. When I worked in the Inpatient Service, my fellow art therapists and I tried to see as many families as time would allow. Sometimes nursing or psychiatry staff were included as co-therapists or as observers. At one point, the Service Chief, a Psychiatrist, and I offered a multi-family art therapy group. Family art therapy was offered on the Inpatient Psychiatry ward if the family was from the DC area. Many were from other areas and their families were not available for treatment. However, when their families came to visit, we would often make time to see them. This always proved an invaluable source of information; they could be a resource and support, or sometimes the source of the problem.

Hanna Kwiatkowska worked with families at National Institutes of Health (NIH) and proposed her family art evaluation (FAE) intervention after identifying the need for a comprehensive evaluative art assessment with this population. Due to the psychosis of a family member, it was difficult to get information verbally. She also discovered that art was a great help with younger children and that oftentimes families would act out their problems in the session. Hanna taught at the George Washington University and I was in one of her first family art therapy classes. In the second semester of this class she required two students acting as co-therapists to conduct an FAE and write up a volunteer family from Walter Reed. The first time I ever met with a family using art was in a class that was held at the child psychiatry clinic in Forest Glen, MD. This was several years before I was employed at Walter Reed and may have influenced my recognizing the FAE as a great resource for the families I was to see there.

Because of the length of the FAE, Barbara Sobol (Sobol & Williams, 2001) began to use a modified version of the FAE in which the family draws five pictures. The five art tasks are presented in the following order: a free theme drawing; a family portrait done as an abstract or a representational drawing; a scribble warm-up exercise and individual scribble drawing; a drawing developed by the whole family from a second scribble drawing; and a final free-theme drawing. The family was given 18 × 24-inch white drawing paper presented on easels and boxes of 12 pastels as well as fine- and medium-line black markers with which to draw. The number of drawings and information gleaned from these pictures and statements about them is always helpful in addressing family concerns and in deciding upon a course of treatment. However, with larger families the evaluation could be further modified to include a free choice picture, an abstract or realistic two- or three-dimensional family portrait, and a family mural. As the evaluation progressed, each family member is asked to briefly describe their artworks and may ask others about theirs. After the session, if the family is available, they are usually scheduled for a follow-up so that the therapists may have time to study the drawings, the family may have more time to process the drawings, and to offer input into further treatment. The case study which follows details a family art therapy intervention.

Impact of Early Trauma and Lack of Validation: Kathy and Her Family

Kathy was in her late forties when she began attending the outpatient art therapy group. She was an accomplished administrator, parent, and wife. She was married to a service member who had recently retired from active military duty and who continued to work for the Military as a civilian mechanic. While on active duty, he had been deployed. Often military families experience the absence of a significant member through deployment, a major stressor for them. About one-third of spouses, who are usually younger than 35 and 95 percent female, suffer from at least one mental health diagnosis. This trend is slightly higher for those whose husbands are deployed (dosomething.org, n.d.). As was common, her husband's absence had a negative impact upon Kathy and her children. Most children are concerned about their parent's deployment. Thirty-seven percent of these children reported that they seriously worry about what could happen to their deployed caretaker (Martin, 2012).

Kathy was diagnosed with major depression and borderline personality disorder. She was intermittently suicidal. A major factor in her depression was that Kathy's father had sexually abused her for years during her early and late adolescence. Kathy was the oldest child and the only female. Kathy's father died of alcoholism when she was still a teenager and, as one might expect, Kathy was furious with him. Unfortunately, after his death, when she got up the nerve to tell her mother and five brothers of her abuse, she was never believed. They accused her of being overly dramatic or exaggerating her memories.

She decided to seek out treatment at this time because a youth minister had seduced her youngest daughter. Kathy had reported this person and, to her chagrin, nothing had been done by the minister or by the bishop. As this was in essence a recapitulation of the lack of belief by her family of her abuse, Kathy became upset and suicidal. Following her hospitalization for suicidal ideation, Kathy was in the long-term outpatient art therapy group. Kathy often drew pictures of monsters and duality, including the light and dark, positive and negative, and good and bad parts of her. She would often try to contain her suicidal feelings and use her creativity to render and validate her feelings, whatever they might be. Sometimes, her art contained very graphic suicidal thoughts. This picture, in response to a tree that symbolizes you, has several unusual aspects (Figure 4.1). The middle of the tree shows a huge hole, sometimes associated with trauma (Wadeson, Durkin, & Perach, 1989) and the branches of the tree almost appear to be hands, making it anthropomorphic. The right part of the tree is green yet losing its leaves, making even the "healthy" part seem sick. The middle and left sides show white branches leading to black ones. The white part holds her intellectual pursuits and some of the areas in which she feels she has been successful. In the black part there are several items related to suicide and self-destructive thoughts, such as a noose, alcohol, and a glue gun. When she drew this picture, Kathy was having a difficult time with nightmares and PTSD symptoms due to family of origin and work stressors. Although not actively suicidal when this was drawn, we can see dissociated aspects of herself, her ego states, or parts. This picture shows how she would dissociate at stressful times, and how her sense of wholeness could fragment. Through externalizing her feelings in her art, Kathy would often attempt to regain a sense of wholeness and perspective so that she might better understand her demons. Kathy received individual therapy from her psychiatrist and individual art therapy when she was feeling at her worst. After seeing her in the outpatient group for about a year,

Figure 4.1 Tree as symbolic of self from group therapy.

it was decided by the treatment team that her family should be seen for family art evaluation and therapy in order to find out whether the family understood the depth of Kathy's illness; to assess the effect of Kathy's depression on them especially as it affected her children; and to ascertain if they might be a source of strength and assistance with her debilitating depression.

Family Art Therapy

The family art evaluation included Kathy, her husband Martin, and two daughters, Shelia and Laura. Her adoptive son was grown up and living in another area. A nurse who was familiar with Kathy's case, having worked with her on the transitional ward 53, acted as a family co-therapist. During their evaluation, they were willing to explore their feelings and to discuss issues with one another. Her husband, although tentative and concerned, appeared reluctant to be present when Kathy was hurting, fearing that he would make her depression worse by his intervention or be unable to diminish her depression if his statements were unintentionally inflammatory.

The week after having completed the FAE, my co-therapist and I met with Kathy, Martin, and Laura. Shelia had to work and was unable to attend. As we looked at all the pictures from the FAE which were pinned to the wall, Kathy seemed less depressed. Laura played an active part, speaking about wanting her "old" mother back, the one who was not depressed, and yet she was realistic in knowing her mother had changed. Kathy began to speak of her wish to please her mother and her determination to do this in spite of the fact that she never could. Kathy wept at one point when talking about the reality of her wishes and her hope of changing the reality of her mother. Martin said that this was the first time he had realized the impact of this wish and expectation upon Kathy, especially since she was so emotional. Both her husband and her daughter talked about unrealistic expectations: "you're a slave mom" when Kathy visits her mother. Laura also said she (grandmother) "has to live her own life, you can't live her life for her." Martin described his passivity and his reluctance to intervene between Kathy and her mother's relationship. He understood mother-in-law's hard life raising six children without a father. Kathy discussed her depression and not wanting to tell her family when she feels bad. Her daughter told her mother not to wear a mask even if she was depressed. Both husband and daughter affirmed they would try to be more alert to Kathy's mood and to check on her when she might be feeling bad.

Kathy, her husband, and their oldest daughter came in for the next session. Laura was absent due to a soccer game. Shelia was angry with Kathy because she was always telling others what their father was angry about by acting as a go-between. Her daughter said she wanted her to stop playing that role. Martin was quiet during much of this intense discussion but, when asked, he said there were both good and bad parts to Kathy playing this role for him. It felt good to have three people rather than two interacting, but he also believed he could deal directly with his children. The therapists normalized this in terms of the military experience in that Martin had been away in the past during deployment or working long hours, when Kathy had to be in charge. This helped Sheila to feel hopeful about this issue in that it had some basis in their reality and it might be open to being changed.

The couple came in with their youngest daughter for the next session. A discussion of the goals behind seeing their family as a unit ensued, and they were asked to draw a picture about a problem they were working on. Martin drew a picture of Kathy going uphill from the home of her family of origin to her current home (Figure 4.2). Kathy is depicted three times in different colors (pink, orange, and blue) to symbolize her development and maturity. Martin talked more during this session than in any previous ones, saying that his physician had told him to be more active with Kathy. Kathy's husband became progressively more and more active and tried more valiantly to help Kathy with her issues when she was around her mom. Martin was worried about Kathy's lack of progress. He asked questions about depression and why it is taking her so long to get better. Kathy drew a picture of herself under the weight of hopelessness, fear, sadness, despair and honesty referring to her abuse (Figure 4.3). She spoke of how it was difficult to tell her family what she is going through. She cried when Martin explained his picture because she realized once again how the family was affected by her illness. Laura painted a picture of a volcano, saying she was angry but did not see her mother that way. We talked about these pictures for several sessions, using them as a way to talk to the family, to illuminate communication patterns, to discuss how anger is expressed and received, and to consider how they can help one another. These pictures proved to be insightful and full of rich symbolism. At the end of our work together, we proposed that Laura see the art therapy intern for individual sessions, as she is the most vulnerable to Kathy's pulling away into her depression.

Figure 4.2 "Life's Baggage" drawn in family art therapy session.

60 P. Howie

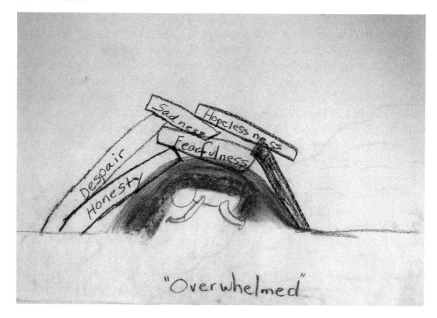

Figure 4.3 "Overwhelmed" drawn in family art therapy session.

Post the family intervention, which lasted a number of months, Kathy continued in the outpatient group. This picture shows one of the issues she spoke of often during family art therapy. It is a picture about the relationship between Kathy and her mom (Figure 4.4). This was drawn during group art therapy showing Kathy and her mother with a minefield between them. Kathy shows herself separated from her mother by many land-mines, depicting the lack of safety and personal threat that exists in relationship with her mom. It also speaks to an insecure attachment, full of fears, and lacking a strategy for getting the love that she needs from her mother. One cannot easily maneuver around those land-mines.

Kathy still grieved that she could not please her mother and that she was the bad one, always trying to do better. Both her children and husband had talked about this in the family intervention. Melanie Klein (Singer, Klein, & Bernard, 1992) postulated the idea of projective identification, which is an important concept for beginning family therapists. It describes our earliest intersubjective experience and basically holds that negative traits and emotions (which are unbearable for the person) and some positive ones are projected onto another person who then accepts these projections as part of their own personality make-up. It seemed clear to the treatment team that Kathy's mother had projected onto her all the angry, self-deprecating, and fearful feelings she could not bear and that Kathy had identified with these feelings. However, Kathy had also identified as intelligent and successful. Transgenerational trauma, as described by Fraiberg, Adelson, and Shapiro (1975), points out the impact upon our

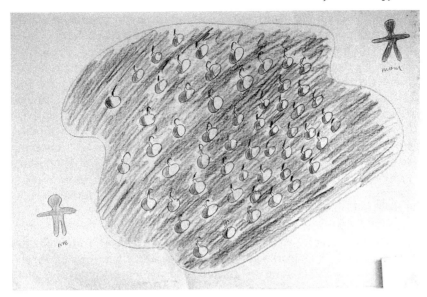

Figure 4.4 Drawn during group art therapy showing Kathy and her mother with a minefield between them.

parenting styles of the "ghosts," or parental introjects, from the past that we must confront as parents. Kathy, who was open to her children's feelings, believed their experience, and endeavored to protect them from harm, provided a markedly different childhood for them than the one she had endured.

Unfortunately, Kathy became ill with stage 4 stomach cancer the following year. The Adverse Childhood Experiences (ACE) study (Feletti, 2002) postulates that childhood trauma is more common than expected and that the traumas have a profound effect on adult health and well-being. Someone who had been sexually abused frequently, as Kathy had, is much more vulnerable to the effects of trauma on physical health. Childhood trauma has been shown to shorten lives by as much as 20 years. I remember vividly the group session in which Kathy discussed her diagnosis of advanced cancer, saying that she felt stupid that she had been suicidal when all she wanted now was to live. This allowed others in the group to think about how fleeting suicidal thoughts could be and that if we feel suicidal one day, we may feel differently the next. Kathy stayed in the group until it ended in 2002 when I left Walter Reed. She worked to enjoy what life was left to her and to spend time with those closest to her. Her family supported Kathy with her wish to have more distance and autonomy from her family of origin.

Conclusion

When one member is hospitalized, has experienced multiple traumas, and manifests deep depression, as Kathy had, we must assume that there is a profound effect on the family. When there is a legacy of trauma, it may be carried on through the generations. Family therapists such as Murray Bowen (1993) have noted the generational transmission of emotional baggage and have designed genograms as a way of tracing the intergenerational transmission of undeclared family problems. In addition, the groundbreaking epigenetic research done by Kellerman (2013) and others has altered our understanding of the costs of trauma for the next generation. His work with the children of Holocaust survivors shows that the trauma of parents may be carried in our genes through the generations. This has dramatically altered our concept of what is health as we endeavor to understand how a system of interlocking relationships drives the life of a family. Family art therapy provides a way to amend some of the effects of trauma, adversity, and military lifestyle stressors on the family and to understand their generational impact. With treatment, the physical consequences of trauma can be ameliorated; and family members can be helped to accept, to see the traumatic event in the past, and to move on with their lives. When working with military members, family treatment can be one of the most important and essential interventions in the art therapist's treatment regimen.

References

Bowen, M. (1993). *Family Therapy in Clinical Practice*. Lanham, MD: Jason Aronson. Retrieved April 5, 2017, from https://www.amazon.com/Family-Therapy-Clinical-Practice-Murray/dp/1568210116

Carter, B., & McGoldrick, M. (1989). *Changing Family Life Cycle: A Framework for Family Therapy* (2nd edition). Boston, MA: Prentice Hall College Division.

dosomething.org. (n.d.). *11 Facts about Military Families*. Retrieved April 4, 2017, from https://www.dosomething.org/facts/11-facts-about-military-families.

Feletti, V. (2002). The relation between adverse childhood experiences and adult health: Turning lead into gold. *The Permanente Journal, 6*(1), 44–47.

Fraiberg, S., Adelson, E., & Shapiro, V. (1975). Ghosts in the nursery: A psychoanalytic approach to the problems of impaired infant–mother relationships. *Journal of the American Academy of Child & Adolescent Psychiatry, 14*(3), 387–421.

Howie, P., Burch, B., Conrad, S., & Shambaugh, S. (2002). Releasing trapped images: Children grapple with the reality of the September 11 attacks. *Art Therapy, 19*(3), 100–105. http://doi.org/10.1080/07421656.2002.10129401

Huebner, A.J. (n.d.). Advice to the therapists working with military families. NCFR. Retrieved June 10, 2016, from https://www.ncfr.org/ncfr-report/focus/military-families/advice-therapists.

Kellermann, N.P. (2013). Epigenetic transmission of Holocaust trauma: Can nightmares be inherited? *The Israel Journal of Psychiatry and Related Sciences, 50*(1), 33–39.

Martin, J.A., & McClure, P. (2000). Today's active duty military family: The evolving challenges of military family life. In *The Military Family: A Practice Guide for Human Service Providers* (pp. 3–24). Westport, CT: Praeger.

Martin, R. (2012, May 27). Military children act out: Performing "deployment." *NPR.org*. Retrieved April 5, 2017, from http://www.npr.org/2012/05/27/153812436/children-act-out-performing-deployment.

Singer, D.L., Klein, R.H., & Bernard, H.S. (Eds.). (1992). *Handbook of Contemporary Group Psychotherapy: Contributions from Object Relations, Self Psychology, & Social Systems Theories*. Madison, CT: International Universities Press.

Sobol, B., & Williams, K. (2001). Family and group art therapy. In J.A. Rubin (Ed.), *Approaches to Art Therapy: Theory and Technique* (2nd edition, pp. 261–280). Philadelphia, PA: Routledge.

Wadeson, H., Durkin, J., & Perach, D. (Eds.). (1989). *Advances in Art Therapy* (1st edition). New York: John Wiley.

Wertsch, M.E. (2011). *Military Brats: Legacies of Childhood Inside the Fortress*. St. Louis, MO: Brightwell Publishing, LLC.

CHAPTER 5

Group Art Therapy: The Evolution of Treatment and the Power of Witness

Paula Howie

>There is no greater agony than bearing an untold story inside of you.
>(Angelou, 2015)

Early in his career, Harry Stack Sullivan appreciated that humans are by nature social beings whose sense of self develops in relationship to one another. In order to become healthy adults we must be validated, accepted, understood, and witnessed by members of our family or of our community. We need to tell our story, as Maya Angelou advises, so that we may be appreciated and confirmed. "Groups are often characterized by intense and personal relationships. This is vital in that personality is almost entirely the product of interaction with other human beings" (Sullivan & Perry, 1974). Our human longing for emotional contact is fundamental to maintaining a sense of personal worth and in defining the meaning of our existence (Burgo, 2012).

Groups teach us about coping with personal and existential factors in life such as being responsible for our choices and that death is a reality of living. Surely war brings home in an undeniable way the importance and brevity of life, the inevitability of death, and the need for the group to provide support, shared history, and common purpose. Since there is strength in numbers, when young men and women band together, there is an almost magical sense of omnipotence that, in the group member's mind, makes him or her invincible. As Daniel Siegel (Siegel, 2010) states, "I" becomes "we." For Siegel, "we" is the culmination of good mother–child interaction and of bearing witness to another's experience. Witnessing becomes a way of processing our life stories, of supporting others, and of providing relief from repressed emotions. One must be mindful and open to the therapeutic relationship however it may develop. Witness, when it is a part of the group experience, allows the person, through another member's empathy, attunement, and mirroring, to feel that he or she was understood in a profound, felt way.

Albert Glass, a WRAMC psychiatrist (in Joellenbeck, Russell, & Guze, 1999), has stated, "perhaps the most significant contribution of World War II military psychiatry was recognition of the sustaining influence of the small combat group or particular members thereof, variously termed 'group identification,' 'group cohesiveness,' 'the buddy system,' and 'leadership'"(p. 26). World War II also helped engender the seminal work of Wilfred Bion, a British psychiatrist, supervisee of Melanie Klein, and military veteran. Bion departed from Klein and Freud's ideas to study large group dynamics. He asserted that in every group two groups are actually present: the work group and the basic assumption group. According to Bion, there are three basic assumptions: dependency, fight–flight, and pairing. The dependency group needs to have members protected by an omniscient and idealized leader so that the group remains passive. In order to preserve itself, the fight–flight group must either flee or be aggressive and fighting. In the pairing group that has met for the purpose of reproduction and two people carry out the work of the group while others remain attentive yet silent. When a group adopts any one of these basic assumptions, it interferes with the task the group is attempting to accomplish (Bion, 1991).

Probably the best-known and most comprehensive discussion of the curative factors in groups and group therapy has been offered by Irving Yalom (1995), an existential psychiatrist whose seminal work provides a classic template for the healing components of groups. The widely researched healing properties of groups include support, instilling hope, universality, altruism, and cohesiveness (Yalom, 1995). Other curative aspects of groups include catharsis and, most importantly, corrective recapitulation of the primary family group (Yalom, 1995). In other words, the group stands in for one's original family which was unsuccessful and gives the opportunity to relive and re-experience intimacy and strong emotions in a safe environment. Groups provide learning by imparting information and imitative behavior (identification, modeling), and didactic instruction about mental health and mental illness, advice, suggestions, etc. Observing another in therapy is helpful and more important in early stages of the group and allows the client an opportunity to experiment with a new behavior. Psychological aspects include insight, interpersonal learning, and existential awareness. The person learns how he or she behaves in the world, what creates his or her core.

While working at Walter Reed, it was helpful to think in terms of Yalom's aspects of group when the group was functioning well and would be considered a "working" group. When there were disruptions such as suicidal ideation, anger displayed between group members, absences, or there was dissension in the group, it was helpful to remember Bion and his basic assumption groups. There were verbal disagreements within the group, which seemed to be fight-and-flight in quality, and there were times when the group was dependent on one person to provide guidance and healing. There were times when pairing was evident.

Art Therapy Groups

Art therapy groups use the potency of group dynamics and art in conjunction with assessment, group development, and growth of its members. Edith Kramer (1990, 2001) worked in groups with children whose emotional issues such as abuse and neglect caused them to be placed in residential or special education settings for at least part of their education until they were able to be returned to the regular classroom. What we learn from reading her descriptions of her work with groups of very disturbed children and guiding their development is that a good outcome is difficult to obtain. Kramer kept in touch with some of the children she saw at Wiltwick School, following their progress into adulthood (see the case studies of Angel and Christopher) and was able to ascertain how the interventions she provided helped. Judith Rubin (1978) discusses treatment in groups and family dyads in her book on child art therapy.

Katherine Williams and Tally Tripp (in J.A. Rubin, 2016) describe working in groups with and without themes. They help us consider when using themes is appropriate. Although a list of potential themes has been delineated elsewhere (Liebmann, 2004; Kim, Kirchhoff, & Whitsett, 2011; Howie, Prasad, & Kristel, 2013), my list of favorites includes a tree as symbolic of yourself, weather as an indicator of your mood, door to my future, bridge to my past and to my future, volcano showing how the individual handles anger and aggression, and mask making using the outside and inside of the mask to portray how I appear to others and how I feel inside. Some examples of these themes follow and may also be found in the e-resource.

Walter Reed Outpatient Art Therapy Group

Jeanne Creekmore and Charlotte Boston describe inpatient groups offered at Walter Reed in Chapter 3. In the inpatient setting there was no consistent group membership, as each group was unique due to patient turnover. Themes were used for the more acutely impaired patients who were seen there. The art therapist must be prepared for anything, including members who were actively hallucinating and the group's unique gestalt. I recall one time on the acute care ward when I was conducting a themes group. The group was held in the dayroom on the fifth floor of the facility, which was ten stories above ground level. After the theme was presented to the group and the members began to draw, a window washer appeared outside of the window. Some members gasped, thinking they might be hallucinating. I did a double take myself as this was something we did not see every day. It was very reassuring to them when we decided that there was indeed a person washing the windows outside and that he was walking on a ledge, which was not visible from where we were sitting. We all walked over and waved to the man who was washing windows.

As part of the development of the activities therapy program, art therapists provided services to outpatient individuals and groups in which the clients were seen over long periods of time. Although inpatient work was always interesting, we found there was a degree of burnout, which was occurring when staff worked exclusively on the inpatient service where patient turnover is constant and the ability to see development and change is more limited. In the outpatient groups or by working with an individual in the outpatient setting, the staff was able to experience the joys and trials of longer term work. In contrast to the inpatient service groups, the art therapist had the option of adding clients with more ego strength to those with less in order to have a more balanced milieu. Some of the case examples which follow demonstrate the effectiveness of having a range of emotional problems and ego strength.

Although suicidality is covered in the next chapter, I must mention the lethality of the group members, many of whom had weapons in their homes and were trained to use them. This could be a difficult problem for the therapist. Sometimes, members who expressed suicidal ideation during a group session were escorted to the emergency room. Although the group would routinely act as a buffer to suicidal feelings, group members could provide a corrective family experience or, on rare occasions, they could make the feelings worse. A group member could be scapegoated when the fight–flight group emerged. Part of the challenge was that the art therapist did not know until the group began which way the emotional tone might go.

I am convinced from my experience and after speaking with my colleague Katherine Williams (personal communication, April 2016) about an ongoing group she and a colleague convene weekly that deep understanding and metamorphosis is possible and occurs in groups where the therapists are attuned to the individual needs of their clients and can model supportive and compassionate behavior. The group I will describe was sometimes structured with themes being brought in or arising from the process. Each person benefitted in their own unique way which often turned out to be a reflection of what they brought to the group.

Case Studies

Alicia was in her mid-forties when she began attending the long-term art therapy outpatient group. She remained in the group for over seven years until it terminated in 2002. She was a non-commissioned officer in the Army. After 20 years of service she decided to retire and pursue other career interests. One of the issues she struggled with in the group was her abusive husband whom she had met in the service. After several years in the group, her 12-year marriage dissolved. She mourned this loss and received much support from other group members, many of whom had been divorced and/or abused in their marriages. During the stress of the dissolution of her marriage, she was intermittently depressed and suicidal. There were others in the group who expressed suicidal feelings. One member in particular, Debby, had attempted suicide once and threatened it several times. She was a former Military Police non-commissioned officer whom I had escorted to the emergency room (ER) on several occasions. Once, because she was so suicidal in group and left before I could take her to the ER, I was forced to call the sheriff in the town in which she lived, who knew her well, to ask him to send a deputy to her house to have her surrender her guns.

When someone was actively suicidal or was having a difficult time, group members would notice but not necessarily interact with them. They would usually respect one another's feelings and listen to their pain. On this particular day, when Alicia was having a difficult time, you can imagine everyone's surprise when Debby, who never said anything to anyone about their suicidal feelings, made Alicia a card which acknowledged her feelings and hoped that she felt better soon (Figure 5.1). When this occurred, I was reminded of the rationale for having a group rather than meeting individually. In sharing their problems, group members could instill hope in their fellow members, in this case hope came from Debby who was probably more suicidal at any given time than anyone else in the group. Debby's altruism also helps her feel more connected to Alicia. If she can help Alicia, perhaps she can help herself. This demonstrates some of the forces acting upon the members such as feelings of warmth, the feeling that they belong, are valued, and are unconditionally supported by group members. The group gave its members the opportunity to relive and re-experience intimacy and strong emotions in a safe environment. It was no coincidence that these women were from similar ranks and had comparable abuse histories. These characteristics are also apparent in a combat unit where the members wear uniforms to tell those in the group from outsiders. They share a commitment, and show mutual support to never leave a comrade behind.

Harry was a high-ranking retired army officer. He had been assigned as an intelligence officer in the Middle East and came with a great deal of knowledge and wisdom about other cultures and parts of the world. He had been diagnosed with a rare type of leukemia which was life threatening. He had lived a long

Figure 5.1 Debby's card for Alicia.

time with this illness and was proud of how he was able to survive, despite others having succumbed to the illness in much less time than he. He was in his early seventies when he began to attend the group and at times he was the only male in the group. Despite this, he said he felt a kinship and understanding from this group, which he had not felt elsewhere or in other settings. Harry would often draw obstacles which would get in his way and he would use cognition to address his illness, fear of future debilitation, and the existential questions about death which one faces with a serious illness. One day, Harry arrived at the group saying that he wanted to draw his lifeline. He produced this picture with colored markers in which he shows a multicolored shape on the top line which reaches to the line marked 80. He said this symbolized his wish to live until he was that age.

Please refer to Plate 3 in the color plate section.

However, he added another line below this one, and was never clear about why he had done so. He said it was his current age, but he was in his early seventies and this line stopped at around the age of 75. Harry remained in the group for several years, adding a great deal to the group with his knowledge and experience. He had a wonderful way of respecting others and helping them to think through problems. Several years after he terminated from the group, I was called to see Harry on the cancer ward where he had been admitted. He was in good spirits but knew he had not long to live. His beloved wife was at his side when he died at age 75 with the same grace with which he had lived. Although this picture has been put away for a couple of years, I wondered, after I had gone to see him that last time on the ward, if Harry's hand, body, and mind had known in that group several years earlier when he was likely to die. Clearly, his second lifeline turned out to be the most accurate account of the time left to him.

Mary Lou was a group member for three years, after which she felt well enough to return to work. Her husband was an enlisted man in the Navy. She was in her early forties when she began treatment. Her history included having been involved in an abusive relationship with a boyfriend for four years beginning at age 13. She was married to a different man when she was in her twenties and, after two decades of marriage, she and her husband had never consummated their marriage. Because of this, she felt she was being punished for her early years with her abusive boyfriend. Mary Lou was diagnosed with borderline personality disorder and would also most certainly have been diagnosed with Type II trauma had trauma been a prevalent diagnosis at the time. She had significant suicidal thoughts and ideation, and talked frequently of the dead person within her. She was quite articulate about her self-mutilation and its meaning in her life. She frequently burned herself with a glue gun and cut herself with razor blades. She described the benefits of this behavior as lessening her emotional pain by refocusing on physical pain, distracting her from suicide by making her emotional pain more tolerable, and allowing her to be punished. I recall that during one group there was a graphic discussion of how to use art to stop this behavior. Others in the group were using markers

70 P. Howie

and drawing on their skin rather than burning or cutting themselves, which offered her an alternative to self-mutilation.

Since she described the dead person inside of her, an example of dissociated parts is demonstrated in the following pictures and shows another way to access this pre-conscious material. Toward the end of treatment, she was drawing lighter pictures of doves and peace which was how she wished to feel. Many of her earlier pictures were like the one shown in Figure 5.2. In this example, Mary Lou shows a demon figure pulling her to her death. After her hospitalizations, Mary Lou would often relate feeling stifled by her illness, which, according to her, was symbolized by the snake. There is also an obvious sexual reference reminding us of those issues from her earlier boyfriend and current marital relationship. She often depicted demons in her art, which symbolized life and death and which were pulling her apart. Her pictures often contained poems in which she explored her feelings of life and death pulling her soul apart, how she often feels trapped by her mental illness, her experience of sadness and loneliness, and the everlasting nature of death. She always blamed herself for her acts of self-destruction, not wanting her family to share any guilt for her suicidal feelings or actions.

Mary Lou used the group for self-expression and for feedback from others. It provided a safe place to express her emotions, even though other members often confronted her about her need for control and her self-destructive behavior. She was able to express and work through many of these feelings with creativity and resilience. Despite her dramatic presentation, others in the group understood her need for validation and acknowledgment. After some time and growing more able to contain these feelings, Mary Lou ultimately left the group and returned to work part-time.

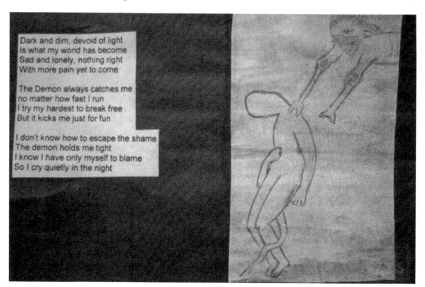

Figure 5.2 Mary Lou being taken away by her demon.

Lila was in her mid-thirties, a married, enlisted officer who suffered from depression, low self-esteem, and a chronic heart disorder. Due to the constant threat of a heart attack and her apprehension of major heart damage, she was concerned about wasting time and uncomfortable in less structured situations. For someone such as Lila who needed space and at the same time needed to delve more inward, mask making was suggested as a possibility. Mask making proved to be a good intervention for her, as she was able to be creative and yet control her self-disclosure. At times, the therapists would make the mask on the patient's face with gauze used to create casts. The person had to trust the therapist or mask maker, as at certain times in this process the person cannot see. This became an even more personal way to get the patients to relate to one another; however, it required extra time and therefore was often not feasible. For this mask, Lila used a ready-made template. I asked her to paint the inside as well as the outside parts of the mask, showing the face that others do not know on the inside and the face she shows to others (her persona) on the outside. If the individual is able to expose some of their internal parts and get to know them, this is extremely beneficial and therapeutic. We became aware that mask making was one of the most helpful interventions for treating dissociation.

Parts have been described by John and Helen Watkins as ego states (Watkins & Watkins, 1997), by Richard Schwartz as internal family systems (Schwartz, 2001), and by Jay Noricks (Noricks, 2011) among others. Acknowledging and working with ego states which were dissociated was a powerful way to elicit integration of the trauma narrative. This mask shows the warrior part of Lila in armor and confidence saying, "Lila can do" (Figures 5.3a and 5.3b).On the inside of the mask she shows her fears, gullibility, and childlike nature. Having her acknowledge these sides of herself allowed Lila to better understand her need to keep others at a distance and to not appear vulnerable to them. She also realized her need to control as an aspect of this and became more open in the group about her physical limitations and fears of the future. Becoming aware of her vulnerable parts, getting to know them through dialogue, sharing them, and being accepted by others was very cathartic for her and others in the group. This can be done with the mask beside the patient on the table for reference so that the patient can speak with it. According to Louis Tinnin (personal communication, July 2012), this mask is an example of a "military" or warrior part. Before integrating this part by acknowledging her other, more hidden parts, this may have been all anyone saw of her—her dedication and dogged adherence to the Military. There are often warrior parts, which may have different aspects of the military experience and may include a part that takes orders, a part that kills, and a shamed part, to name a few.

In my current practice I often ask to people map their parts and have a dialogue with them (Howie in Gussak & Rosal, 2016). They are asked to take a round piece of paper and think about those parts of themselves, which they are aware of, and to adhere them with tape in some way relating them onto a larger piece of paper. This also allows the individual to acknowledge and become aware of potential hidden and unknown parts. It is very important for the therapist to

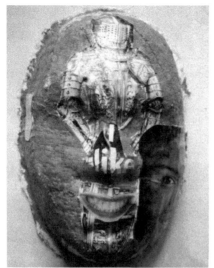 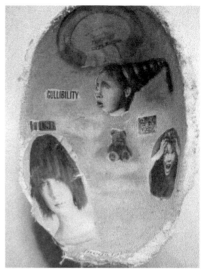

Figures 5.3a and 5.3b Outside and inside of her mask.

assist the client to have a dialogue with their parts. Tinnin and Gantt (2013) recommend using a technique they call the "externalized dialogue" when dealing with parts. This is an elegant and powerful approach to helping the individual contact and begin to reintegrate the part and therefore the past. The therapist has the person write down a dialogue using one color for the unknown part and another color for the unifying self. When a person creates a mask today, I use the externalized dialogue to help integrate the mask into the person's known parts. This is helpful for disembodied voices as well (Tinnin & Gantt, 2013).

Conclusion

Group art therapy proved to be one of the most effective interventions with military personnel. Not only could we see and treat more service members in groups, but this venue allowed some of the strengths of military culture to be utilized for the benefit of the patient. The person is not alone in their problems; they have hope; and they are able to help others by giving oneself for the healing of the other. The group can help alleviate social isolation. Bearing witness and sharing our experiences are valuable ways to process an experience, to obtain empathy and support, and to lighten our emotional load via sharing it with a witness. Although the human experience of trauma may be ubiquitous, it contains unique elements for each of us and we continue to be able to explore it through the stories we tell each day. While some stories are easier for us to share than others, we all long for the benefit of a witness, since a witness assures us that our stories are heard, contained, and transcend time; for it can be said that one is never truly forgotten when one is shared and carried in the hearts of others. The attraction of the group for its members includes feelings of warmth; and that they belong, are valued, unconditionally supported, and accepted by the others. These characteristics are most apparent in a combat unit where the members also wear uniforms to tell those in the group from others and share a commitment to protect one another and to never leave a comrade behind. With the addition of art to the benefits of group therapy, each person was allowed to have hope and given the opportunity to begin to heal.

References

Angelou, M. (2015). *I Know Why the Caged Bird Sings*. New York: Random House.
Bion, W.R. (1991). *Experiences in Groups: And Other Papers* (Revised edition). London: Routledge.
Burgo, J. (2012, July 1). Bearing witness and being seen. Retrieved April 5, 2017, from http://www.afterpsychotherapy.com/bearing-witness-and-being-seen/.
Gussak, D.E., & Rosal, M.L. (2016). *The Wiley Handbook of Art Therapy*. Chichester, UK: Wiley-Blackwell. Retrieved April 5, 2017, from http://www.amazon.com/Handbook-Therapy-Clinical-Psychology-Handbooks/dp/1118306597/ref=sr_1_1?s=books&ie=UTF8&qid=1464197284&sr=1-1&keywords=rosal+and+gussak.
Howie, P., Prasad, S., & Kristel, J. (Eds.). (2013). *Using Art Therapy With Diverse Populations: Crossing Cultures and Abilities* (1st edition). London: Jessica Kingsley.
Joellenbeck, L., Russell, P., & Guze, S. (Eds.). (1999). *Strategies to Protect the Health of Deployed U.S. Forces: Medical Surveillance, Record Keeping, and Risk Reduction*. Washington, DC: National Academies Press.
Kim, J.B., Kirchhoff, M., & Whitsett, S. (2011). Expressive arts group therapy with middle-school aged children from military families. *The Arts in Psychotherapy*, 38(5), 356–362. http://doi.org/10.1016/j.aip.2011.08.003.
Kramer, E. (1990). *Art Therapy in a Children's Community: A Study of the Function of Art Therapy in the Treatment Program of Wiltwyck School for Boys*. New York: Schocken Books.
Kramer, E. (2001). *Art as Therapy: Planning and Setting Up Groups*. London: Jessica Kingsley.
Liebmann, M. (2004). *Art Therapy for Groups: A Handbook of Themes and Exercises* (2nd edition). Hove, East Sussex; New York: Routledge.
Noricks, J. (2011). *Parts Psychology: A Trauma-based, Self-state Therapy for Emotional Healing*. Los Angeles, CA: New University Press.
Rubin, J. (1978). *Child Art Therapy*. New York: Van Nostrand Reinhold.
Rubin, J.A. (Ed.). (2016). *Approaches to Art Therapy: Theory and Technique* (3rd edition). New York: Routledge.
Schwartz, R.C. (2001). *Introduction to the Internal Family Systems Model*. Oak Park, IL: Trailheads Publications.
Siegel, D. J. (2010). *The Mindful Therapist: A Clinician's Guide to Mindsight and Neural Integration* (1st edition). New York: W.W. Norton & Company.
Sullivan, H.S., & Perry, H.S. (1974). *Schizophrenia as a Human Process*. New York: W.W. Norton. Retrieved April 5, 2017, from http://www.amazon.com/Schizophrenia-Human-Process-Norton-Library/dp/0393007219/ref=sr_1_sc_1?s=books&ie=UTF8&qid=1461091886&sr=1-1-spell&keywords=schizophrenis+as+a+human+process.
Tinnin, L., & Gantt, L. (2013). *The Instinctual Trauma Response And Dual-brain Dynamics: A Guide for Trauma Therapy*. Linda Gantt.

Watkins, H.H., & Watkins, J.G. (1997). *Ego States: Theory and Therapy* (1st edition). New York: W.W. Norton & Company.

Yalom, I.D. (1995). *The Theory and Practice of Group Psychotherapy* (4th edition). New York: Basic Books.

CHAPTER 6

Managing Suicide in the Military
Paula Howie

In his book *The Savage God,* Alvarez (1990) discusses the suicide of his colleague and friend Sylvia Plath, one of the most lauded poets of the twentieth century. He believes her suicide, unlike the attempt described in her book *The Bell Jar,* was a call for help and that, on some level, she wished to be saved. In an introductory note to the BBC about "Daddy," one of her many poems rife with her wishes to reunite with her dead father, Plath writes of the narrator, "she has to act out the awful little allegory once over" (p. 39). As therapists, we see clients who act out over and over pondering the idea of death daily, and making the decision to live or die as they discuss their choices in a creative and unselfconscious way. Alvarez (1990) believed that Plath was able to keep her unhappiness in check at times because she was able to write about her despair and suicidal thoughts and to put them symbolically in her poetry. As art therapists, we believe that if people draw about and discuss suicide and death we can make a difference in their choosing to live. We can define our intervention as providing a dialogue with the suicidal part, finding the part that wishes to live, and allowing ambivalence to emerge in order to opt for living and to combat the wish of dying. In the ensuing years since Sylvia Plath's tragic demise, healthcare professions have been privy to much improved suicide treatment regimes to include risk assessment, medications, and a variety of psychotherapy interventions. Despite these strides, suicide continues to be a major quandary for clients and therefore for their caregivers.

Facts about Suicide

What most of us don't realize is that the majority of deaths from firearm violence are suicides, not homicides. Garen J. Wintemute (2015), Professor of Emergency Medicine and Director of the Violence Prevention Research Program at University of California at Davis, has revealed that suicide by firearm is far more common than homicide. Since 2006, homicides have decreased, but suicides have increased, so that by 2012, nearly two-thirds of deaths from firearm violence were suicides. White males are most likely to commit suicide with the mortality rate gradually increasing with age.

In terms of the Military, an average of 20 veterans a day committed suicide in 2014, a trend that reflects record high rates among young men fresh out of the military and among growing numbers of women taking their own lives (Zoroya, 2016). The VA found the worst suicide pattern among male veterans aged 18 to 29. Their suicide rate was 86 per 100,000 people, nearly four times the rate among active duty service members in 2013. By contrast, the overall US suicide rate is 13 per 100,000 people. In addition, in a space of two years, more active duty soldiers have died by self-inflicted wounds than in combat, averaging nearly one a day for the past year (Zoroya, 2016). Family breakups, depression, repeated deployments in a war zone, and post-traumatic stress disorder (PTSD) were designated as major causal factors for active duty and retired military personnel. To add to this, the wars in the Middle East have increased the number of veterans diagnosed with PTSD or combat stress reactions. The rates of PTSD for veterans of the wars in Afghanistan and Iraq are conservatively estimated at between 9 and 24 percent, with a higher rate for veterans of the war in Iraq because of greater combat exposure (longer and more frequent deployments). PTSD increases in a linear manner with the number of active combat a soldier experiences (Hoge, Auchterlonie, & Milliken, 2006; Hoge et al., 2004).

Suicide is surely one of the most complicated and alarming aspects of working with individuals in the Military. It brings up many existential questions, such as how responsible is the therapist for protecting someone else's life, who is responsible for the individual's choices, how far should one go to save another human being who wishes to end his or her pain, and how guilty would one feel if a patient were to complete a suicide? Much as working in the Military setting brings questions of how you see the Military and what you think of our country's sometimes destructive policies, suicide requires one to confront one's own personal thoughts about it, to challenge depressive affect, in the patient and, perhaps, in oneself, and to consider whether suicide is a viable option or an unnatural act against religious teachings, or something in between. Against this backdrop, there is no question that those with a military background are trained in the use of firearms and in the use of other self-destructive implements such as knives and explosives. This makes the therapist's job more difficult, as one can almost assume, whether the person is in the Military or a family member, that there are lethal weapons available to the suicidal person.

There are many good suicide risk-assessment tools online which are offered by governmental and mental health associations such as the Centre for Applied Research in Mental Health and Addiction (The Centre for Applied Research in Mental Health and Addiction (CARMHA), & for the Ministry of Health, 2007) and the American Psychological Association (Firestone, n.d.). These tools lay out the way one must go about assessing the individual on several levels and cover what one must ask and assess to ascertain the level of suicide risk and the appropriate steps one must take to get them into the level of treatment required. They include questions such as: do you have a gun or a weapon? Do you have a plan? Do you use mind-altering non-prescription substances? If so, the therapist must offer further inquiry and evaluate their level of care, which may include outpatient, inpatient, day treatment, partial hospitalization, etc. Many resources and descriptions of working with suicidal clientele also address therapist self-care and burnout.

In addition to general assessment tools and increased evaluation of suicidal ideation, as art therapists we have the visual symbols, which give us non-verbal clues about the client's state of mind. The art therapist may see subtle signs of suicidal ideation even though the person is not voicing it. This is not magic; it is merely being tuned into non-verbal clues. If the therapist is concerned or is seeing something and knows the person has been depressed, it is better to say something and to be wrong than to say nothing and risk missing suicidal ideation. An inquiry may be asking about their color choice and their symbols. One can say to the client, "This may sound far-fetched, but I have seen symbols like that used by people who were thinking of hurting themselves. I just wanted to check it out with you to make sure we are not missing something. If you have noticed any disturbing feeling or thoughts even if the feeling may have been a fleeting one, we can talk about it here." This way, the art therapist provides an opening that may never have existed before. The person may feel heard and seen. If the person has been thinking about self-harm, they will be relieved or they could be suspicious that you could read their minds. You can assure them that you cannot, but that you have been trained to notice certain aspects and non-verbal behavior in art.

Suicidal Indicators in Artwork

Art therapists see indicators of depression and suicidal wishes in artwork in indirect, subtle, or overt ways. One service member with whom I worked individually in the studio did a very sketchy but easily discernible picture of herself hanging. When I escorted her back to the ward and informed the nursing staff, they put her on suicide watch. During one of the checks, the staff found her later in her room trying to affix her belt to a shower rod. Although clearly a cry for help, we now know that we must take cries for help seriously. She might have accidentally injured or asphyxiated herself before anyone found her if not for the visual information she had provided to the art therapist.

Debby, who was mentioned in Chapter 5, had to be walked to the emergency room on several occasions due to threatening pictures or statements she made. Her messages were usually blatant and full of self-hatred. She would sometimes put guns or other implements of destruction in her pictures. Once, when she had threatened self-harm, she refused to be escorted to the ER. Instead, she left the group and I was forced to call the sheriff's department in the county in which she lived to ask an officer to go to her home and remove her guns.

Mary Lou, also mentioned in Chapter 5, would make contracts to insure that she would not harm herself. Once she refused hospitalization and I had to have her call when she got home making sure her daughter had arrived from school. Mary Lou often talked about how upset her adopted daughter would be if she hurt herself. This is reminiscent of Sylvia Plath who put out milk for her children and made sure the nanny was coming before she put her head in the oven and turned on the gas. Oftentimes, family members, wives, husbands, or children can provide the support or the rationale needed for stemming the urge to self-harm or for managing suicidal ideation outside the hospital setting.

Art often taps into a deeper level of emotion, and the person may be informing the art therapist what they are thinking, whether they want to or not. Patients can be savvy enough so that they can deny suicidal ideation or a self-harm plan when asked in order to avoid hospitalization. Harriett Wadeson (1987) discusses a case in which a man whom others on the treatment team had evaluated as not suicidal went home on pass over the weekend and hung himself. She had noticed that his artwork contained a covert message of his intentions.

A similar case that riveted my attention and made me forever sensitive to suicide was one of subtle lethality and deadly resolve, and one which contained a message of her intentions. I was supervising a student while her usual supervisor was on vacation. The student had an uneasy feeling about her client's newest picture, although she couldn't quite put into words what troubled her about it. The patient, Sophie, who was diagnosed with bipolar illness, was in her late twenties (about the age of the art therapy student) and was medically trained. The patient's drawings in early groups showed stream-of-consciousness and primary process thinking, and contained different, random elements such as a rainbow which appears hooked to a psychedelic sun, a rooster head, a plant, and black puzzle pieces among other items (Figure 6.1). The picture that was disturbing to the student was of a colorful, well-drawn rooster, a cocky bird shown next to her usual drawings. What we know from hindsight is that this picture showed a focus and energy not seen in her earlier, less focused work. The later picture shows her determination and strength. The student's concern turned out to be prophetic in that Sophie went to a nearby isolated park while on pass and cut her wrists. She was dead by the time the police found her. As a result of this experience and others, we began to look at any artwork of those patients who had committed suicide successfully and at those who we had saved by alerting the nursing staff. What we found was that when someone was successful there were very subtle changes in their work. Although one must report when suicidal ideation is overt as a cry for help, by far the most lethal attempts were signaled by subtle changes in one's art, which made them more difficult to discern. Subtle changes in energy level, focus, colors from dark to bright or bright to dark, and the inclusion of suicidal symbols (overt and covert), become the basis for follow-up inquiries and concern. In her chapter on recognizing suicide, Wadeson (1987), who saw many such patients in her work at the National Institutes of Health, organizes suicidal pictures into those containing messages, anger, feelings of harmfulness toward others, self-hatred, hopelessness, communication or isolation, and spiral symbols (p. 85). Herman (1989), in her study of suicide, points out aspects that comprise most reliable content in suicide assessment, which include hopelessness, isolation, anger, aggression, and low self-esteem (p. 112). The art therapist must be aware of these elements and themes in order to assess her patient's suicide risk.

Figure 6.1 Sophie's earlier drawing (left) and later picture (right) prior to her suicide.

Mary Huntoon (1953), who worked with World War II service members in the Winter VA, describes a self-portrait that a suicidal patient completed and then obliterated by crossing out: self-hatred leading to self-destruction. She calls this "art as release" and explains that by symbolically destroying himself the person may no longer need to act on self-destructive impulses (p. 30). She further states, "[A]ny change in the use of colors either toward black or toward brilliance and greater use of color, is watched carefully and reported" (p. 30). This change is significant as an indication of someone's increased energy and resolve. This statement certainly applies to Sophie's pictures, although we were too inexperienced and self-doubting to alert the staff to the art therapy student's feeling of unease. There is clearly a shift in her use of color both in the boldness and structure of the picture after she had resigned herself to suicide.

John

An active duty enlisted soldier, John was seen in the acute care and on the transitional ward for several months until he received his discharge papers from the Army. He was diagnosed with major depressive disorder and schizoid personality. It is no wonder that his family history included distant parents, and that he was frustrated by his inability to have significant, long-term relationships. He had been married twice and was estranged from his children. Before coming to the acute care ward, he voiced depression, hostility toward others, hopelessness, and self-destructive thoughts. He was seen in art therapy as he was able to use art for self-expression and to monitor his suicidal ideation. Although his pictures and sculptures were very dramatic, he rarely had much to say about what he drew except that he wasn't sure what it meant or he didn't know why he chose his subjects. Although a part of his schizoid personality, this lack of connection to his art may have also been due to dissociation. However, during the course of his several months of treatment, his art spoke volumes about his view of women, whom he alternatively saw as frightening or needing protection, his efforts to handle his depressed feelings, and his constant suicidal thoughts. Although never openly endorsing suicidal intent or a plan, John's art was full of symbols of death and destruction. Art was truly a window into his passion, distress, and a way for him open up and at the same time remain somewhat aloof. He drew a series of skulls, which were evolving into men and women with partial flesh covering their bone structure. He had a series of chess pieces with skull like heads rather than castles or knights. He often used found objects and newspapers. John could depict the softer side of women, as he did in a soft pastel drawing of Camille Claudel, Auguste Rodin's mistress, or their more frightening aspects, as when he drew Medusa, the fearsome Gorgon who could turn men into stone with her gaze. One of his most disturbing pictures, completed about halfway through his treatment, was of the grim reaper (See Figure 6.2). John uses black pastel to draw this skull-like, floating specter of death holding a large scythe. The placement of this gruesome figure on newspaper gives the picture a human context, making the reaper a little less formidable. John was put on watch status and followed carefully until his art showed fewer symbols of death. He was sent home after his hospitalization and was looking forward to making a life beyond his military career. When he left, the treatment team made sure that he had follow-up services at the VA in the Midwest where he could continue his treatment.

Lisa

Lisa was in her mid-forties and had a history of bipolar disorder, suicidal ideation, and alcohol abuse when she joined the outpatient group. Her husband was an officer in the Army. Lisa had a special interest in art therapy since she had taken art classes, and was a serious artist. Sometimes she was angry, became self-destructive, and expressed suicidal thoughts. When Lisa began treatment, she filled out the Pearson-Marr archetypal inventory (PMAI) (Pearson & Marr, 2007). This is a self-assessment using 12 Jungian archetypes and is a complement to the Myers-Briggs. It is a method for developing an appreciation of the properties of these archetypes in order to assist with personal growth and group psychological health. On the PMAI, Lisa's highest scoring archetypes were the Lover and the Destroyer. She completed a picture depicting these archetypes and talked about how similar these were for her, almost twins. Indeed, she described them as two sides of the same person. Differentiated only by their color, the figure of the Lover is drawn in pink and yellow pastel on the right side, while the Destroyer is drawn on the left side in gray and black pastel. In both figures their eyes are unseeing and blank. These figures do not appear to have mouths. This picture was helpful in that we could talk about the positive parts of both these archetypes. The Lover is alive, vital, and in love with the

Managing Suicide in the Military 81

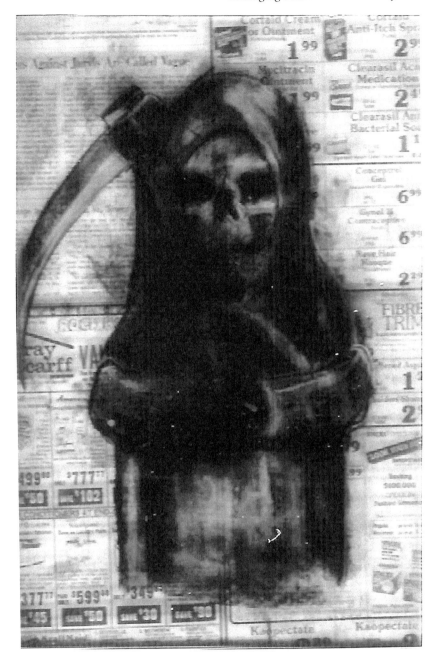

Figure 6.2 John's depiction of the grim reaper.

world while the Destroyer is able to deal successfully with loss and to move on. It also allowed an understanding of the negative aspects of each archetype: the Lover may include indiscriminate sexuality, sometimes associated with bipolar illness, and the Destroyer, with self-destructive behavior. This destruction was linked to her suicidal thoughts and it became a way for me to ask about these feelings without sounding accusing or suggestive.

Please refer to Plate 4 in the color plate section.

Lisa was in a verbal therapy group and discussed eloquently how she sometimes shows a "together front" to her therapy groups and then falls apart when she goes home, saying she cannot stop herself. To illustrate this, she drew a picture of a large foot getting caught in a rope and about to trip. She said this was like the old saying "Give them enough rope and they will hang themselves." This was a subtle but worrisome association. She had succeeded in using suicidal ideas and couching them in such a way that no one would know that she was suicidal. Lisa had said earlier that she did not want to use suicidal imagery because she did not want to be escorted to the acute care unit. This was passed on to her primary physician who worked out a contract with her and followed her closely for the next two weeks.

Later in her treatment, Lisa produced this graphic picture of her pain, saying no one could understand it, especially not her therapists (Figure 6.3). She seemed angry and talked about not wanting to explore her layers of pain or go through them because she does not know what is there and how deep her pain may go. The picture shows Lisa cutting her legs, and she discussed with the group how this made her feel alive. This resonated with others in the group, some of whom also burned themselves with glue guns. There ensued a helpful discussion about what one could do besides cutting, to include getting one's family to stay around and using red marker to make the lines but not penetrating the skin. Lisa denied that she did this often, saying it wasn't yet a habit because she had done it infrequently. This was also a springboard for group discussion about her shame, guilt, and anger about self-mutilation; we were able to put this into context as needing to change her life when the negative manifestation of the Destroyer was active. Lisa had a great way of asking others about themselves and letting them give her straight feedback. During this time I often assigned Lisa homework, since she had a home studio and liked to work alone. The homework could stretch the therapeutic effect of the group. She would often bring her pictures in to art therapy to discuss them.

One of her last pictures was a self-portrait. Lisa had done other, more distorted self-portraits but this one shows a close-up of her head partially hidden behind a game board structure. She filled the spaces of the game board with such daily chores as ironing, grocery shopping, tools, painting, clothes drying on the line, and cooking, among other things. Although there are still hidden parts we could have worked on, the treatment team had monitored her cutting and suicidal ideation and deemed her to be healing well. Lisa was ready to leave the group and saw herself as more hopeful than when she first began. She was able to say goodbye to us without anger or hostility. She also planned to continue to take art classes and resume her painting in her home studio.

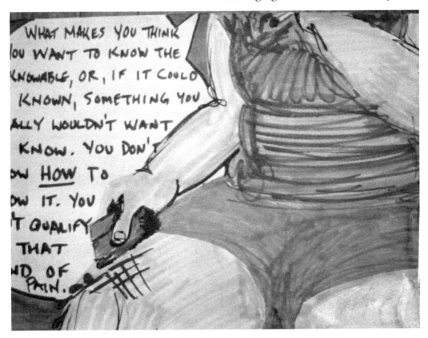

Figure 6.3 Lisa's destructive impulses.

Conclusion

All of the individuals described above had some aspects of a suicidal message in their art, although at times these messages could be disguised and convoluted. They also demonstrated some of the issues discussed by Wadeson (1987), including anger, self-hatred or low self-esteem, and hopelessness. Those patients who were successful at isolating rather than communicating their suicidal thoughts were the most lethal and the most difficult to reach. Depression was manifest in each person's behavior and artwork in a variety of ways. Plath (Alvarez, 1990) talked about the repetitive nature of suicidal ideation. There do seem to be times when the patient is stuck and has trouble moving on. Lisa's anger compelled her to cut herself and to think of self-injury time and again. John's self-loathing and distrust of others was manifest in his constant use of death symbols. Both denied these feelings at the same time that they were asking for help. Ambivalence was observed in all the patients' work as they wished for and pushed away help from the group and therapists. Surely, one demonstrable fact in all that we have seen is that drawing these feelings can make a difference between living and dying.

Working with those who threaten self-harm is some of the most difficult work a therapist can undertake. Therefore, we must be continually vigilant for signs of hopelessness and depression in our own lives. Self-care, which includes meditation, making sure one has time for personal artwork, physical exercise, adequate sleep, support, and sometimes therapy for the caregiver, are keys to ensuring one's continued health. We can seek out supervision, especially if we become aware of self-blame or seeing suicide as a personal failure. Despite its difficulty, there are great rewards in working with this population, especially when one can help patients modulate suicidal wishes and feelings, sustaining them enough so that they may take part in what life has to offer.

References

Alvarez, A. (1990). *The Savage God: A Study of Suicide*. New York: W.W. Norton & Company.

Firestone, L. (n.d.). Suicide: What therapists need to know. Retrieved August 28, 2016, from https://www.apa.org/education/ce/suicide.pdf.

Herman, D.A. (1989). *Suicide and Art Therapy: Exploring the Pictorial Expression of Features Related to Suicidal Intent*. Concordia, Montreal, Quebec, Canada. Retrieved April 5, 2017, from http://spectrum.library.concordia.ca/4360/1/ML51396.pdf.

Hoge, C., Auchterlonie, J., & Milliken, C. (2006). Mental health problems, use of mental health services, and attrition from military service after returning from deployment to Iraq or Afghanistan. *JAMA*, 295(9), 1023–1032. http://doi.org/10.1001/jama.295.9.1023.

Hoge, C.W., Castro, C.A., Messer, S.C., McGurk, D., Cotting, D.I., & Koffman, R.L. (2004). Combat duty in Iraq and Afghanistan mental health problems, and barriers to care. *New England Journal of Medicine*, 351(1), 13–22.

Huntoon, M. (1953). Art Therapy for patients in the acute section of Winter VA hospital, Topeka, Kansas. *Department of Medicine and Surgery Information Bulletin*, 10, 29–32.

Pearson, C.S., & Marr, H.K. (2007). *What Story Are You Living? A Workbook and Guide to Interpreting Results from the Pearson-Marr Archetype Indicator* (1st edition). Gainesville, FL: Center for Applications of Psychological Type.

The Centre for Applied Research in Mental Health and Addiction (CARMHA), & for the Ministry of Health. (2007). Working with the client who is suicidal: A tool for adult mental health and addiction services. Retrieved August 28, 2016, from http://www.health.gov.bc.ca/library/publications/year/2007/MHA_WorkingWithSuicidalClient.pdf.

Wadeson, H. (1987). *Art Psychotherapy*. New York; Chichester: John Wiley.

Wintemute, G.J. (2015). The epidemiology of firearm violence in the twenty-first century United States. *Annual Review of Public Health*, 36(1), 5–19. http://doi.org/10.1146/annurev-publhealth-031914-122535.

Zoroya, G. (2016, May 4). U.S. military suicides remain high for 7th year. *USA TODAY*. Retrieved April 5, 2017, from http://www.usatoday.com/story/news/nation/2016/04/01/us-military-suicides-remain-stubbornly-high/82518278/.

PART II

Current Trends in Art Therapy Treatment in Military Settings and the Expansion of Treatment Settings

CHAPTER 7

Treating the Wounded Warrior: Cognitive and Neural Aspects of Post-Traumatic Stress Disorder

Paul Newhouse and Kimberly Albert

Introduction

The neural and cognitive components of post-traumatic stress disorder (PTSD) are embedded in impairment of the overall stress management system of the brain. While much remains to be learned regarding the pathophysiology of PTSD and its development, for the purposes of therapeutic strategies, PTSD may be seen primarily as a cognitive disorder that includes a disruption of stress management systems and emotional and non-emotional memory systems. These systems are dependent on various neural processes and brain structures involving an interaction of regulatory systems.

Trauma exposure is a common experience, with the type of trauma that would meet criteria for a post-traumatic stress disorder (PTSD) diagnosis being experienced by over 55 percent of respondents in the National Comorbidity study (Kessler, Sonnega, Bromet, Hughes, & Nelson, 1995) and up to nearly 90 percent of respondents in studies of higher risk populations (Breslau et al., 1998; de Vries & Olff, 2009). However, only a fraction of those exposed to traumatic events develop PTSD, with prevalence generally between 7 and 9 percent (Kessler et al., 1995).

Maintaining emotional and neuroendocrine function following trauma exposure may require a careful balance of acute and long-term brain responses. The diagnostic criteria for PTSD include four symptom clusters: intrusive memories and re-experiences, changes in arousal, negative emotions, and avoidance of trauma-related stimuli (Gentes et al., 2014). These symptoms highlight the multiple brain systems that are involved in PTSD: neuroendocrine response, cognitive, and emotion regulation systems. Each of these systems likely has a unique contribution to PTSD symptoms and presents a possible target for intervention.

Currently, the most rigorously studied PTSD treatments include approaches aimed at decoupling the experience of trauma-related stimuli from stress system and negative emotion response (Jorge, 2015). These commonly include training in changing cognitive and emotional processing of stimuli, suggesting that the involvement of cognitive-emotional brain systems may be integral to

PTSD etiology. However, the success of these treatments may be limited by low adherence (Bisson & Andrew, 2007) and the challenge of altering adverse cognitive emotional responses once they have become generalized beyond trauma-related stimuli.

Future effective treatments will likely benefit from a multi-system approach, combining interventions aimed at altering the stress response, changing the cognitive emotional processing of both trauma-related and generalized anxiety-provoking stimuli, and emotional responding. Art therapy approaches may be useful for modifying some of these factors. Further, an understanding of the cognitive and neural components of PTSD will contribute to the development and application of art therapy and other novel approaches.

Cognitive Aspects of Post-Traumatic Stress Disorder

PTSD patients experience intrusive thoughts about the traumatic event and have emotional responses to re-experiences and trauma-related stimuli that provoke anxiety and negative mood. Abnormal cognitive–emotional interactions are common to mood and anxiety disorders, including PTSD. Intrusive memories are most often of the antecedents (predictors) (Ehlers & Clark, 2000) of the trauma and are generally visual, although occassionlly kinesthetic, auditory, and olfactory (Hackmann, Ehlers, Speckens, & Clark, 2004).

Early cognitive theories of PTSD posit that the traumatic event disrupts schemas about the justness/safety of the world, and the personal worth of the individual, especially in people with rigid worldviews (Kushner, Riggs, Foa, & Miller, 1993). Rather than face this dilemma, the individual avoids memories of the event (and stimuli that provoke these memories) (Janoff-Bulman, 1992). Emotional processing theory adds to the cognitive theory that avoidance prevents habituation and extinction of the anxiety-provoking memories and responses to related stimuli. Avoidance increases and reinforces fear, and reinforces the belief that the individual is incapable of normal functioning (Kushner et al., 1993). Avoidance or disruption of specific memories for the traumatic event can produce a generalized feeling of threat; anxiety is not associated with a particular traumatic event (because the cognitive process of association is avoided), and becomes generalized and constant (Ehlers & Clark, 2000). Interpretation of PTSD symptoms following trauma predicts the maintenance of PTSD. People who interpret flashbacks and intrusive thoughts, or physical symptoms (startle, sleep disturbance), as abnormal reactions are more likely to develop and maintain PTSD (Halligan, Clark, & Ehlers, 2002).

PTSD symptoms are related to a negative attributional style in interpersonal trauma. Attribution of events to external sources and understanding those events as stable and uncontrollable is related to increased PTSD symptoms (Mikulincer & Solomon, 1988). Rumination is related to PTSD symptom severity; however, rumination in PTSD tends to be about the antecedents and consequences of the trauma and not about the actual traumatic event (Ehlers & Steil, 1995). Rumination may contribute to the perception of ongoing threat and maintain PTSD (Ehlers & Clark, 2000). Anxiety sensitivity (AS), the fear of anxiety and seeing anxiety symptoms as being harmful, is associated with PTSD symptom severity, and may be a vulnerability or maintenance factor for PTSD. Anxiety sensitivity predicts PTSD symptoms over time, with reductions in PTSD symptoms related to reductions in AS, specifically in women (Feldner, Zvolensky, Schmidt, & Smith, 2008).

PTSD patients complain about their ability to concentrate and remember events from their own lives, and demonstrate learning and memory deficits, particularly for verbal information. Similar to individuals with depression, PTSD patients have difficulty recalling specific life events, and provide general instances or periods of time when asked to recall life events (McNally, 2006). This may serve as a protective measure to avoid memories or thinking about specific life events (Hermans, Defranc, Raes, Williams, & Eelen, 2005).

These cognitive and emotional aspects of PTSD may be related to structural and functional changes in the neurobiological networks that are important for regulating cognitive emotional processes and stress response.

Ventral and Dorsal Systems in the Stress Response

The cognitive characteristics of individuals with PTSD can be explained in the dorsal (top) and ventral (underside) of the brain system model of emotion regulation. This model separates the brain into ventral regions that are responsible for the rapid appraisal of emotional information, and dorsal regions that are responsible for allocating resources to cognitive tasks, and goal-directed behavior (Phillips, Drevets, Rauch, & Lane, 2003). Dorsal regions include anterior dorsomedial pre-frontal cortex (dmPFC; emotion regulation), dorsolateral prefrontal cortex (dlPFC) and lateral parietal (task-related activity). The ventral system is responsible for appraising the salience of stimuli and generating emotional reactions. The ventral system includes ventromedial pre-frontal cortex (vmPFC) and orbito-frontal cortex OFC (self-referential processing of stimuli and evaluation of outcomes of goal-directed behavior) and amygdala (rapid generation of emotional responses to high-salience information).

During the healthy stress response, activity in the brain shifts from dorsal system mood regulation to ventral system threat evaluation and management as cognitive resources are preferentially allocated to automatic processes for responding to threat (Arnsten, 2009). Enhanced ventral activity results in acute dysphoria which is a normal and necessary component of the stress response as negative mood motivates managing stressors (Gold, 2015). There are two regulatory components of the dorsal system: activity of the hippocampus (in the deep temporal cortex of the brain) is automatically enhanced in response to amygdala (the amygdala is important in fear response and fear memory) activity, while frontal activity is recruited through later stage or voluntary processes (Phillips, Ladouceur, & Drevets, 2008). In the unstressed state the subgenual pre-frontal cortex inhibits amygdala activity and consequently attenuates amygdala-driven attention (Gold, 2015). During stress, dorsal system function is down-regulated in favor of automatic, rapid emotional responses in the ventral (limbic) system. Once dorsal activity is decreased the amygdala is released from inhibition (Drevets et al., 1997).

The amygdala, which is part of the ventral threat evaluation system, plays a central role in both the mood and cognitive response to stress, through reciprocal projections (i.e., connections) with dorsal system structures. It also orchestrates endocrine secretion and autonomic nervous system responses through projections to the hypothalamus and central autonomic centers (Gold, 2015). In a recent expert review, Gold posits that an unregulated feed-forward system decreases dorsal system activity and increases amygdala activation leading to a prolonged dysphoric state and biasing cognitive processes toward negative emotionally valenced information (Gold, 2015). Because of this cascade, the stress response system may become dysregulated following prolonged activity or severe trauma exposure.

The changes in ventral and dorsal activity that occur during the normal stress response result in altered cognitive processing of emotional information, including memory (McGaugh, 2004) and bias of attention for threatening or negatively valenced stimuli (Arnsten, 2009). Normally in the short term, giving priority to potentially threatening or negative information serves to efficiently process and manage stressors; however, in a dysregulated stress system persistent negative bias may become established and contribute to cognitive vulnerability for depression or PTSD.

Neural Correlates of PTSD Symptoms and Emotional Memory

When symptoms are triggered in individuals with PTSD, activity increases in amygdala and insula and declines in portions of the pre-frontal cortex (Liberzon & Martis, 2006). PTSD subjects show greater amygdala activity (important in fear response and memory) and less medial pre-frontal activity (i.e., less top-down control) to fearful faces (Shin et al., 2005), as well as to trauma-related images and sounds (Bremner et al., 2004). The more severe the PTSD symptoms, the more activity there is in the amygdala and the less activity there is in the pre-frontal cortex. In addition, certain pre-frontal brain regions (e.g., anterior cingulate) are actually smaller in PTSD subjects than in trauma-exposed but not symptomatic subjects, or in PTSD recovered subjects (Rauch, Shin, & Wright, 2003). This suggests that reduced anterior cingulate volume may be a vulnerability factor (trait); or it may be a consequence of PTSD that remains as a scar.

The neurocognitive differences associated with PTSD may indicate a disruption in functional communication between the medial pre-frontal cortex and the amygdala. There is reduced activity in some pre-frontal areas during emotional tasks (Bremner et al., 2004; Shin et al., 2005). In addition, PTSD subjects (compared to only trauma-exposed subjects) showed delayed time in naming the color of words related to their trauma compared to the time to name either negative words or neutral words (McNally, 2006).

Phelps (Phelps, 2006) has noted that the amygdala is responsible for the emotional contribution to declarative memory. Specifically, she suggests that the amygdala can modulate both the encoding and storage of hippocampal-dependent memories and that bidirectionally the hippocampus, by forming episodic representations of emotional significance, can influence the amygdala response when emotional stimuli are encountered (Phelps, 2004). Thus, there is an overlapping system of brain regions that function in anxiety and mood regulation, the response to psychosocial stress, and memory for emotional events.

Memory for negative emotional information appears to be directly linked to the degree of amygdala activation during encoding and to the interaction between the amygdala and medial temporal lobe memory systems. In addition, psychosocial stress may impair learning by suppressing the activity of these structures. Memory processes for emotional information appear to be altered in PTSD, but the underlying neurobiology of these changes is currently unknown. Traumatic stress may produce the suppression of limbic (e.g., amygdala, hippocampus) activity and impair memory, particularly for emotional information that requires amygdala input.

Stress Vulnerability

The stress exposure model suggests that affect/anxiety disruption is the result of a biological vulnerability combined with the trigger of stressful life events (Hankin, Mermelstein, & Roesch, 2007; Kendler, Thornton, & Gardner, 2000; Liu & Alloy, 2010). Altered stress responses, and abnormal function of the brain regions important to the stress response, have been consistently found in individuals with PTSD and depression (Korszun, 2009). These alterations resemble an unregulated stress response (Lupien, McEwen, Gunnar, & Heim, 2009), including hyperactivity of the stress hormone control system (hypothalamic–pituitary axis or HPA) and difficulty regulating the stress hormone cortisol (Lupien & Lepage, 2001).

The hippocampus is an important regulator for cortisol and of HPA axis activity (Herman & Cullinan, 1997; Jankord & Herman, 2008). Alterations in hippocampal structure and function may result in stress system dysregulation as hippocampal control of the HPA axis is reduced. Reduced ability of the hippocampus to regulate stress responding and modify its activity in response to acute stress may result in dysregulation of the entire stress system.

As noted above, mood and anxiety dysregulation may result from an imbalance in functional activity in the dorsal and ventral divisions of the limbic system and pre-frontal cortex (Drevets, Price, & Furey, 2008; Mayberg, 1997). The dorsal and ventral systems also have roles in the response to psychosocial stress (Pruessner et al., 2008, 2009). Stress hormone activity following psychosocial stress is associated with increased activity in ventral system structures, paired with decreased activity in the dorsal system (Dedovic, Duchesne, Andrews, Engert, & Pruessner, 2009).

There seem to be important sex differences in responses to stress and PTSD. Women with depression and/or PTSD have higher basal levels of the stress hormone cortisol and blunted responses to psychosocial stressors than women without these disorders (Burke, Fernald, Gertler, & Adler, 2005). The cortisol response to stress also decreases during certain phases of the menstrual cycle (Kirschbaum, Wust, & Hellhammer, 1992; Kirschbaum et al., 1999). Women remain more sensitive than men to lower levels of cortisol following repeated stressors (Vamvakopoulos, 1995; Wang et al., 2007). Women may be more sensitive to mood and anxiety dysregulation following traumatic stress than men because of changing ovarian hormone effects on the HPA axis and brain circuits important for the stress response.

There is also clear evidence that there are significant male/female differences in the modulation of fear and fear extinction tied to estrogen (estradiol) levels that modulate frontal brain and amygdala activity during fear extinction (Milad, Igoe, Lebron-Milad, & Novales, 2009; Zeidan et al., 2011). In fact, the use of hormonal contraceptives blocks the production of endogenous estrogen and impairs the extinction of fear (Graham & Milad, 2013), which may be relevant to the development of PTSD. Blunted fear extinction may contribute to the development of PTSD (Milad et al., 2009) and recent work that has examined extinction deficits in women with PTSD showed that low estrogen may be a vulnerability factor for the development of PTSD (Lebron-Milad, Graham, & Milad, 2012), particularly during or after the occurrence of trauma. As the role of women in the Military is expanding, the implications of these findings will require further study.

Fearful stimuli activate the amygdala in the service of increasing vigilance and attention to the environment, and may not require cortical (i.e., cognitive) involvement. Thus, traumatic stress and fearful stimuli may activate different neural circuits that may be affected differentially, and in turn may affect emotional memory differently. Kim and Diamond (2002) have proposed a model in which stress, by acting indirectly through elevations in cortisol levels and directly through excess amygdala input to the hippocampus, impairs hippocampal plasticity and subsequently cognitive functioning. While amygdala involvement is essential to emotional learning, excess amygdala activation or activation combined with stress appears to impair hippocampal functioning.

PTSD is a highly co-morbid disorder, often appearing with other mood and anxiety disorders, including major depression. Mood/anxiety dysfunction is characterized by increased attention and memory for negative information (Suslow et al., 2010; Watkins, Martin, & Stern, 2000), and decreased memory and attention for positive stimuli (Sloan, Strauss, & Wisner, 2001). The cognitive model of depression/anxiety posits that emotional processing circuits in the brain are altered so that there is a bias toward negative information, and attenuated processing of positive information (Disner, Beevers, Haigh, & Beck, 2011). This bias for the negative remains during remission (Thomas et al., 2011). The emotional cognitive changes that are associated with depression are similar to those seen following acute stressors. For example, stress decreases the retrieval of neutral and positive information (Kuhlmann & Wolf, 2006; Roozendaal, 2002; Roozendaal, Barsegyan, & Lee, 2008).

Conclusions

The neural and cognitive components of PTSD are embedded in impairment of the overall stress management system of the brain. While much remains to be learned regarding the pathophysiology of PTSD and its development, some broad conclusions and implications for treatment may be drawn from this overview. For the purposes of therapeutic strategies, PTSD can and should be seen primarily as a cognitive disorder that includes a disruption of stress management systems and emotional and non-emotional memory systems.

The activation of emotional circuits within the brain coupled with the activity of stress and sex hormones during stressful life events serve a positive purpose to motivate self-preservation and to respond appropriately to threat and dangerous situations. Encoding of memory for these situations and events is also valuable in that it leads to the appropriate avoidance of repeated situations of danger or threat and in some ways may be thought to "immunize" against dangerous situations in much the same way that the immunologic system "remembers" foreign invaders, bacteria, etc. and protects against those threats.

Ideally, such protection systems become active during times of threat and then return to a baseline level of activity that does not disturb the equilibrium of the organism and restores normal functioning. However, when such protection systems do not deactivate, long-term damage and corrosive effects may occur and normal functioning is not restored. Just as a dysregulated or persistently activated immunological system can produce autoimmune disease, a stress management and emotional memory system that does not return to a baseline level of activity after a stressor or threat is no longer present may produce long-term dysregulation of emotional processing, persistent activation of threat response systems, and biological and cognitive changes necessary to adapt to this persistent activation. This may lead to long-term psychopathology (e.g., PTSD).

Thus it would seem that the goal of treatment in PTSD would be to (1) reduce the persistent over activation of stress response systems, (2) change the interpretation of normal everyday experiences as threat, (3) ameliorate mood and anxiety disruption, and (4) decouple the episodic memory for traumatic events from the emotional and stress response components of that memory. While the full treatment of these four components is beyond the scope of this chapter and may require biological as well as psychological approaches, art therapy may be particularly applicable to the fourth component, since it can serve as an intermediary between the cognition of the traumatic event as separate from the emotional memory. Art therapy may also address the second treatment goal with intentional fine motor activity that can mitigate fearful responses which are grounded in the interface of the motor system and fight, flight, or freeze response, assisting in the exploration of basic emotion (Hass-Cohen et al., 2015, p. 226). Military-associated trauma may be particularly suitable for such approaches, as such events may have high visual content and visual information may be a critical piece of traumatic memories. Because these sensations are often visual and kinesthetic, art therapy appears unique among psychological therapies because of its capacity for visualization which may be a particularly powerful method for recalling traumatic memories within a safer context, exploring the emotional reaction to the manifest content of the traumatic memory and perhaps desensitizing or limiting the emotional content associated with these memories and the ensuing fear, anxiety, and activation of stress response systems.

Continuing research will be necessary to fully understand the interplay between emotion systems in the brain, episodic memory, and traumatic events. Nonetheless, advances in our understanding of the cognitive and neural aspects of the brain's response to stressful life events and trauma have been considerable. It is time that these advances are applied in a thoughtful and proactive way to the design of therapeutic strategies, including novel art therapy interventions.

References

Arnsten, A.F.T. (2009). Stress signalling pathways that impair prefrontal cortex structure and function. *Nature Reviews Neuroscience, 10*(6), 410–422.

Bisson, J., & Andrew, M. (2007). Psychological treatment of post-traumatic stress disorder (PTSD). *Cochrane Database of Systematic Review* (3), CD003388. doi: 10.1002/14651858.CD003388.pub3.

Bremner, J.D., Vermetten, E., Vythilingam, M., Afzal, N., Schmahl, C., Elzinga, B., & Charney, D.S. (2004). Neural correlates of the classic color and emotional stroop in women with abuse-related posttraumatic stress disorder. *Biological Psychiatry, 55*(6), 612–620.

Breslau, N., Kessler, R.C., Chilcoat, H.D., Schultz, L.R., Davis, G.C., & Andreski, P. (1998). Trauma and posttraumatic stress disorder in the community: The 1996 Detroit Area Survey of Trauma. *Archives of General Psychiatry, 55*(7), 626–632.

Burke, H.M., Fernald, L.C., Gertler, P.J., & Adler, N.E. (2005). Depressive symptoms are associated with blunted cortisol stress responses in very low-income women. *Psychosomatic Medicine, 67*(2), 211–216.

de Vries, G.J., & Olff, M. (2009). The lifetime prevalence of traumatic events and posttraumatic stress disorder in the Netherlands. *Journal of Traumatic Stress, 22*(4), 259–267.

Dedovic, K., Duchesne, A., Andrews, J., Engert, V., & Pruessner, J.C. (2009). The brain and the stress axis: The neural correlates of cortisol regulation in response to stress. *Neuroimage, 47*(3), 864–871.

Disner, S.G., Beevers, C.G., Haigh, E.A., & Beck, A.T. (2011). Neural mechanisms of the cognitive model of depression. *Nature Reviews Neuroscience, 12*(8), 467–477.

Drevets, W.C., Price, J.L., & Furey, M.L. (2008). Brain structural and functional abnormalities in mood disorders: Implications for neurocircuitry models of depression. *Brain Structure and Function, 213*(1–2), 93–118.

Drevets, W.C., Price, J.L., Simpson, J.R., Jr., Todd, R.D., Reich, T., Vannier, M., & Raichle, M.E. (1997). Subgenual prefrontal cortex abnormalities in mood disorders. *Nature, 386*(6627), 824–827.

Ehlers, A., & Clark, D.M. (2000). A cognitive model of posttraumatic stress disorder. *Behaviour Research and Therapy, 38*(4), 319–345.

Ehlers, A., & Steil, R. (1995). Maintenance of intrusive memories in posttraumatic stress disorder: A cognitive approach. *Behavioural and Cognitive Psychotherapy, 23*(3), 217–249.

Feldner, M.T., Zvolensky, M.J., Schmidt, N.B., & Smith, R.C. (2008). A prospective test of anxiety sensitivity as a moderator of the relation between gender and posttraumatic symptom maintenance among high anxiety sensitive young adults. *Depression and Anxiety, 25*(3), 190–199.

Gentes, E.L., Dennis, P.A., Kimbrel, N.A., Rissling, M.B., Beckham, J.C., Workgroup, V.A. M-A.M., & Calhoun, P.S. (2014). DSM-5 posttraumatic stress disorder: Factor structure and rates of diagnosis. *Journal of Psychiatric Research, 59*, 60–67.

Gold, P.W. (2015). The organization of the stress system and its dysregulation in depressive illness. *Molecular Psychiatry, 20*(1), 32–47.

Graham, B.M., & Milad, M.R. (2013). Blockade of estrogen by hormonal contraceptives impairs fear extinction in female rats and women. *Biological Psychiatry, 73*(4), 371–378.

Hackmann, A., Ehlers, A., Speckens, A., & Clark, D.M. (2004). Characteristics and content of intrusive memories in PTSD and their changes with treatment. *Journal of Traumatic Stress, 17*(3), 231–240.

Halligan, S.L., Clark, D.M., & Ehlers, A. (2002). Cognitive processing, memory, and the development of PTSD symptoms: Two experimental analogue studies. *Journal of Behavior Therapy and Experimental Psychiatry, 33*(2), 73–89.

Hankin, B.L., Mermelstein, R., & Roesch, L. (2007). Sex differences in adolescent depression: Stress exposure and reactivity models. *Child Development, 78*(1), 279–295.

Hass-Cohen, N., & Findlay, J., Cozolino, L., and Kaplan, F. (2015). *Art Therapy and the Neuroscience of Relationships, Creativity, and Resiliency: Skills and Practices.* New York: W.W. Norton & Company.

Herman, J.P., & Cullinan, W.E. (1997). Neurocircuitry of stress: Central control of the hypothalamo–pituitary–adrenocortical axis. *Trends in Neuroscience, 20*(2), 78–84.

Hermans, D., Defranc, A., Raes, F., Williams, J.M., & Eelen, P. (2005). Reduced autobiographical memory specificity as an avoidant coping style. *British Journal of Clinical Psychology, 44*(4), 583–589.

Jankord, R., & Herman, J.P. (2008). Limbic regulation of hypothalamo–pituitary–adrenocortical function during acute and chronic stress. *Annals of the New York Academy of Science, 1148*, 64–73.

Janoff-Bulman, R. (1992). *Shattered Assumptions: Towards a New Psychology of Trauma.* New York: Free Press; Maxwell Macmillan International.

Jorge, R.E. (2015). Posttraumatic stress disorder. *Behavioral Neurology and Neuropsychiatry, 21*(3), 789–805.

Kendler, K.S., Thornton, L.M., & Gardner, C.O. (2000). Stressful life events and previous episodes in the etiology of major depression in women: An evaluation of the "kindling" hypothesis. *American Journal of Psychiatry, 157*(8), 1243–1251.

Kessler, R.C., Sonnega, A., Bromet, E., Hughes, M., & Nelson, C.B. (1995). Posttraumatic stress disorder in the national comorbidity survey. *Archives of General Psychiatry, 52*(12), 1048–1060.

Kim, J.J., & Diamond, D.M. (2002). The stressed hippocampus, synaptic plasticity and lost memories. *Nature Reviews Neuroscience, 3*(6), 453–462.

Kirschbaum, C., Wust, S., & Hellhammer, D. (1992). Consistent sex differences in cortisol responses to psychological stress. *Psychosomatic Medicine, 54*(6), 648–657.

Kirschbaum, C.K.B., Gaab, J., Schommer, N.C., & Hellhammer, D.H. (1999). Impact of gender, menstrual cycle phase, and oral contraceptives on the activity of the hypothalamus–pituitary–adrenal axis. *Psychosomatic Medicine, 61*(2), 154–162.

Korszun., E.Y., & Korszun, A. (2009). Sex, trauma, stress hormones and depression. *Molecular Psychiatry, 15*, 23–28.

Kuhlmann, S., & Wolf, O.T. (2006). A non-arousing test situation abolishes the impairing effects of cortisol on delayed memory retrieval in healthy women. *Neuroscience Letters, 399*(3), 268–272.

Kushner, M.G., Riggs, D.S., Foa, E.B., & Miller, S.M. (1993). Perceived controllability and the development of posttraumatic stress disorder (PTSD) in crime victims. *Behaviour Research and Therapy, 31*(1), 105–110.

Lebron-Milad, K., Graham, B.M., & Milad, M.R. (2012). Low estradiol levels: A vulnerability factor for the development of posttraumatic stress disorder. *Biological Psychiatry, 72*(1), 6–7.

Liberzon, I., & Martis, B. (2006). Neuroimaging studies of emotional responses in PTSD. *Annals of the New York Academy of Science, 1071*, 87-109. doi:10.1196/annals.1364.009.

Liu, R.T., & Alloy, L.B. (2010). Stress generation in depression: A systematic review of the empirical literature and recommendations for future study. *Clinical Psychology Review, 30*(5), 582–593.

Lupien, S.J., & Lepage, M. (2001). Stress, memory, and the hippocampus: Can't live with it, can't live without it. *Behavioural Brain Research, 127*(1–2), 137–158.

Lupien, S.J., McEwen, B.S., Gunnar, M.R., & Heim, C. (2009). Effects of stress throughout the lifespan on the brain, behaviour and cognition. *Nature Reviews Neuroscience, 10*(6), 434–445.

Mayberg, H.S. (1997). Limbic–cortical dysregulation: A proposed model of depression. *Journal of Neuropsychiatry and Clinical Neuroscience, 9*(3), 471–481.

McGaugh, J.L. (2004). The amygdala modulates the consolidation of memories of emotionally arousing experiences. *Annual Review of Neuroscience, 27*, 1–28.

McNally, R.J. (2006). Cognitive abnormalities in post-traumatic stress disorder. *Trends in Cognitive Science, 10*(6), 271–277.

Mikulincer, M., & Solomon, Z. (1988). Attributional style and combat-related posttraumatic stress disorder. *Journal of Abnormal Psychology, 97*(3), 308–313.

Milad, M.R., Igoe, S.A., Lebron-Milad, K., & Novales, J.E. (2009). Estrous cycle phase and gonadal hormones influence conditioned fear extinction. *Neuroscience, 164*(3), 887–895.

Milad, M.R., Pitman, R.K., Ellis, C.B., Gold, A.L., Shin, L.M., Lasko, N.B., … Rauch, S.L. (2009). Neurobiological basis of failure to recall extinction memory in posttraumatic stress disorder. *Biological Psychiatry, 66*(12), 1075–1082.

Phelps, E.A. (2004). Human emotion and memory: Interactions of the amygdala and hippocampal complex. *Current Opinion in Neurobiology, 14*, 198–202.

Phelps, E.A. (2006). Emotion and cognition: Insights from studies of the human amygdala. *Annual Review of Psychology, 27*–53.

Phillips, M.L., Drevets, W.C., Rauch, S.L., & Lane, R. (2003). Neurobiology of emotion perception I: The neural basis of normal emotion perception. *Biological Psychiatry, 54*, 504–514.

Phillips, M.L., Ladouceur, C.D., & Drevets, W.C. (2008). A neural model of voluntary and automatic emotion regulation: Implications for understanding the pathophysiology and neurodevelopment of bipolar disorder. *Molecular Psychiatry, 13*(9), 829, 833–857.

Pruessner, J., Dedovic, K., Pruessner, M., Lord, C., Buss, C., Collins, L, … Lupien, S. (2009). Stress regulation in the central nervous system: evidence from structural and functional neuroimaging studies in human populations. *Psychoneuroendocrinology, 35*(1), 179–191.

Pruessner, J.C., Dedovic, K., Khalili-Mahani, N., Engert, V., Pruessner, M., Buss, C., … Lupien, S. (2008). Deactivation of the imbic system during acute psychosocial stress: Evidence from positron emission tomography and functional magnetic resonance imaging studies. *Biological Psychiatry, 63*(2), 234–240.

Rauch, S.L., Shin, L.M., & Wright, C.I. (2003). Neuroimaging studies of amygdala function in anxiety disorders. *Annals of the New York Academy of Sciences, 985*(1), 389–410.

Roozendaal, B. (2002). Stress and memory: Opposing effects of glucocorticoids on memory consolidation and memory retrieval. *Neurobiology of Learning Memory, 78*(3), 578–595.

Roozendaal, B., Barsegyan, A., & Lee, S. (2008). Adrenal stress hormones, amygdala activation, and memory for emotionally arousing experiences. *Progress in Brain Research, 167*, 79–97.

Shin, L.M., Wright, C.I., Cannistraro, P.A., Wedig, M.M., McMullin, K., Martis, B., … Rauch, S.L. (2005). A functional magnetic resonance imaging study of amygdala and medial prefrontal cortex responses to overtly presented fearful faces in posttraumatic stress disorder. *Archives of General Psychiatry, 62*(3), 273–281. doi:10.1001/archpsyc.62.3.273.

Sloan, D.M., Strauss, M.E., & Wisner, K.L. (2001). Diminished response to pleasant stimuli by depressed women. *Journal of Abnormal Psychology, 110*(3), 488–493.

Suslow, T., Konrad, C., Kugel, H., Rumstadt, D., Zwitserlood, P., Schoning, S., … Dannlowski, U. (2010). Automatic mood-congruent amygdala responses to masked facial expressions in major depression. *Biological Psychiatry, 67*(2), 155–160.

Thomas, E.J., Elliott, R., McKie, S., Arnone, D., Downey, D., Juhasz, G., … & Anderson, I.M. (2011). Interaction between a history of depression and rumination on neural response to emotional faces. *Psychological Medicine, 41*(9), 1845–1855.

Vamvakopoulos, N.V. (1995). Sexual dimorphism of stress response and immune/inflammatory reaction: The corticotropin releasing hormone perspective. *Mediators of Inflammation, 4*(3), 163–174.

Wang, J., Korczykowski, M., Rao, H., Fan, Y., Pluta, J., Gur, R.C., … Detre, J.A. (2007). Gender difference in neural response to psychological stress. *Social Cognitive and Affective Neuroscience, 2*(3), 227–239.

Watkins, P.C., Martin, C.K., & Stern, L.D. (2000). Unconscious memory bias in depression: Perceptual and conceptual processes. *Journal of Abnormal Psychology, 109*(2), 282–289.

Zeidan, M.A., Igoe, S.A., Linnman, C., Vitalo, A., Levine, J.B., Klibanski, A., … Milad, M.R. (2011). Estradiol modulates medial prefrontal cortex and amygdala activity during fear extinction in women and female rats. *Biological Psychiatry, 70*(10), 920–927.

Plate 1 Pastel drawing entitled "God's promises are True."

Plate 2 Group mask project from Creative Arts Therapy (CAT) group.

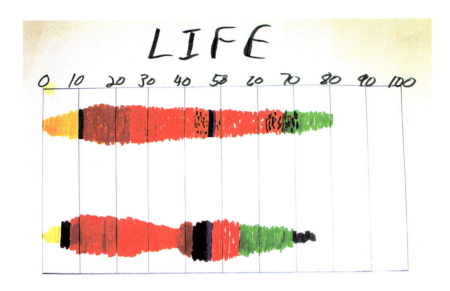

Plate 3 Drawing entitled "Life."

Plate 4 Lisa's picture of the destroyer and the lover.

Plate 5 Commemoration/memorial box.

Plate 6 Drawing by individual experiencing nightmares following a blast injury.
Source: (Originally published in "Art therapy for PTSD and TBI: A senior active duty military service member's therapeutic journey," *Arts in Psychotherapy*. Vol. 49, July 2016. Reprinted with permission.)

Plate 7 Service members accessing their strengths.

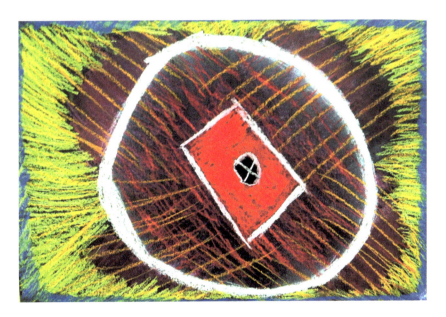

Plate 8 Inner demons.

Plate 9 A sketching artist.
Source Photograph by Belinda Carr of Arts of the Covenant, California, printed with permission.

Plate 10 Monsters on the Bus—Tiny.

Plate 11 Graphic expression of MST and the survivor's representation of the experience.

Plate 12 Untitled, colored pencil on paper, 18 × 24 inches.

CHAPTER **8**

Complicated Grief: Considerations for Treatment of Military Populations

Jacqueline P. Jones

When someone, a civilian, dies here, in America, there's a place to go to visit, to think of the person, to leave notes or flowers. There, on the battlefield, your battle buddy is shot. You keep runnin' and gunnin' because you have to, and someone else drags their body to safety. They're loaded onto the bird, and the spot of land where they were killed just blends into the rest of the Afghan landscape. Their body is flown back to their home state, where a funeral is held, while you're still deployed, pretending like it didn't affect you.

(Compilation of quotes by service members discussing common experiences with grief)

Death affects us all. Every life will eventually end in death and everyone will experience the effects of death and loss of significant others. Our nation's warriors are especially familiar with this reality. Despite the fact that military occupations require service members to encounter, confront, and accept the very real possibility of death and dying, many factors contribute to the complication of service members' grief processes. This chapter will provide definitions of grief and manifestations of complicated grief as well as military-specific contributing factors that place service members at risk for complicated grief. The author has provided clinical art therapy to active duty service members in treatment for traumatic brain injury (TBI) and psychological health (PH) conditions at Intrepid Spirit One (ISO), the National Intrepid Center of Excellence satellite at Fort Belvoir. It became apparent that complicated grief was a significant phenomenon that should be taken into consideration and addressed while providing behavioral health treatment to this population.

Grief

Despite the universality of grief as part of the human condition, its manifestation is unique for each individual. In order to address various presentations of grief, basic components must be defined. Bereavement refers to loss; grief describes the emotional response to a loss; grief work allows an individual to progress through the pain brought on by the loss; and mourning refers to the practices and behaviors displayed by an individual in response to a loss which are shaped by societal norms and expectations (Brabant, 2002).

Expression of grief is extremely variable and involves "physical, emotional, cognitive, spiritual, and social" elements (Drenth, Herbst, & Strydom, 2010, p. 1) that oscillate (Bonanno, 2009) and change over time (Shear, 2015). During acute grief, an individual typically responds to the separation from the loved one as well as to stress caused by the loss. The bereaved often experiences yearning, sadness, shock, thoughts of the deceased, confusion regarding identity, and withdrawal from activities (Shear, 2015).

The Dual Process Model of Coping with Bereavement posits that bereaved individuals deal with bereavement-related stressors by undertaking loss- and restoration-oriented coping strategies (Stroebe & Schut, 1999). Loss-oriented coping involves processing aspects of the loss itself, such as focusing on the person who died, life together, and circumstances of the death. Restoration-oriented coping involves focusing on identifying what consequences need to be dealt with and how. George Bonanno (2009) suggests that there are three potential courses for bereavement: (1) resilience, found to be the most commonly experienced, in which an individual is able to process the pain associated with the grief with minimal effect on functioning; (2) recovery, in which an individual may be acutely overwhelmed by grief but gradually progresses back to a functional state; and (3) chronic grief, in which an individual struggles with grief symptoms and impairments that are longer lasting (pp. 6–7).

Complicated Grief

A bereaved person is considered to be experiencing complicated grief when a grief response is particularly severe and prolonged according to social norms and chronically impairs functioning in various domains. Complicated grief is characterized by chronic yearning and sadness, persistent thoughts of the deceased, and an inability to accept the reality of the death. The bereaved may obsess over consequences of the loss or personal feelings of anger and guilt associated with the death, may oscillate between avoiding reminders of the death and constantly seeking physical proximity via their belongings, and self-isolate as he or she develops a belief that positive feelings were linked strictly with the person who died (Shear, 2015). Shear (2015) further states that complicated grief is more likely to occur following the death of a significant other or a child, or a death that occurred suddenly and violently. Additional risk factors for a bereaved person to develop complicated grief include pre-loss factors such as a history of mood or anxiety disorders, substance abuse, numerous losses, insecure attachment styles, acting as a caregiver for the deceased, and post-death stressors such as financial problems, social conflicts, and lack of support in the aftermath of the loss (Shear, 2015). These factors perpetuate the longing for the deceased and prevent the loss- and restoration-oriented processing in grief work.

Grief Involving Violent Death

When the circumstances that surround a death are traumatic, the bereaved individual is faced with the overwhelming task of processing both their grief and their reaction to trauma simultaneously. A healthy grieving process can be impeded by typical responses to trauma, such as denial, avoidance of any reminder of the event or loss, and shattered worldviews and images of self, thus prolonging the initiation of grief work, thereby establishing a complicated grief trajectory. Responding to grief and trauma requires coping strategies that are often contradictory, further complicating an individual's ability to resolve either. The intolerable nature of post-traumatic stress symptoms such as re-experiencing and hyperarousal cause the survivor to avoid the event, thus preventing sufficient processing of the traumatic event (Brewin & Holmes, 2003; Dalgleish, 2004; Ehlers & Clark, 2000, cited in Smith, Abeyta, Hughes, & Jones, 2015) as well as processing the deaths that occurred (Smith et al., 2015). In addition to intrusive images of violent death, lowered self-efficacy and disruptions in worldview caused by the traumatic event (Smith et al., 2015) make the process of acknowledging loss and developing productive strategies to deal with trauma and grief more challenging.

Disenfranchised Grief

Grief may become complicated if the bereaved individual experiences disenfranchised grief. Disenfranchised grief occurs when an individual experiences a loss and is not afforded the opportunity to grieve (Doka, 2002). The grief experienced is not acknowledged publicly, nor is it validated by others, due to the grieving norms established by the society in which the bereaved individual lives. The grief may be disenfranchised for several reasons: not recognizing the relationship with the deceased; the loss not being acknowledged as significant; the exclusion of the griever from mourning practices; the circumstances of the death (i.e., if the nature of the death is stigmatized); and the manifestations of grief (Doka, 2002). In addition, grief may become disenfranchised as a result of lack of empathy from oneself, family, community, or transcendent reality (Neimeyer & Jordan, 2002).

Disenfranchised grief exacerbates grief symptoms and complicates grieving processes. The circumstances that disenfranchise the grief intensify the emotions already inherent in grief and have been shown to result in greater severity of anger, guilt, and feeling powerless (Doka, 2002). Disenfranchised grief often leads to private grief, resulting in the griever experiencing a lack of social support and not engaging in helpful mourning rituals within society. Isolated from grieving within a social context, the griever's focus may become fixated on the past, inhibiting the ability to develop senses of pleasure and meaning in a world in which the deceased no longer exists (Jordan & Litz, 2014).

Aspects of Military Service Which Place Service Members at Risk for Complicated Grief

Artworks created in art therapy at the ISO frequently express struggles with prolonged and disenfranchised grief. Losses that frequently lead to complicated grief include sudden, violent deaths, especially when the survivor needed to continue to fight for his own survival, deaths that could not be overtly mourned, deaths of civilian women and children living in the midst of war, deaths of comrades that occur after service members had been reassigned to other units, deaths of family members while an individual is deployed, and loss of aspects of self or career, especially when caused by invisible injuries.

Military personnel are continually at risk for contact with violent death (Benedek & Ursano, 2006). Combat deployment settings are extremely conducive to complicated and disenfranchised grief as service members routinely face situations that would cause grief while not accorded the opportunity to process their emotions. Combat infantry Army and Marine units who served in Operation Iraqi Freedom (OIF) and Operation Enduring Freedom (OEF) include: "being attacked or ambushed" (58–95%); "being responsible for the death of an enemy combatant" (12–65%); "being responsible for the death of a noncombatant" (1–28%); "seeing dead bodies or human remains" (39–95%); "handling or uncovering human remains" (12–57%); "knowing someone seriously injured or killed" (43–87%); "seeing ill or injured women or children whom you were unable to help" (46–83%); "had a buddy shot or hit who was near you" (22–26%) (Hoge et al., 2004, p. 18). Such experiences occur within a military culture that "explicitly regulates the expression of emotion" (Christian, Stivers, & Sammons, 2009, p. 31). An effective means of conditioning service members to suppress emotions is by engraining a sense of weakness associated with an expression of sadness. Shay (1994) presents an example of an American soldier in Vietnam who, while holding a dead buddy, was told by his company commander to "'Stuff those tears' and 'Don't get sad, get even!'" (p. 63); "To weep was to lose one's dignity among American soldiers in Vietnam," (p. 63), and this is seen commonly in current conflicts as well.

Oftentimes combat environments involve situations in which the individual's life is also at imminent risk, leaving him psychologically unavailable to grieve. While engaged in a firefight, for instance, an infantryman must continue to manage or extinguish threat, oftentimes utilizing instinctual processes, thereby prolonging the opportunity to work through his grief. When violent deaths occur within traumatic contexts, an individual's "psychological commitment to survival" may deny him the "luxury of grief" (Raphael, Stevens, & Dunsmore, 2006, p. 9). Service members are on constant alert, which requires ongoing externally focused awareness. Grief requires individuals to be inwardly focused on their internal emotions, which would leave service members and others around them at greater risk for vulnerability and potential death (Shay, 2004). After reviewing his own graphic narrative of a combat trauma in which he was shot (saved by his flak jacket) and then ran over to a buddy who had also been shot and was killed in action, a Marine Sergeant stated: "I was hit … then later stood frozen as I watched someone so close to me die. When I got back to the PB, I had an hour to sulk in it, then I was told to get back to work. That's not normal grieving" (personal communication, May 8, 2015).

OIF and OEF have placed service members in war theaters in which enemy insurgents and other threatening persons are difficult to distinguish from non-threatening civilians, which has required service members to make quick decisions in ambiguous situations. Grief becomes complicated when emotional responses to these quick decisions set in. Knowing that the rules of engagement have been followed may only go so far to psychologically comfort a service member who has killed a woman or child. Ambiguity of warfare and questioning one's actions leads to intensified feelings of self-judgment, anger, guilt, and hopelessness of mankind (Drescher et al., 2009) which complicate the grief process.

It is not uncommon for bereaved service members to miss the opportunity to communalize grief. Community-based rituals allow people to collectively acknowledge grief and provide venues for people to receive and give social support to others who share in the loss. According to Doka (2002), "rituals that connote loss are critical to mourning. These rituals provide structure and support for the expression of grief" (p. 8). However, when referring to opportunities to collectively grieve fallen soldiers in Vietnam, Shay (1994) writes: "communal recognitions of deaths were … conducted by rear-echelon officers who had no emotional connection to the dead or their comrades" (p. 66), and "mourning was dreaded, perfunctory, delayed, devalued, mocked, fragmented, minimized, deflected, disregarded, and sedated" (p. 67).

According to Commander Matthew Stevens, Chief of the Pastoral Care Department at Fort Belvoir Community Hospital, the transient nature of the Military is an institutional factor that results in disenfranchised grief. A service member may train with a unit, deploy with that unit, and then be reassigned to another unit shortly after returning stateside, thereby leaving a unit where grief could be shared and mutually supported to go to a new unit in which the bereaved becomes isolated in their grief (personal communication, April 2015). The transient nature of a military career further isolates bereaved service members when fellow comrades are killed in action or die by accidents or suicide as time passes, or members of units disperse through reassignments or retirements, leaving survivors often isolated and apart from others who would otherwise share in the grief. It is also common for service members to miss grieving rituals when family members die either because they were deployed and unable to return home to attend the funeral, or they are not informed of a death until they return home.

Even after service members return home from war zones and would seemingly have an opportunity to grieve more fully, society's general lack of understanding of the depth of one's love for a buddy further prolongs the grief process. Military culture emphasizes collectivism and teaches that "an individual is of limited value, whereas the unit can accomplish anything" (Christian et al., 2009, p. 32). From training in harsh environments to fighting in combat, service members establish close friendships, develop unit cohesion, rely on others for their own survival, develop commitment and accountability for the survival of group members, and instinctually place buddies' lives ahead of their own on the battlefield (Christian et al., 2009). Despite the fact that service members often describe feeling deep love for comrades that has no equal outside of the warrior sector, they are often faced with a lack of empathy when exhibiting symptoms of grief over the loss of military brothers. In the United States, as in many other societies, grieving rules are typically limited to loss of family members (Doka, 2002). Grieving mores and society's lack of understanding of military comradeship further disenfranchise a service member's grief for the loss of a fellow warrior. The felt lack of sympathy and external and internal disenfranchisement often lead to feelings of anger and hurt which further one's isolation, increasing the severity of complicated grief (Shear, Gorscak, & Simon, 2006).

As medical care in combat zones improves, resulting in fewer mortalities and an increase in wounded casualties, loss of aspects of self and career is a category of grief that is growing in prevalence among returning service members. Physical, cognitive, and psychological injuries leave affected service members faced with the challenge of accepting lost abilities and their "new normal." Approximately one-third of service members returning from conflicts in Iraq and Afghanistan suffer from post-traumatic stress disorder (PTSD), major depression, or report probable TBI due to exposure to blasts (Tanielian & Jaycox, 2008)—a significant number returning with invisible injuries of war. Psychosocial loss refers to loss that occurs when an individual changes markedly from the person he or she once was (Doka & Aber, 2002). When a person continues to maintain the same physical appearance, the bereaved persons (the individual and those surrounding him or her) maintain denial of the loss for a greater period of time than more apparent physical injuries and losses. Grieving psychosocial loss is especially difficult because there are no societal rituals with which to recognize the change (Doka & Aber, 2002).

A by-product of grief that is silenced down range and at home is the development of negative coping strategies that perpetuate complicated grief. Silenced grief causes feelings of guilt and shame to develop within the survivor, which inhibit grief by giving the bereaved further reason to suppress their grief and focus on feelings of shame instead of on the loss itself (Kuhn, 2002). Feelings of self-blame and survivor's guilt may also stem from traumatic death. Service members often share feelings of guilt associated with failing to protect their brothers, their leadership, those under their command, or innocent civilians. Feeling at fault for deaths of others causes the survivor to maintain utilization of defense mechanisms such as silence, avoidance, and suppression. Self-blame for the death of a comrade may be viewed as a way to keep the deceased in the present (Shay, 1994). Maintaining feelings of intense pain associated with a loss can act as evidence of the intensity of the love shared in the relationship with the deceased; letting pain subside would feel like a betrayal (Shear et al., 2006). While the utilization of avoidance defense mechanisms is understandable, traumatic

104   J.P. Jones

grief needs to be processed, as using avoidant-based strategies to cope with stressors is associated with increased psychological distress and decreased resilience (Holahan & Moos, 1987, cited in Kelly & Vogt, 2009).

Art Therapy as Vehicle to Process Complicated Grief

Art therapy is demonstrating value as an especially effective means of processing complicated grief for service members seeking care at ISO. Patients report that art therapy enables them to deal comfortably with subject matter that they have been suppressing and avoiding. Jordan and Litz (2014) describe core elements of treatment for prolonged grief as: psychoeducation on grief; emotional processing of the loss; social engagement and confrontation of activities that have been avoided for being reminders of the loss; identification of goals to promote greater sense of life meaning; and challenging cognitions that impede success with the previously stated tasks. Shear (2015) describes treatment for complicated grief as addressing two main tasks: working to reduce negative feelings that promote complicated grief so that the loss can be focused on, and working to restore one's own functioning, thereby successfully adapting to the loss. It has been shown that patients in treatment for prolonged grief show greater improvement in grief symptoms, sociability, and cognitive change when their treatment involves exposure to, and a format for, the emotional processing of the distressing event prior to cognitive restructuring tasks (Bryant et al., 2014).

Utilizing art expression to process loss is effective because it allows for exposure to subject matter otherwise avoided, the expression of painful feelings, and a means for managing chaos and meaning making. Since art making naturally utilizes sensory processes, and thus accesses the limbic system's storage of sensory memories linked to events that are traumatic or stressful, art expression is emerging as a critical element of trauma processing (Malchiodi, 2003). Art expression provides a means for re-exposure to a traumatic event, which is essential in trauma processing since it allows for the suppressed material to be brought forth into consciousness, where it can then be restructured into a way the survivor finds more manageable (Steele, 2003). Art making not only assists service members in bringing factual elements of events into consciousness; it also provides a means to express, acknowledge, and consciously feel emotions that have been suppressed regarding the losses. According to existential art therapist Bruce Moon (2009), "Creation does not ease pain but, rather, ennobles it. It does not cure it, it accepts. … Art embraces people's deepest fears, loneliness, pain, and guilt" (p. 117). Through art expression, service members are able to externalize and sit with their feelings of self-blame, guilt, anger, and sadness—the avoidance of which exacerbates complicated grief. Once facts and feelings associated with events are externalized through visual means, service members are faced with a reflection of their internal experience of grief. Art products then create a platform for them to begin to develop insight into which feelings are complicating their grief; face, bring order to, and resolve internal conflicts; make meaning as a result of the loss; and assume a role as creator of progress that can come out of the event and loss—all while honoring the significance of the life lost, creating permanent objects that keep the spirit of the loss alive in present awareness, in a means that can be shared with and received by others, promoting essential social connections.

Case Example

M is a 31-year-old active duty United States Marine Corps Gunnery Sergeant who was referred to ISO for evaluation for TBI after exhibiting chronic headaches and noticeable memory loss. In addition to these symptoms, M presented with dizziness, blurred vision, sleep disturbances, a history of mild traumatic brain injury (mTBI), irritability, and mood swings. He has been diagnosed with war-related mTBI, cognitive disorder, tinnitus, and PTSD. M has been an active duty Marine for 11 years, has deployed to Iraq twice, in 2004 and 2005, to Afghanistan in 2011, and to Japan, Korea, and Thailand in 2012. His history of mTBI is the cumulative result of injuries sustained while playing football, during martial arts instructor training, and nearly daily encounters with nearby blasts from IEDs, rocket-propelled grenades (RPGs), and mortars while in Iraq and Afghanistan. His PTSD is mainly rooted in his 2004 and 2005 deployments to Iraq, as 20 of his friends were killed during his first deployment and a Major he was responsible for protecting was killed when he stepped on an IED during his second deployment. M was referred to art therapy when his physiatrist at ISO recommended he engage in interdisciplinary treatment offered throughout the clinic to address his cognitive, physical, and emotional impairments and symptoms that affect his ability to handle responsibilities at work and at home without becoming cognitively exhausted and emotionally irritated, angry, and reactive.

M engaged in many art therapy opportunities, including both group-based and individual art therapy. From the first session, the prevalence of complicated grief processes became evident in M's artistic expressions. He participated in art therapy group sessions which allow service members to openly express themselves using a variety of creative arts media and modalities. M first wrote a poem expressing how the light of life breaks down the stones of pain of the past, then began acknowledging the impact of grief upon his life as he constructed a montage painting to express how stones, which represent fellow soldiers who died during deployment, create ripples that lead to chaos in his life.

M created a mask in individual art therapy sessions. The cover of the mask presents an American flag design with a bullet hole through the forehead, which M described as a representation of his patriotism while acknowledging pain that comes along with his military career. M utilized the inside of the mask to confront the primary source for his complicated grief. He depicted the dead, torn-apart body of the Major who was killed when he stepped on an IED right behind M, who had been tasked with protecting his life (Figures 8.1a and 8.1b). In this event, M's sense of self-efficacy was destroyed as he had failed at his job of protecting the Major; his worldview was shattered as everyone believed the

106 J.P. Jones

Figure 8.1a and 8.1b Outside and inside of mask.

Major to be invincible and this event proved that no one was immune to the dangers of combat; he lost faith in God, which had been his primary source of resiliency up until that point; he developed self-hatred for not protecting the Major and for questioning God; and he was injured in the blast and sustained an mTBI himself. After utilizing art to expose the event and to allow associated feelings to surface, M became ready to address conflicts with feelings that complicated his grief.

In level two art therapy groups in which service members are provided with more specific directives that enable them to express and process concepts of identity, one's soul, grief and loss, and transitions, M began to use creative processes to externalize his internal conflicts related to his losses, specifically the traumatic loss of the Major. In a drawing of his greatest fear, M depicted the "epic battle" within his mind in which he has been unable to trust in his greatest desire to provide protection for his family since he was unable to protect the Major. When group members were asked to write a dialogue between themselves and an entity of their choice, M wrote a dialogue between himself and his inner soul and/or Jesus. This exercise allowed M to express his anger at God for the events that had happened in Iraq, his disappointment in himself for allowing the Major to die and for projecting that anger onto God, being deserving of inwardly directed anger onto himself, and acknowledgment of risks associated with self-punishment. In a depiction of his soul, M drew an image of an ocean to represent how he feels constantly "pounded, pounded, pounded" and unable to reach calmer waters which he related to his inability to reconcile the traumatic death of the Major and his consequential relationship with God. In a depiction of what his soul needs, M represented the peace he finds when snuggling up with his daughters and watching cartoons. M recognized the importance of working toward acceptance, as his current state of anger prevented him from always being the father figure he wanted to be for his daughters.

Later, service members were asked to create commemoration/memorial boxes with the option to make the outsides celebrate aspects of self/career and the insides to memorialize or grieve aspects of self/career. On the outside of his box, M placed his division symbols as well as photos and references to two commanding officers who had played pivotal roles in taking over Fallujah who were killed in Iraq. On the inside, M created a Sculpey model of the Pendleton cross, which his unit constructed to mourn Marines whose lives were lost in Iraq and Afghanistan, so that he could figuratively visit the site whenever he wants to honor the deceased. After speaking with his mother-in-law about his grief, she responded by sharing a quote to assist with his grieving process, which he then added as the finishing touch to the inside of his box: "There are stars whose radiance is visible on Earth though they have long been extinct. There are people whose brilliance continues to light the world even though they are no longer among the living. – Hannah Senesh."

Please refer to Plate 5 in the color plate section.

In individual sessions, M continued to explore various ways in which art could be used in his recovery. These included depicting images of combat trauma, to drawing portraits of those killed in action, to developing a sketch for a tattoo design that he plans to get (Figure 8.2). M's tattoo design incorporates the tree of life whose roots will acknowledge all the Marines he had known and lost throughout his career, whose leaves will acknowledge his own family members, and whose trunk is surrounded by animal symbols of the Major who was killed as well as a his personal military self. M spent the remainder of his art therapy treatment creating an 18 × 24-inch mixed-media grief processing book in which he dedicated each page to creating an image to memorialize each comrade who had died.

Summary

Art therapy has provided a vehicle for M to process complicated grief. He has been able to address the effects of pain caused by losses he has survived throughout his military career, to externalize traumatic circumstances surrounding deaths, and to express and process feelings of self-blame and self-hatred that have fueled his unstable moods and issues with anger. He has been able to connect with group members also working through complicated grief, to open communication with family members who support him in his grief, to honor those lost while finding purpose in his own survival, and to cognitively restructure how he should deal with his grief. M has shifted from a belief that he needs to be punished for the Major's death to the point of physical and emotional self-destruction, to a belief that productively processing the complicated grief and working toward healing and recovery from mTBI and PTSD will allow him to become the person he wants to be for

Figure 8.2 Tree of life tattoo.

his family. M continues to utilize art therapy as a primary means for recovery and reconciliation.

Service members are at increased risk for disenfranchised and complicated grief due to military-related factors and the warrior's place within society at large. It is imperative that complicated grief issues be better understood and identified in order to provide improved care for our service members. Since loss is permanent, grief is never completed or resolved. Art therapy demonstrates value as a therapeutic modality that can support bereaved individuals in their progression through complicated grief.

The views expressed in this chapter are those of the author and do not reflect the official policy of the Department of Defense, or the U.S. Government.

References

Benedek, D.M., & Ursano, R.J. (2006). Mass violent death and military communities: Domains of response in military operations, disaster, and terrorism. In E.K. Rynearson (Ed.), *Violent Death: Resilience and Intervention beyond the Crisis* (pp. 295–309). New York: Routledge.

Bonanno, G.A. (2009). *The Other Side of Sadness: What the New Science of Bereavement Tells Us about Life after Loss.* New York: Basic Books.

Brabant, S. (2002). A closer look at Doka's grieving rules. In K.J. Doka (Ed.), *Disenfranchised Grief: New Directions, Challenges, and Strategies for Practice* (pp. 23–38). Champaign, IL: Research Press.

Bryant, R.A., Kenny, L., Joscelyne, A., Rawson, N., Maccallum, F., Cahill, C., Hopwood, S., Aderka, I., & Nickerson, A. (2014). Treating prolonged grief disorder: A randomized clinical trial. *JAMA Psychiatry, 71*(12), 1332–1339. doi: 10.1001/jaapsychiatry.2014.1600.

Christian, J.R., Stivers, J.R., & Sammons, M.T. (2009). Training to the warrior ethos: Implications for clinicians treating military members and their families. In S.M. Freeman, B.A. Moore, & A. Freeman (Eds.), *Living and Surviving in Harm's Way* (pp. 27–49). New York: Routledge.

Doka, K.J. (2002). Introduction. In K.J. Doka (Ed.), *Disenfranchised Grief: New Directions, Challenges, and Strategies for Practice* (pp. 5–22). Champaign, IL: Research Press.

Doka, K.J., & Aber, R.A. (2002). Psychosocial loss and grief. In K.J. Doka (Ed.), *Disenfranchised Grief: New Directions, Challenges, and Strategies for Practice* (pp. 217–231). Champaign, IL: Research Press.

Drenth, C.M., Herbst, A.G., & Strydom, H. (2010). A complicated grief intervention model. *Health SA Gesondheid, 15*(1), Art. #415, 1–8. doi: 10.4102/hsag.v15i1.415.

Drescher, K.D., Burgoyne, M., Casas, E., Lovato, L., Curran, E., Pivar, I., & Foy, D.W. (2009). Issues of grief, loss, honor, and remembrance: Spirituality and work with military personnel and their families. In S.M. Freeman, B.A. Moore, & A. Freeman (Eds.), *Living and Surviving in Harm's Way* (pp. 437–465). New York: Routledge.

Hoge, C.W., Castro, C.A., Messer, S.C., McGurk, D., Cotting, D.I., & Koffman, R.L. (2004). Combat duty in Iraq and Afghanistan, mental health problems, and barriers to care. *The New England Journal of Medicine, 351*(1), 13–22.

Jordan, A.H., & Litz, B.T. (2014). Prolonged grief disorder: Diagnostic, assessment, and treatment considerations. *Professional Psychology: Research and Practice, 45*(3), 180–187. doi: 10.1037/a0036836.

Kelly, M.M., & Vogt, D.S. (2009). Military stress: Effects of acute, chronic, and traumatic stress on mental and physical health. In S.M. Freeman, B.A. Moore, & A. Freeman (Eds.), *Living and Surviving in Harm's Way* (pp. 85–106). New York: Routledge.

Kuhn, D.R. (2002). A pastoral counselor looks at silence as a factor in disenfranchised grief. In K.J. Doka (Ed.), *Disenfranchised Grief: New Directions, Challenges, and Strategies for Practice* (pp. 119–126). Champaign, IL: Research Press.

Malchiodi, C.A. (2003). Art therapy and the brain. In C.A. Malchiodi (Ed.), *Handbook of Art Therapy* (pp. 16–24). New York: The Guilford Press.

Moon, B.L. (2009). *Existential Art Therapy: The Canvas Mirror.* Springfield, IL: Charles C. Thomas.

Neimeyer, R.A., & Jordan, J.R. (2002). Disenfranchisement as empathic failure: Grief therapy and the co-construction of meaning. In K.J. Doka (Ed.), *Disenfranchised Grief: New Directions, Challenges, and Strategies for Practice* (pp. 95–117). Champaign, IL: Research Press.

Raphael, B., Stevens, G., & Dunsmore, J. (2006). Clinical theories of loss and grief. In E.K. Rynearson (Ed.), *Violent Death: Resilience and Intervention beyond the Crisis* (pp. 3–29). New York: Routledge.

Shay, J. (1994). *Achilles in Vietnam: Combat Trauma and the Undoing of Character.* New York: Scribner.

Shear, K., Gorscak, B., & Simon, N. (2006). Treatment of complicated grief following violent death. In E.K. Rynearson (Ed.), *Violent Death: Resilience and Intervention beyond the Crisis* (pp. 157–174). New York: Routledge.

Shear, M.K. (2015). Complicated grief. *The New England Journal of Medicine, 372*(2), 153–160. doi: 10.1056/NEJMcp1315618.

Smith, A.J., Abeyta, A.A., Hughes, M., & Jones, R.T. (2015). Persistent grief in the aftermath of mass violence: The predictive roles of posttraumatic stress symptoms, self-efficacy, and disrupted worldview. *Psychological Trauma: Theory, Research, Practice, and Policy, 7*(2), 179–186. doi: 10.1037/tra0000002.

Steele, W. (2003). Using drawing in short-term trauma resolution. In C.A. Malchiodi (Ed.), *Handbook of Art Therapy* (pp. 139–151). New York: The Guilford Press.

Stroebe, M., & Schut, H. (1999). The dual process model of coping with bereavement: Rationale and description. *Death Studies, 23*(3), 197–224.

Tanielian, T., & Jaycox, L.H. (2008). *Invisible Wounds of War: Psychological and Cognitive Injuries, Consequences, and Services to Assist Recovery.* Retrieved April 5, 2017, from http://www.rand.org.

CHAPTER 9

Integrative Approaches to Treating PTSD and TBI: Art Therapy Approaches within the National Intrepid Center of Excellence at Walter Reed National Military Medical Center

Melissa S. Walker

The National Intrepid Center of Excellence (NICoE)

The NICoE is the Military Health System (MHS) institute for complex, co-morbid traumatic brain injury (TBI) and psychological health (PH) conditions. Located on the base of Walter Reed National Military Medical Center in Bethesda, MD, the NICoE delivers comprehensive and holistic care, conducts focused research, and exports knowledge to benefit service members, their families, and society. Combat- and mission-related TBI with PH conditions affect countless service members and their families each year. Although each condition can cause specific symptoms, a complex constellation of symptoms may emerge that requires a unique treatment plan (NICoE One Pager, n.d.). According to the National Center for PTSD, mild traumatic brain injury (mTBI) is often referred to as the "signature injury" of the conflicts in Iraq and Afghanistan, and service members who have experienced mTBI are at increased risk of depression and underlying PH conditions to include post-traumatic stress disorder (PTSD) (Summerall, 2014).

Active duty service members of all branches, ranks, and ages are referred to the NICoE by their primary care providers and then guided through a four-week intensive outpatient care program which includes conventional and complementary/integrative treatment. Over the course of the four weeks, service members are exposed to 18 different clinical specialties and attend an estimated 115 appointments with providers (W. Greenhalgh, personal communication, July 2015). This immersion allows for the service member to be cared for holistically, through the integration of cognitive (speech and language pathology, neurology, assistive technology), physical medicine and rehabilitation (internal medicine, physical therapy, occupational therapy, audiology, ophthalmology), behavioral health (psychiatry, neuropsychology, family therapy, art/music therapy), and wellness (Western and mind/body medicine, nutrition, dance/movement therapy, Chaplain services) treatments. The facility operates on the premise that the psychological, physical, and spiritual parts of an individual do not operate exclusively of one another, but rather affect one another.

While at the NICoE, service members are introduced to the creative arts therapies as a means to express themselves and process their identities, stressors, transitions, and traumatic memories. Art therapy, as well as music therapy and therapeutic writing, is the standard of care at the facility, and group and individual art therapy sessions are integrated into every service member's four-week treatment plan. This format provides the opportunity for service members who wouldn't usually opt to partake in art therapy to be exposed to and explore the process, often surprising themselves and eventually fully integrating the arts into their treatment regimen and lives. Based on observation of benefit from art therapy by the treatment team, as well as service member feedback and request, service members may be scheduled for follow-up sessions in their third and fourth weeks. It is observed that many service members also opt to visit the art therapy studio space during their lunch-hours, breaks in care, and after-care hours to work on projects autonomously.

The following list includes treatment goals of art therapy at the NICoE, as well as the improvements observed after the sessions, with guidance from Collie, Backos, Malchiodi, and Spiegal, (2006; Walker (2013):

- *Traumatic brain injury (TBI):* Increased stamina and frustration tolerance, increased dexterity and hand–eye coordination, improved initiation of sequential activities, increased on-task duration, task completion improvement.
- *Post-traumatic stress disorder (PTSD):* Reduction of arousal and hyper-vigilance, reconsolidation of memories, increased ability to externalize and process traumatic memories, reactivation of positive emotion.
- *TBI and PTSD (overlap):* Decreased anxiety, reduction of agitation/anger, increased self-esteem, reconnection with a repair of sense of self and identity, increased sense of control and self-efficacy.

Standardized art therapy sessions at the facility include group art therapy mask making in the first week of care, individual art therapy evaluations and follow-ups in the second and third weeks of care, and a culminating group art therapy session in the fourth and final week during which the service members create montage paintings. Interwoven throughout the four weeks are also music therapy group and individual sessions, a clinical expressive writing session, and a weekly creative writing workshop facilitated by professional writers who are also military veterans. The NICoE's creative arts therapy program expansion has come about in part as a result of a partnership with the National Endowment for the Arts (NEA), another federal agency. Creative Forces: The NEA Military Healing Arts Network has been developed to explore how creative arts therapy and arts engagement programs can improve health and well-being in military healthcare settings (NEA/Walter Reed Healing Arts Partnership, n.d.). Service members are given the opportunity to advocate for the treatments they believe work best, and the integration of all three of the creative arts modalities allows for deeper work surrounding meaning making and catharsis. Art therapy pioneer Elinor Ulman (Ulman & Dachinger, 1975) was onto something when she recognized the power of the creative experience to bring order out of chaos, and help the artist—in this case the service member—to better understand himself and his world in times of war and its aftermath.

Mask Making

Service members who come through the NICoE's program are introduced to art therapy in their first week of care, as part of a two-hour group art therapy mask-making session. They visit a designated art therapy space, the walls of which are lined with the artworks of past service members who have come through the program. The presence of artworks made by their peers seems to make the service members feel more comfortable to explore the art therapy process, and many have also shared that they were able to relate to the content and become motivated by it to create their own work. While service members have the option to take their artwork home after the NICoE program, many opt to leave theirs behind so that they may inspire the next service members to come through. The art therapy studio has become a visual community, symbolically enveloped by the experiences, thoughts, and feelings of service members with TBI and PTSD.

It is during this first mask-making session that the art therapist must introduce the space as safe for exploration without judgment and gently coax the service members—many of whom have never engaged in art making before—into the creative process. Service members are first asked whether or not they have created art recently, the majority of whom respond with "no" or a shake of the head. The art therapist then normalizes this for the service member, identifying the reasons why individuals move away from art making—factors that include self-consciousness ("I don't want to engage in something I'm not 'good' at"), space, time, funding—and perhaps that nasty first-grade art teacher who told them their sky should be blue and not purple. The difference between art therapy and an arts and crafts "class," for example, is then explained. Service members are assured that there will be no critiquing or grading, and the focus is not on aesthetics or technique, but on the symbolism and the process of the creation of the product.

Service members are given pre-made papier mâché masks and invited to transform them however they would like. The concept of identity is discussed, but the theme of the mask is left open.

The service member may depict something concrete or abstract and may use the mask to focus on a particular memory or to free their minds of intrusive thoughts. During the group art therapy sessions at the NICoE, it is observed that socialization occurs naturally as part of the art-making process. Service members begin sharing stories and joking with each other, creating a sense of community. Yalom (1985) discusses how group therapy aids in healing through the development of socializing techniques, imitative behavior, interpersonal learning, and group cohesiveness. Fluctuation between re-experiencing and avoidance of scenarios that may lead to flashbacks or panic attacks seen in PTSD may engender social isolation and distrust in others (Collie et al., 2006); however, the group process affords individuals the opportunity to immediately reconnect to others and to discover similarities with peers (Dunn-Snow & Joy-Smellie, 2000). Service members are invited to share the symbolism behind their artwork at the end of the session, and interaction with the art therapist and other group participants promotes social skills and ultimately self-understanding for the client with TBI (Sell & Murray, 2006). In his article on the paradox of expressing speechless terror, Harris (2009) describes the need for the traumatized to "rejoin the world of others" following exposure to extreme stressors or mass violence. He acknowledges that this is hampered by the PTSD psychological numbing symptoms that can lead to alexithymia, namely the inability to describe or identify emotions. Withdrawal from social interaction challenges recovery, and alexithymia hinders the success of verbal psychotherapeutic interventions. Van der Kolk (1996) offers up creative arts techniques as an alternative "language" that may bypass these issues.

Mask making is the directive chosen for the first art therapy group for a variety of reasons. Having a pre-made structure to work with seems to be less intimidating than introducing the service members to a directive that involves a blank sheet of paper or canvas. Because the masks are moldings of human faces, which literally and symbolically encapsulate the area of injury and focus of the NICoE program—the brain—the form easily translates for the service member and allows for the expression of their psychological and physical states. In Dunn-Snow and Joy-Smellie's (2000) case study on mask making as an art therapy technique, mask work was observed to facilitate the functions of identification, concealment, protection, and transformation.

Throughout history, masks have been used in the military—most often to conceal or protect during combat (gas masks, for instance). Kluge Fellow Tappert's culminating research presentation at the Library of Congress references the work of Anna Coleman Ladd, an American sculptor who created masks to cover up the faces of men who had been disfigured during World War I so that they may reintegrate into society without judgment (C-Span, 2015). While Ladd's work seems to have an opposite intention from the NICoE's art therapy process (to cover up versus expose), the goal of reintegration is the same. The masks created at NICoE give the service members a visual voice. They provide an outlet for making the invisible wounds of war visible. And when viewed by others—their peers, their family members, or society—they validate the service members' experiences and give a concrete face to intangible pain. This became most evident when National Geographic published a blast injuries article in the February 2015 edition, including photographs of masks created at the NICoE (Alexander, 2015). Service members were followed to their homes and photographed wearing the masks they had created while at the

NICoE—juxtaposing their depictions of the effects of war onto their personal lives. The worldwide response of the public indicated that while one may read and hear about these effects, *seeing* them provoked a whole new level of empathy and emotion for the viewer.

In the first six years of the NICoE art therapy program, over 1,000 masks were created. Examples of themes depicted in the masks include the split sense of self—or dual identity (see Figures 9.1a, 9.1b, and 9.1c). Service members at the NICoE are often grappling with the different parts of themselves that they feel either need to stay separate from their home/family lives, the parts of themselves that they might feel ashamed of, or perhaps the parts of themselves that they feel they have lost, and are therefore mourning, due to their injuries. Service members develop a strong sense of identity within the communal military culture. When this identity is disrupted by injury, the service members must revisit the phase associated with identity formation and reconfigure their new selves into their lives (Erikson, 1959). The struggle between the reality of their functional level and the service members' abilities to operate at what they consider full capacity creates what Erikson (1959) describes as an identity crisis. Art therapy allows them to work through an identity crisis and begin to understand and assimilate the parts of their new identities into their lives. Other themes present in the masks include patriotism, death, grief and loss, pain, and the injury itself. A thematic analysis of close to 400 of the masks explores these themes in depth, and discusses the use of mask-making to process identity as an individual, in relationships, in the community, in society, and over time (Walker et al., 2017).

Reoccurring symbolic content has also been observed. Many service members depict masks whose mouths have been locked, stitched, or gagged—to represent their inability to open up due to either the fear of judgment and stigma, even punishment. Protocol may prohibit the service member from sharing what he has experienced due to a mission's sensitive or secretive nature, especially in the special operations community. An inability to "open up" may also be attributed to the physiological change that occurs in an individual's brain following a traumatic event. In a healthy brain, the left and right hemispheres are constantly communicating. According to van der Kolk (2003), neuroimaging scans suggest that when an individual attempts to recall the traumatic event, the left frontal cortex of the brain shuts down. This includes the Broca's area of the brain, which is the center of expressive speech and language. In contrast, the areas of the brain that are activated during trauma light up. These include areas in the right hemisphere of the brain that control emotional and autonomic arousal and detect a threat (Crenshaw, 2006). According to Klorer (2005), art making activates the same parts of the brain as trauma—indicating that art therapy can bypass the left frontal cortex and stimulate the area of the brain responsible for encoding the traumatic memory. When an individual then processes the meaning behind their artwork with the therapist, they are reactivating the frozen speech area of the brain, and therefore reintegrating its two hemispheres (Walker, 2013).

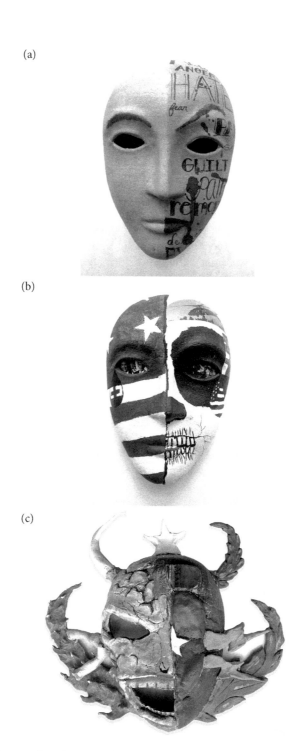

Figures 9.1a, 9.1b, and 9.1c Masks made in art therapy.

Individual Art Therapy

During the individual art therapy sessions at the NICoE, service members are asked about their progress and current goals for treatment within the program. Individual projects may then be implemented based on these goals. These sessions also allow for the development of a rapport between the art therapist and the service member. The service members feel more comfortable delving into their personal lives, joking with the therapists, and opening up about the meaning behind their artwork. In short, it is the moment when the service member and art therapist can begin to trust one another. It is not uncommon for service members to choose to externalize a traumatic memory. Bessel van der Kolk (2003) describes this as the service member putting into pictures a speechless terror (the trauma that is frozen in the somatic memory) that cannot be described by words (Talwar, 2007).

Please refer to Plate 6 in the color plate section.

A detailed case study of a service member's individual art therapy treatment at the NICoE, "Art therapy for PTSD and TBI: A senior active duty military service member's therapeutic journey", may be found through open access in *The Arts in Psychotherapy* journal (Walker, Kaimal, Koffman, & DeGraba, 2016). Plate 6 is an example of an art therapy project created by the service member and one of the individual art therapy projects highlighted in the study. During a mortar attack on his base in Iraq, the service member crawled to safety into a bunker. Dazed by the blast, the service member lay on his side and stared at an imaginary bloody face looking back at him. This image continued to haunt him and remained a secret for seven years. The service member was unable to describe what he was seeing and why until he came through the NICoE program. Although somewhat wary of alternative and integrative therapies, he chose to attend art therapy after finding benefit from acupuncture. He successfully externalized the image of the bloody face during mask making and after leaving the program noted that the face was no longer an intrusive memory. He saw it only a few times in a year-and-a-half post discharge, and both times the service member did not feel anxious because he knew the mask was still safely contained in the NICoE art therapy studio.

The service member returned for individual follow-up and shared that though the image of the bloody face was gone, he was still having flashbacks of the mortar attack. Herman (1992) explains that trauma survivors often suffer from intrusive thoughts surrounding the experiences and relive the events as if they were occurring in the present. The traumatic moment becomes encoded as an abnormal form of memory that often breaks spontaneously into consciousness both as flashbacks during waking hours and as nightmares during sleep (Pifalo, 2007). Over the course of a few weeks, the service member visited the art therapy studio and carefully depicted the blast that resulted in his TBI. Each time the patient visited the studio, he would share that while he was having flashbacks of the blast, instead of feeling upset, he was motivated to focus on what parts of the painting he needed to change to accurately depict the moment.

After completing the painting, the service member brought in dirt from the compound where the trauma occurred, shrapnel that had been removed from his body, as well as other found objects from the scene. The patient integrated these objects into the piece, hanging them from fishing wire to create the illusion of a blast. The objects the service member was holding onto found a safe place to be stored, and in turn created a sense of closure for the service member. Instead of leaving the completed project behind, the patient felt comfortable enough to take the piece with him and hang it in his home. This gesture supports Solomon and Siegel's belief (2003) that "the arts are powerful tools in the processing, metabolizing, and assimilating of the toxic effects of trauma that linger, fester, and affect the developing brain" (Rubin, 2006, p. 10). The service member was not only able to re-create the traumatic memory, but he was able also to integrate the moment and the symbolic objects associated with the moment into his everyday life. Although the service member needed to leave his initial mask piece behind, he was able to bring this painting home with him, symbolizing assimilation of the event into his life and identity as well as a sense of mastery achieved through the successful creation of the artwork. Via externalization, and by taking control of the memory, it was transformed from an intrusion into a life experience he could be proud of surviving.

The service member later processed his art therapy experience via a writing reflection and then shared it with the art therapist (Walker et al. 2016). He stated:

> I would continue making paintings of my hauntings, and each time I see them less, or not at all. In my opinion, I am bringing some compartmentalized fear into the open and admitting I was in fact afraid. Being afraid is something I have always denied ... to other people ... and to myself. Realizing fear is not weakness has helped me, and realizing weakness is not failure is something I am still working hard to engrain in my thought process.

Pifalo (2007) states that art therapy gains access to the traumatic images and brings them into the consciousness where they can be addressed. Because of the visual nature of trauma, image-based therapy offers efficient means of accessing, processing, and integrating split-off fragments of memory that result in flashbacks and nightmares.

Initially, service members engaging in individual art therapy need more assistance during the art-making process. Sell and Murrey (2006) state: "It is essential to allow clients the opportunity to feel a sense of control over the process. During the initial art therapy sessions, the [therapist] lends client his/her ego strength and guides the client through the session process" (p. 31). Over time, however, the need for an art therapist to carefully or directly guide the session will fade as the independence and confidence of the patient increases (Sell & Murrey, 2006). This autonomy was observed with the case example above who has continued to visit the art therapy studio and externalize images he sees during his acupuncture treatments—often pulling out all of the materials on his own. He has also recently mentioned the desire to set up an art studio at home. Worth noting but not conclusive is the observed change in the discussed service member's Magnetoencephalography (MEG) scans pre and post treatment. Neurologists at the NICoE observed increased activity in the right parietal and occipital regions. The occipital lobe is where the primary visual cortex is located, the area which contains the modules of cells that respond to direction, movement, texture, and color of visual stimuli (Lusebrink, 2004). This may indicate that treatments such as art therapy and acupuncture are literally "waking up" that area of his brain. Lusebrink (2004) states, in her attempt to understand art therapy and the brain, that "brain structures provide alternate paths for accessing and processing visual and motor information and memories" (p. 133). She adds that art therapy is uniquely equipped to take advantage of these alternate paths and to activate them through the use of various art media. In Lobban's (2012) article on military veteran art therapy in the UK, she reiterates that research has shown that "traumatic memories are held in the non-verbal right brain which can be accessed by art therapy using its own language of symbols and sensations, then externalized and decoded in order to create a narrative" (pp. 14–15). She also believes that the art therapy process results in new neural pathways that can alter function and improve communication between brain hemispheres, assisting in the processing and reintegration of traumatic material, as evidenced in Plate 6 when the service member was able to describe the moment of his injury in a complete narrative.

When appropriate, family members are incorporated into the service members' sessions. Family art therapy projects are designed according to family dynamics and needs. For instance, post injury of a service member, the spouse often becomes the caregiver. It is important for the spouse to have time to him- or herself, and also for the spouse to encourage the service member to learn to function on his or her own. In this case, the art therapist would guide the service member and spouse to work on individual projects alongside each other, stepping in when assistance is needed so that the spouse may focus on him- or herself while slowly letting go of concern for the service member. In instances where the service member has become isolated from the family, a collaborative project may be introduced so that the service member can relax and become comfortable engaging and communicating with the family. This interaction can improve the overall dynamics of the family unit as they move forward, and many service members continue to create art with their children after they leave the NICoE program (Walker, n.d.).

Montage Painting (and Beyond)

In the fourth week of care, service members engage in a final art therapy group during which they are invited to create montage paintings. This directive allows for the layering of materials to depict a theme—either about the self, beliefs, or the symbolic representation of the passage of time (before treatment/after treatment; before war/after war). The layering allows for the integration of the many facets of a service member's life. They may flip through magazines, clip out words and images that resonate with them, and then collage these onto their canvas. Canvases are often first painted with a relevant background scene. In general, service members are observed to have brighter affects, are more at ease with the art materials, more autonomous during the process (can "dive right in"), and more social and comfortable around each other and the art therapist.

Figure 9.2 eloquently displays this healthy change in both physical and psychological presence. The figure, an abstract portrait of the service member, approaches the door slumped over in a dark and colorless place. The service member described the door as his entrance into treatment at the NICoE. The figure is then shown standing upright and proud to the right of the door. The atmosphere is now bright blue and sunny. Above the scene are magazine clippings of letters that spell out the word "repairs."

The majority of montage paintings created by the NICoE service members focus on the future as they prepare to leave the program and move forward. While these products depict hopeful futures and positive outcomes, the NICoE program is perhaps only one stop in a service member's journey to recovery. It is important to pay attention to what the service member's canvas might look like post discharge, but follow-up with an art therapist at a service member's home base is not always possible. Exit surveys conducted pre discharge from the NICoE

Figure 9.2 Healthy change.

consistently suggest that while many service members found art therapy to be one of the most beneficial treatments they engaged in, it is also one of the treatments they fear they will have the least access to once returning home. However, clinicians who follow up with the service members have access to the NICoE art therapy notes in AHLTA and have commented on their ability to continue the exploration of the meaning behind the service members' artwork in their sessions.

All service members at the NICoE are encouraged to continue exploring the creative arts post discharge. Whether this occurs in a formal art therapy setting or on their own depends on the resources available within the service member's community, as well as his or her desire to continue with a therapist or engage in art making autonomously. Service members often reach back to the NICoE art therapist—sharing that they have created studios in their homes, hung artwork created as a family, sold works of art for military-focused charities, or have gone back to school to pursue careers as artists. Some share that while they don't believe they will pursue the arts on their own, they feel their engagement in the art therapy at NICoE assisted them in opening up about difficult content and will allow them to engage better in traditional talk therapies moving forward. In the words of a Marine who completed the NICoE program, "I would say art therapy has not only been my way to cope, but it saved me. I don't talk about it but I was in a dark place. … It's amazing that a few people and expressing yourself will change your life." These words echo the sentiments of many service members who have come through the NICoE since it opened in 2010, and they provide a glimpse into the reason behind the art therapy program's success in becoming an integral part of the NICoE treatment model.

Art therapists specializing in treating the military population on military bases, medical centers, including the Veterans Health Administration, and in surrounding communities are necessary to extend to service members and their families throughout the nation the benefits noted above. Expansion has already begun via the aforementioned partnership with the NEA. The NEA first assisted in integrating creative writing and music therapy into the NICoE treatment model. In 2013, the NEA funded and placed a contract art therapist at Intrepid Spirit I at Fort Belvoir—one of nine satellite facilities built by the Intrepid Fallen Heroes Fund to extend the care provided at the home bases of many of the troops suffering from the effects of TBI and PH (Intrepid Fallen Heroes Fund, n.d.). The art therapy program was successfully integrated into the Intrepid Spirit I's model, and the art therapist was converted from a contractor to a full-time government employee with the Department of Defense. Additional placements of creative arts therapists within the MHS will support access to integrative treatment for service members and their family units. This also allows for additional research and expansion efforts across the MHS. For instance, images of the masks, as well as all other art therapy session observations and products, are stored in the Armed Forces Health Longitudinal Technology Application (AHLTA)—the electronic medical record system used by providers within the Department of Defense. The NICoE plans to conduct a thematic analysis of these mask images and correlate them to service member data collected over the span of the four-week treatment, as it has become apparent that many service members were focused on similar themes.

The NICoE's former Commander continues to stress the need for the nation to shift its regard for art therapy in the military setting from a "nice to have," to a "need to have"—and the NICoE model is but one example of how this idea has been put to (best) practice.

The views expressed in this chapter are those of the author and do not reflect the official policy of the Department of the Army/Navy/Air Force, Department of Defense, or U.S. Government.

References

Alexander, C. (2015, February). The invisible war on the brain. *National Geographic*, 30–53.

Collie, K., Backos, A., Malchiodi, C., & Spiegal, D. (2006). Art therapy for combat related PTSD: Recommendations for research and practice. *Art Therapy: Journal of the American Art Therapy Association, 23*(4), 157–164.

Crenshaw, D. (2006). Neuroscience and trauma treatment. In L. Carey (Ed.), *Expressive and Creative Arts Methods for Trauma Survivors* (pp. 21–38). Philadelphia, PA: Jessica Kingsley.

C-Span. (2015). World War I veterans and art therapy. Retrieved April 5, 2017, from http://www.c-span.org/video/?323952-1/discussion-world-war-veterans-art-therapy.

Dunn-Snow, P., & Joy-Smellie, S. (2000). Teaching art therapy techniques: Mask-making, a case in point. *Art Therapy: Journal of the American Art Therapy Association, 17*(2), 125–131.

Erikson, E. (1959). Identity and the life cycle: Selected papers. *Psychological Issues, 1*, 1–171.

Harris, D. (2009). The paradox of expressing *Speechless Terror*: Ritual liminality in the creative arts therapies' treatment of posttraumatic distress. *The Arts in Psychotherapy, 36*(2), 94–104.

Herman, J. (1992). *Trauma and Recovery*. New York: Basic Books.

Intrepid Fallen Heroes Fund. (n.d.). Intrepid Spirit Centers. Retrieved April 5, 2017, from https://www.fallenheroesfund.org/Intrepid-Spirit-Centers.aspx.

Klorer, G.P. (2005). Expressive therapy with severely maltreated children: Neuroscience contributions. *Art Therapy: Journal of the American Art Therapy Association, 22*(4), 213–220.

Lobban, J. (2012). The invisible wound: Veterans' art therapy. *International Journal of Art Therapy: Formerly Inscape, 19*(1), 3–18

Lusebrink, V. (2004). Art therapy and the brain: An attempt to understand the underlying processes of art expression in therapy. *Art Therapy: Journal of the American Art Therapy Association, 21*(3), 25–135.

National Endowment for the Arts. (n.d.). NEA/Walter Reed Healing Arts Partnership. Retrieved April 5, 2017, from http://arts.gov/partnerships/walter-reed.

National Intrepid Center of Excellence. (n.d.). NICoE One Pager. Retrieved April 5, 2017, from http://www.nicoe.capmed.mil/About%20Us/SitePages/Home.aspx.

Pifalo, T. (2007). Jogging the cogs: Trauma-focused art therapy and cognitive behavioral therapy with sexually abused children. *Art Therapy: Journal of the American Art Therapy Association, 24*(4), 170–175.

Rubin, J. (2006). Foreword. In L. Carey (Ed.), *Expressive and Creative Arts Methods for Trauma Survivors* (pp. 9–13). Philadelphia, PA: Jessica Kingsley.

Sell, M., & Murrey, G. (2006). *Alternative Therapies in the Treatment of Brain Injury & Neurobehavioral Disorders: A Practical Guide* (pp. 29–39). New York: Routledge.

Solomon, M.F., & Siegel, D.J. (Eds.). (2003). *Healing Trauma: Attachment, Mind, Body, and Brain.* New York: W.W. Norton.

Summerall, E.L. (2014). Traumatic brain injury and PTSD. Retrieved April 5, 2017, from http://www.ptsd.va.gov/professional/co-occurring/traumatic-brain-injury-ptsd.asp.

Talwar, S. (2007). Accessing traumatic memory through art making: An art therapy trauma protocol (ATTP). *Arts in Psychotherapy, 34*(1), 22–35.

Ulman, E., & Dachinger, P. (Eds.). (1975). *Art Therapy in Theory and Practice.* New York: Schocken Books.

van der Kolk, B.A. (1996). The complexity of adaptation to trauma: Self-regulation, stimulus discrimination, and characterological development. In B.A. van der kolk, F.A.C. McFarlane, & L. Weisaeth (Eds.), *Traumatic Stress: The Effects of Overwhelming Experience on Mind, Body, and Society* (pp. 182–213). New York: The Guilford Press.

van der Kolk, B.A. (2003). *The Frontiers of Trauma.* Presentation at the Psychotherapy Networker Symposium, Washington, DC.

Walker, M. (2013). Understanding the value of art therapy [Blog post]. Retrieved April 5, 2017, from http://blog.americansforthearts.org/2013/05/13/understanding-the-value-of-art-therapy.

Walker, M. (n.d.). Art therapy programming at the National Intrepid Center of Excellence (NICoE). Retrieved April 5, 2017, from http://www.arttherapy.org/upload/toolkitmedicalsettings/intrepedcenter.pdf.

Walker, M., Kaimal, G., Gonzaga, A., Myers-Coffman, K., & DeGraba, T. (2017). Active duty military service members' visual representations of PTSD and TBI in masks. *International Journal of Qualitative Studies on Health and Well-being.* DOI: 10.1080/17482631.2016.1267317.

Walker, M., Kaimal, G., Koffman, R., & DeGraba, T.J. (2016). Art therapy for PTSD and TBI: A senior active duty service member's therapeutic journey. *The Arts in Psychotherapy, 49,* 10–18. doi: 10.1016/j.aip.2016.05.015.

Yalom, I. (1985). *The Theory and Practice of Group Psychotherapy* (3rd edition). New York: Basic Books.

CHAPTER 10

The Giant Steps Program: Creating Fellowship and Meaning

Martha Haeseler

Giant Steps is a long-term outpatient group treatment program for veterans within the psychiatric service at Veterans Administration (VA) Connecticut Healthcare System. I was involved in the Giant Steps program from its expansion in 1996 until I left in the winter of 2015. What follows is a description of this unique and comprehensive program.

History

Giant Steps was formed in the 1990s as a "therapeutic holding" group for veterans who took clozapine, a new antipsychotic medication. The intention was to provide an outpatient group which would be attractive to them and induce them to stay in treatment. It met on two mornings a week, included an art therapy group, and utilized a psycho-educational approach. The founding psychiatrist named it Giant Steps after a jazz tune by Charlie Parker.

In 1996, three psychiatric nurses and I expanded Giant Steps to become a full-time program. Eventually, the nurses left and I became program director and conducted the program alone, except for one morning section, which was (and continues to be) led by advanced practice nurses. I enlisted the aid of art therapy interns and other resources in VA: psychology interns, a music therapist, a chaplain, and volunteer artists. A few years later, I was able to hire a part-time art therapist, and we grew the program from 45 to 70 veterans with a staff of 1.33 FTEs.

The Program

Giant Steps meets on five mornings for two-and-a-half hours, and three afternoons for two hours per week. Most veterans come for two mornings or afternoons. Veterans attend the same sections each week so that the groups are consistent. Veterans are referred by clinicians, and many veterans ask for a consult. Most groups are large, averaging 15, and we have a waiting list. Veterans can stay in Giant Steps as long as it remains therapeutic for them; some have been in the program for 19 years.

There is art therapy in all our sections, and one afternoon and four mornings are devoted entirely to art. Other sections include psycho-education about managing problems and emotions, music therapy, social skills, spirituality, PTSD, gardening, and other topics.

The Veterans

Veterans in Giant Steps have a full range of psychiatric diagnoses, including PTSD. In addition, many have physical challenges, a history of substance abuse, and/or military sexual trauma (MST). In the past few years more women have joined Giant Steps, and younger veterans from Iraq and Afghanistan. Although increasing numbers of veterans have been able to go back to school or to work, or leave Giant Steps because they feel able to be out in the world without the program's support, some more symptomatic veterans have stayed in the program for years. For many of them there has been slow but steady progress, mostly in gaining self-respect and a sense of meaning and pleasure in life; managing symptoms; relating to other people; and expanding their connections to their communities. One such veteran often says: "Giant Steps is the best job I ever had!"

Clinical Approaches

The initial mission for Giant Steps included promoting fellowship; helping veterans deal with challenges and symptoms through psycho-education; promoting self-expression and self-discovery through art therapy; promoting healthy lifestyles and community reintegration; and helping veterans enjoy their lives. Of these, one of the most important has been promoting fellowship; veterans experience a deep sense of belonging within the program, care for one another, and often speak of Giant Steps as "home." When people feel cared for, they are more able to care for themselves and others.

Since many Giant Steps veterans are socially isolated, without vocation, and feel of little value to society, another main goal has been to empower them, and give them a sense of self-respect, purpose, and meaning. We do this in many ways, including the following:

- Encouraging them to develop identities as artists and take pride in their work. We organize art shows both at VA and in the community, and encourage veterans to participate independently in community art events. We make a calendar featuring veterans' artwork and sell it to raise money for special events. We helped several veterans self-publish art books. Giant Steps veterans are often asked to paint murals or other projects at VA, whereby they can give something back to the VA community.
- Helping them focus on their strengths and abilities, take leadership in their lives, and have confidence in using their skills to help others. Many begin to rely more on resources in their communities and less on

institutional support. Some veterans have used skills learned in Giant Steps to get jobs or develop businesses.
- Teaching them crafts, and conducting sales at VA. Veterans make and sell anything they want, such as wreaths, mosaics, silk painting, silk screen, and jewelry. The garden group sells plants, succulent gardens, and nature-based crafts. Veterans are proud that people buy what they produce and that they can raise funds for their program.
- Developing a garden group (described below), in which veterans can do meaningful work that makes a difference in the life of the VA community.

Fellowship, belonging, meaning, empowerment, and hope are all words inherent in the Recovery Model (SAMHSA, 2015). They are also tenets of positive psychology (Seligman, 2002). Our primary goal is to create a supportive community within which all of these concepts can grow. Another applicable concept is post-traumatic growth, "positive psychological change experienced as a result of the struggle with highly challenging life circumstances" (Baker, Kelly, Calhoun, Cann, & Tedeschi, 2008).

Art Therapy

The room is set up so that 16 veterans can sit in a circle at tables. There are also tables at the side, and easels in the back, for those who need extra space or are not ready to join the group at the tables. We have a large collection of art, photography, and poetry books; many art materials, including supplies for collages, mosaics, and printmaking; a veterans' computer with Photoshop; a large-screen TV for artwork and art history films; and an iPad for veterans whose use of hands is compromised.

Groups begin with discussion of upcoming events, messages, or issues concerning group members. Then, most of the time is devoted to art making. For the last half hour, veterans have the opportunity to show their artwork and discuss it with the group. In one section, most of the veterans have shorter attention spans, and we find that they invest more in their artwork when we provide a warm-up activity, discussion, or theme. Other art therapy groups are usually non-directive, so that veterans can explore issues when they are ready, at their own pace. Veterans help themselves to whatever art materials they wish, and work independently. Staff members are available if help is asked for, or if someone is upset, needs inspiration, or wants technical assistance. However, if staff initially holds back, veterans will turn to each other and provide the needed support, guidance, and inspiration. At times, we provide stimulation via discussing artists and trips to art galleries, introducing new materials, or demonstrating techniques. When discussing artwork, veterans' comments to each other are usually supportive and often very insightful. Because we occasionally model comments or questions designed to encourage veterans to look more closely at their own art and think about why the image came up at that particular time, most new members soon understand that lines, shapes, and colors might lead to self-understanding. If veterans would prefer to not show or discuss their artwork, that is also fine.

From Edith Kramer, my mentor; I learned how to build a program where veterans feel accepted, inspired, and empowered to develop their abilities and bring forward their best selves. Her passion for art; close attention to multicultural considerations; focus on helping children develop their strengths and find pleasure in creative work; ability to put her whole self in support of children, with unconditional positive regard and a caring structure; and emphasis on the importance of children helping each other have all inspired aspects of Giant Steps. Her psychoanalytic viewpoint has been affirmed by current research in neuroscience, which asserts that traumatic memories are stored in the deep brain (like Freud's unconscious), inaccessible to the frontal lobes, the thinking and reasoning parts of the brain (like the ego). Van der Kolk and Fisler (1995) wrote that traumatic material is stored as sensory images, not accessible through words. Therefore images, sounds, touch, or smells can trigger a flashback, a reliving of the original trauma. Since art making is a complex process which activates all parts of the brain (Perry, 2008), art therapy is an ideal treatment for veterans with PTSD. Creating images can tap into the traumatic material without overwhelming the artist. When traumatic material emerges in the artwork, the cognitive, integrative functions of the brain come into play, helping the traumatic experience become less toxic, turning it into a memory which can be integrated into the sense of self. Edith Kramer wrote: "Art can absorb and contain more raw affect than most other equally complex and civilized endeavors" (Kramer, 1971, pp. 185–186).

In a recent interview, van der Kolk (2014) said,

> Trauma is not the story of something that happened back then—it's the current imprint of that pain, horror, and fear living inside people. Trauma isn't something that lives outside clients. The job for therapists is to help them feel safe inside themselves.

He quotes a line from W.H. Auden: "Truth, like love and sleep, resents approaches that are too intense." Kramer wrote: "The art therapist's actions and attitudes were geared to conveying to the children the feeling that the unconscious meaning of their efforts was understood and accepted, without bringing more of the problem to consciousness than they could tolerate" (1958, p. 71). In Giant Steps, safety is a high priority; there is no push to address traumatic material in the artwork. Veterans are encouraged to use art for any purpose that seems helpful to them. For some, balancing shapes and lines and colors seems to help them organize their scattered thoughts. Some seem to be soothing themselves in a meditative manner through colors and rhythmic movements with the materials; some focus on creating beauty as a way to be in the moment and stop attending to frightening thoughts or voices. Some challenge themselves to master new techniques; some use humor in their art, or seem to be constructing cultural identities or life narratives. Some connect to the natural world, and many express feelings in a productive and non-threatening way through art making. There are also some who, at their own time and pace, depict their traumatic material and talk about it; this creates a model for others who may eventually wish to do the same. Veterans are more inspired by each other than by staff.

When positive psychology became popular, I realized that this was what Kramer was teaching all along. She believed that helping children develop their strengths and focus on their artwork would help them deal with conflict and challenges and would promote maturation in general. Similarly, Seligman wrote (2002) that if people find their own signature strengths and develop those strengths, they will become more resilient.

There is a magical feel to a group when all you hear are the movements of chalk on paper, or paint on canvas, with occasional conversations breaking out. Sometimes there are lively discussions about current or individual issues, but the focus is mostly on the art making, and staff intervenes only if conversations become loud or heated. Conflicts within the group are rare and handled with a gentle touch, and often the relevant veterans meet with staff outside of the group space so that an optimal environment for creative work can be maintained. Within a setting of creativity, mutual support, and relatively low stimulation, veterans with schizophrenia or PTSD, who often become tense when emotion is expressed, become able to tolerate higher levels of openness and expression of feelings. Veterans who have trouble tolerating being in groups of people can work comfortably and come to find mutuality in relationships.

One veteran did a series of explosive abstract colored drawings. When he said he wanted to do a self-portrait, I gave him a mirror and suggested he look closely at his features, such as his eyes, to see the shapes, lines and shadows. He came back the next day with a drawing of many eyes, then did a series of paintings of eyes. He said he realized they were Viet Cong eyes watching him from the jungle in Vietnam, while he sat up all night whittling a stick so that the enemy would not catch him unawares. For his final painting in the series, "Vietnam – My Mind's Eye," he wrote:

> By trying to block out my experience as a Marine rifleman in Vietnam I became unable to perform as a complete individual. I thought my inadequacies were innate in me. Now I can see the compelling nature of that experience. I have trouble in crowds; I watch my back. I was afraid to fear the fear. Through my art I can address things I don't have access to. I sketch and paint without thinking. Maybe 2/3 of the way in I start to understand what and why I'm painting. Presently it's eyes. I know they are related to my Vietnam experience. Enemy eyes in the jungle. The 4 layers of the crying eye show that 4 decades passed before I could "see" the pain and fear of Vietnam. This I have experienced in the Giant Steps art and therapy group. I now am starting to feel lucky that I have a method of

overcoming or at least breaking even in my journey to feel comfortable within myself.

(Haeseler, 2012, p. 22)

In subsequent paintings he dealt with themes of aggressor and victim, PTSD and machismo, and longing to develop the softer, artistic side of himself.

After painting colorful landscapes and flowers, another Vietnam veteran spent a long time drawing his combat boots, and entitled the picture "Vietnam Experience." A few years later, after painting a series of swamps, he told of a traumatic event in Vietnam when he and his platoon had to spend several days and nights crouching in a swamp, boots full of water and mud, in deathly fear of a sniper. After this painting, he was able to paint scenes from his childhood, his current life, and his hopes and dreams.

Another veteran created a three-dimensional piece in which a hand reaches out from broken glass, trying to grab some origami heroin. He wrote:

> The hand of addiction is a demon, insidious. The hand is always there. You could be the taker, you could be the giver, and you're the loser either way. It could be your hand or my hand. The bag of cocaine is so close, it hovers right there, waiting, for a capitalist or a victim. As soon as you grab it, you lose. The broken mirrors represent broken dreams. If you look in the mirrors, you will see there are two of you. One of you is clean, but the addicted inner self is always there, wanting to get that hit. … Creating this brings it all back but it was constructive, shows me how far I've come. This picture says more than I can say. Through God's Grace I am finally free from the powerful hand of addiction. My hope is that this art work will help people come in touch with the reality and consequences of substance abuse.

Special Art Projects

At times, when Giant Steps was faced with challenges, I initiated group projects so that we could come together in the art and deal with our experiences. The first challenge was the 9/11 terrorist attack. Veterans and staff painted individual tiles and mounted them in checkerboard fashion on a plywood board 42 × 54 inches. Between the tiles, we grouted a mosaic from broken tiles, stones, shells, and found objects brought by veterans and staff, and entitled the work "In Remembrance" (Plate 7). VA mounted it in a public place and we held a VA-wide remembrance ceremony. At the time I wrote:

> As we put our pieces together, I felt that our individual feelings were given context and came together to create a whole. Also, the physical process of constructing something from nothing, and of bringing lost and broken pieces together in a work of art, felt like a powerful antidote to the powerlessness I experienced when witnessing the shattering of buildings

and sorting through of broken pieces looking for human life. I felt as though we were rebuilding and creating beauty from the rubble.

(Haeseler, 2002, p. 123)

Many of Seligman's (2002) signature strengths are represented in the tiles: spirituality, love, patriotism, nature, hope, peace, tolerance, honor, and duty. Veterans were accessing strengths which would help them remain resilient in that challenging time.

Please refer to Plate 7 in the color plate section.

Another challenge was moving out of our space in 2012. It was a difficult transition, because for a long time we knew we would have to move but did not know where, or whether the new space would be adequate. The move had a lot of meaning for us, and raised anxiety, fear, and issues of loss for both veterans and staff. I suggested two art projects designed to help us focus on what was positive within ourselves and the program, and to remind ourselves that we would be taking the positives with us, even though we were leaving the room behind.

When we had a date to move, I told the veterans that Buddhists inscribe flags with prayers and symbols for things that are important to them, such as health, peace, compassion, good fortune, and other positive things. With every breath of air, the flags gently send the blessings into the space around them.

I said that we too could make prayer flags. I suggested that we put on them something special about ourselves, our space, and Giant Steps, things we wanted to take to the new space. Then, when we moved, we would find our flags filling the air with all those good things.

I made flags out of fabric, watercolor paper, and canvas. I set out, in addition to fine art materials, beautiful collage papers, fabrics, ribbons, buttons, glitter, and more. The resulting images were as diverse as the veterans creating them, including landscapes, flags, and positive characteristics of the program; one veteran wrote: "Giant Steps, my salvation." We felt comforted and empowered when we finally saw our flags in the new space (Figure 10.1).

Months later, we still hadn't moved. I suggested we make artists' trading cards as gifts for people who would come to our opening reception: family, friends, VA community. I suggested that the theme of the cards could be something about Giant Steps, to educate guests about our program. Since we were in suspense about when we would move, I thought it would be useful for us to look forward to a time when we would be in our new room, ready to receive guests, giving them gifts relating to our strengths. Giving gifts is a strategy for promoting resilience.

The project exceeded my expectations. Even veterans with short attention spans embraced the project with gusto, each making several cards. Some women took materials home and made dozens of cards each. One of them later received a grant to make empathy cards about MST for the waiting room of the women's clinic. Again, the words and imagery on the cards show a wide variety of strengths, hope, and good feeling for the program and themselves.

Figure 10.1 Veterans' flags hanging in the new group space.

Garden Group

Wishing to share my interests with veterans, during my first year at VA we created a small garden. The following year I received a grant to build a large garden with stone paths between the beds, and a raised bed in the center for wheelchair gardening.

In 2009, the Chief of Psychiatry persuaded me that we needed a garden in the courtyard, a central meeting place. The Director approved and gave me funds. Creating it with a few veterans was challenging, and I realized I needed to form a separate garden group. Since then, garden group has been asked to create a new garden every year, including a "Welcome Garden" at the main entrance; a private viewing garden for veterans receiving dialysis; a women's garden; an herb garden for patients' meals; and others. The last of eight gardens was a walking garden labyrinth (Figure 10.2).

Through the Incentive Work Therapy Program, veterans in garden group can receive modest payment for their work. They maintain the gardens and harvest the herbs for the kitchen through our hot and dry summers. Veterans find gardening therapeutic for the following reasons: being close to nature; caring for living things; getting fresh air and exercise; working collaboratively; and giving back to VA by creating something enjoyed by many veterans, staff, and visitors. Research has shown that gardens in healthcare institutions improve health and morale for patients, families, and staff, and reduce healthcare costs (Americans for the Arts, 2009, p. 18).

Figure 10.2 Walking garden labyrinth.

The Future

The current Giant Steps Director has just hired someone into my position and will be able to conduct more groups and grow the program. As it evolves, there may be some changes: The new VA Director let us know that we may need to shorten our length of stay. We came up with some strategies for the future such as offering time-limited groups; hiring peer mentors; and having alumni groups led by veterans. Some veterans would still benefit from an indefinite stay in the program, but many others could transition more quickly to utilizing resources in their communities outside VA.

Conclusion

Art therapy has been essential to veterans' treatment in Giant Steps; most veterans tell us they prefer art making to other aspects of our program. Many have said that art therapy saved their lives. Art can be a crucible for transforming trauma, challenging experiences, and inner conflict into something life-enhancing, and for empowering veterans to lead more independent lives.

I close with a group artists' statement for an exhibition of their art at a local college. Each veteran contributed a sentence or two. Their statements follow:

> Artwork can take you into combat, show what war is all about, what it does to individuals, and how they recoup and start to see the light through the tunnel. Our artwork shows the gamut from despair to love, from past to future, from darkness to light. It is rewarding to each veteran to be in the

exhibition. It gives us the opportunity to express ourselves and personalities and how we interpret reality. We rediscover ourselves through the art and find that we have talent and that we can put down what we really want to say, in our hearts. It is very gratifying that others appreciate our art. It makes us feel that we are worth something. We are the soldiers who came back alive. Although we have problems, when we do art we work on our issues and find reasons to live. Because people care about us, instead of living in a world of violence and fear, we can show our love and peace. With the help of others, we try to do the best that we can. It's nice to witness the fruit of our labors. We feel honored to be here today.

References

Americans for the Arts. (2009). *2009 State of the Field Report: Arts in Healthcare* (updated March 2014). Americans for the Arts. Retrieved April 5, 2017, from http://www.americansforthearts.org/sites/default/files/ArtsInHealthcare_0.pdf

Baker, J.M., Kelly, C., Calhoun, L.G., Cann, A., & Tedeschi, R.G. (2008). An examination of posttraumatic growth and posttraumatic depreciation: Two exploratory studies. *Journal of Loss and Trauma, 13*, 450–465.

Haeseler, M. (2002). In Remembrance, September 11, 2001. *Art Therapy: Journal of the American Art Therapy Association, 19*(3), 122–23.

Haeseler, M. (Ed.). (2012). *Workbook: Resiliency through Art, Training by the American Art Therapy Association for the United States Army Arts and Crafts Managers.* Alexandria, VA: American Art Therapy Association.

Kramer, E. (1958). *Art Therapy in a Children's Community* (2nd edition). New York: Schocken Books.

Kramer, E. (1971). *Art as Therapy with Children* (2nd edition). Chicago, IL: Magnolia Street Publishers.

Perry, B. (2008). The healing arts: The neuro-developmental impact of arts therapies. Keynote address, *Thirty-eighth Annual Conference of the American Art Therapy Association,* Cleveland, OH.

SAMHSA (2015). SAMHSA's working definition of recovery. Retrieved April 24, 2015, from http://store.samhsa.gov/shin/content//PEP12-RECDEF/PEP12-RECDEF.pdf.

Seligman, M.E.P. (2002). *Authentic Happiness: Using the New Positive Psychology to Realize your Potential for Lasting Fulfillment.* New York: Free Press.

van der Kolk, B. (2014). When talk isn't enough: Easing trauma's lingering shock. Interviewed by R. Howes, *Psychotherapy Networker,* July/August. Retrieved April 5, 2017, from http://www.psychotherapynetworker.org/magazine/currentissue/item/2522-point-of-view/2522-point-of-view.

van der Kolk, B., & Fisler, R. (1995). Dissociation and the fragmentary nature of traumatic memories: Overview & exploratory study. *Journal of Traumatic Stress, 8*(4), 505–525.

CHAPTER 11

Art Therapy with Substance Abuse and Co-occurring Disorders in Military Populations

Eileen A. McKee

According to tradition and legend, the United States Marine Corps was founded in a bar. Many Marines like to tell this story, and will joke good-naturedly, "Well, the Marines started in a bar, so that explains a lot about us." Tun Tavern, a favorite Philadelphia watering hole for American revolutionaries during the 1700s, is considered the "Birthplace of the Marines" for its role as the site of the first recruitment drive for the Corps in 1775. At the National Museum of the Marine Corps in Quantico, Virginia, there is even a "Tun Tavern"-themed restaurant that replicates the colonial-era pub, complete with a well-stocked bar and draft list (Sturkey, 2002).

This story of the local tavern, which has taken on almost mythological significance, offers us some insight into the relationship between drinking and military culture. Tun Tavern is a symbol of camaraderie, of the bonds formed around a table set with tankards of ale, the trust and familiarity that comes with having a regular meeting place, a ritual of loosening tongues and muscles at the end of the day with a drink and good company. Alcohol is, after all, the great equalizer. In an organization as diverse as the US military, with thousands of individuals from all walks of life, having a drink together is a quick way of bonding and finding common ground with someone who may hold your life in their hands during battle.

According to a 2012 review of alcohol use within the military conducted by the National Institute on Alcohol Abuse and Alcoholism (NIAAA), a division of the National Institutes of Health, military service members are significantly more likely than their civilian counterparts to engage in heavy or problematic drinking (Schumm & Chard, 2012). What starts as casual, social drinking can shift into substance abuse and addiction in the absence of adequate oversight and preventative measures. The NIAAA report also states that in addition to cultural and demographic factors, "military-related stressful events also may contribute to the high rates of problem drinking" by active duty service members (p. 402). "Military-related stressful events" may include exposure to combat, military sexual trauma, and certain types of training and deployment exercises, among other factors. The development of mental health conditions in service members such as depression, trauma disorders, or anxiety often create new and more complex presentations in those seeking treatment for addiction (Substance Abuse and Mental Health Services Administration, 2007).

Addiction carries with it a tremendous amount of stigma. Medical and therapeutic disciplines have come a long way from dismissing addiction as a problem of moral failure, but there continues to be reluctance among the general public to treat substance abuse with the same compassion and understanding as other mental health or medical diagnoses. Individuals who enter into treatment for substance use disorders have taken a difficult step toward changing their lives, and when it comes to addressing this change therapeutically, professionals have a responsibility to remain aware of the implications such steps have for those individuals and for their wider communities. In the case of changing maladaptive behaviors such as substance abuse, the most effective therapeutic interventions make change compelling and desirable, while remaining aware of challenging subtleties such as handling resistance, unraveling the tangles between emotion and biology, or considering the dynamics of culture and communities.

Art therapy with military substance abuse and co-occurring disorder populations can serve to illuminate solutions to these challenges, using the art process and artwork as another way of bringing some light to the murkiness and uncertainty that alcohol and drugs can cause. In this chapter, a model for art therapy with military substance abuse and co-occurring disorders is outlined which addresses common elements that arise in treatment, and ways to address them creatively and compassionately. The terms "patient" and "service member" are used here to refer to individuals receiving treatment, as the majority of this chapter will focus on treatment in a medical or controlled outpatient setting. The terms "substance abuse," "substance use disorder," and "addiction" are used throughout this chapter with some fluidity, taking into account common vernacular around alcohol and drug use as well as clinical diagnoses and definitions.

The current DSM-V categorizes substance use disorders as "mild," "moderate," or "severe," with each having its own set of criteria. This is a shift from the earlier DSM-IV-TR definitions of "abuse" of versus "dependence" on a specific substance. This chapter will also discuss conditions that are diagnosed in addition to a substance use disorder. The term "co-occurring disorders" refers to mental health diagnoses that are concurrent with a diagnosis of a substance use disorder, such as a diagnosis of post-traumatic stress disorder or major depressive disorder in addition to an alcohol use disorder or stimulant use disorder. According to the DSM-V, these diagnoses must be distinct from each other, rather than a cluster of symptoms resulting from the same disorder (American Psychiatric Association, 2013). Sometimes also referred to as "dual diagnosis" or "dual disorders," the term "co-occurring disorders" is used in this chapter for consistency. Addressing addiction or substance abuse involves a delicate dance of approaches that are sensitive to the interactions of brain, body, spirit, and environment. Integrated care for substance use disorders—care that addresses substance abuse and mental health issues as interrelated and influenced by each other—is now considered an industry standard (Gulliver & Steffen, 2010; Substance Abuse and Mental Health Services Administration, n.d.).

Service members who seek or enroll in substance abuse treatment come from a variety of backgrounds, with different expectations for care, as well as varying levels of motivation or engagement in treatment. Within the active duty military population, there are special considerations to take into account if service members are receiving treatment for substance abuse and co-occurring disorders. Substance abuse treatment can be recommended by an active duty service member's command, a service member can be referred due to disciplinary action as a result of substance abuse, or an individual may self-refer for treatment. Substance abuse, and substance abuse treatment, may carry different associations for service members based on a patient's military occupational specialty (MOS), substance of choice, branch of service, or rank.

Many military patients enter treatment for substance abuse as their first foray into mental healthcare, and may be unfamiliar with therapy as a general concept. Despite industry recommendations of integrated care for substance abuse and mental health treatment, a 2012 Institute of Medicine report analyzing Department of Defense policies and programs relating to substance use disorders found "a lack of integration of SUD [substance use disorder] care with other behavioral health and medical care" and "highly variable" rates of implementation of evidence-based practices in treatment of substance use disorders (Institute of Medicine, 2012, pp. 4–8). This is perhaps due, in part, to the military's traditional practice of addressing substance use through legal and administrative channels. This frequently results in service members' reluctance to seek help due to the potential lack of confidentiality related to substance abuse treatment. Command-ordered substance abuse treatment within military treatment facilities has specific parameters; namely that commands of service members enrolling in such treatment options (whether voluntarily or not) have a "right and need to know the progress and outcome of treatment," as well as additional information that may affect mission integrity, the service member's fitness for duty, or factors that may affect the safety of the unit or command (Department of Defense/Military OneSource, 2015, par. 4).

Service members seeking help for addiction or co-occurring disorders often discuss ambivalence about how their treatment may affect their career or their relationships with peers and superiors. It is important to be sensitive to the many different subtle associations of substance abuse and addiction within the broader military culture. Offering opportunities to address these subtleties, and allowing patients to explore them in ways that are productive and personally relevant, is the key component of art therapy with this population.

This chapter outlines three elements of substance abuse and co-occurring disorders treatment which are either uniquely engaged through the arts therapies or that are further enriched when they are addressed through non-verbal and creative interventions: building group cohesion and social support, developing independent self-regulating skills, and expressing and exploring resistance or ambivalence. Considering substance abuse treatment within both military and civilian settings is predominantly structured around group interventions, these elements are presented here through a group art therapy lens. They may certainly be adjusted to individual art therapy when time and resources permit and as the art therapist feels is appropriate.

Structuring Approaches: Directive and Non-directive Engagement

Treatment for substance use disorders and co-occurring disorders at the inpatient, residential, or partial hospitalization level is typically short term and time limited. Addressing patients' needs through a combination of directive and non-directive art therapy approaches is most effective in these settings. As Feen-Calligan (1995) found while working to integrate spirituality and addiction treatment through art therapy, providing occasional unstructured art-making opportunities allows patients to engage with their treatment at their own pace, taking control of their expression in a setting that is otherwise highly regimented and structured. However, many patients are at a loss about how to begin the process of expression, and may not trust their own experiences enough to risk engaging with an unfamiliar modality. The structure and containment of a clear directive, presented with encouragement for each patient to make it their own, may be seen as a reassuring "assignment" to be completed, while allowing individuals the flexibility to deviate from the directive as they become more comfortable with the expressive process.

Generally, substance abuse treatment incorporates a large degree of education and skill development as part of the recovery process. This may involve topics such as the disease model of addiction, how different substances affect the brain and body, the stages of change, and improving life skills such as effective communication, time management, and stress management. "Relapse prevention" is a substance abuse treatment approach that seeks to arm patients with practical tools to recognize, address, and manage triggers for substance use in order to avoid relapse and relapsing behaviors. This approach is also commonly utilized in co-occurring disorder treatment, though the focus may be slightly adjusted to address unsafe or maladaptive behaviors and patterns (such as social isolation or self-harming) in addition to the use of substances.

Due to the structured learning process and general educational ethos of many substance abuse treatment programs, providing some similarly modeled art therapy interventions helps integrate creative modalities in a way that is consistent and inclusive within multidisciplinary settings. However, the reality of the world outside of treatment centers and structured programs can be ambiguous, confusing, and full of gray areas to the newly sober. Many patients, once they grow comfortable with peers and staff, find a sense of safety and containment in an inpatient, residential, or partial hospitalization treatment setting. The threat of triggering situations is dramatically reduced, access to substances is removed or significantly restricted, and patients have ready access to qualified support and therapeutic interventions to address their emotional needs in real time.

For military service members, transition is a guaranteed experience across the span of a career. Preparing service members with substance abuse and co-occurring disorders to better manage transitions in general sets the stage for better management of service-specific transitions, whether that is a change in duty assignment, retirement, or separation from military service. Art therapy and engagement with the creative arts in general during times of transition can help patients navigate the gray areas between identities—between "addict" and "sober," "service member" and "veteran," "military" and "civilian." Because art making is an open-ended and flexible process, it gives patients a chance to consider possibilities beyond right and wrong or black and white. Supported opportunities to engage with non-directive art making while actively in treatment offer patients a chance to begin the process of developing a sober and recovery-minded identity according to their own needs and abilities. By providing therapist-directed *and* open or patient-directed engagement in art making, the art therapist provides space for patients to experience safety while also exploring their own individual recovery processes.

Building Group Cohesion and Social Support

Decreasing isolation and increasing the role of peer involvement in an individual's treatment can be implemented through art therapy interventions focusing on group cohesion, skill development, and providing more senior group members with opportunities to impart knowledge or guide newer members through processes. For patients who are new to the creative arts, skeptical of the role art and art making may play in their treatment, or ambivalent about treatment in general, it is helpful to have more experienced peers introduce the general concept of art therapy during an opening check-in at the start of a group session. Not only does this give group members a sense of ownership and agency over their involvement in the art-making process, it also implicitly sets expectations for participation and connection with each other. Reducing the power differential between therapist and patient allows for more comfortable exploration of treatment objectives within a supportive peer framework—the "we" so strongly and effectively advocated by 12-Step programs. In addition, having patients introduce what art therapy "is" to each other, in their own words, gives the art therapist a real-time sense of how interventions and processes are being interpreted, understood, and integrated by the patient milieu.

Treatment of substance use disorders tends to be heavily structured in favor of group-based interventions. Group psychotherapy, education, and mutual support groups like Alcoholics Anonymous and Narcotics Anonymous emphasize the importance of community and interdependence in recovery. Community and camaraderie is also of key importance in military culture. Many service members respond positively to group interventions in substance abuse treatment, and form strong bonds with their fellow patients. These bonds are vital to building a supportive recovery network and maintaining progress initiated in treatment. Residential or inpatient settings for substance abuse and co-occurring disorders are likely to strongly emphasize community and milieu interactions as key components of treatment. For many patients addressing addiction and other mental health diagnoses, learning to engage with others in a sober and healthy way is an important step in recovery.

Group art therapy interventions, such as completing group murals or engaging in partnered drawing, build these skills through productive collaboration. As in any group, conflict or tension may arise between members in the process, especially as patients learn to better manage conflict, communicate their feelings and needs, and interact constructively with others in a sober and contained environment. The quality of a group's interactions can set the stage for more in-depth work on emotion management and communication, essential skills in recovery.

Developing Independent Self-regulating Skills

In managing emotions, being able to properly connect with and identify specific emotions is the first step toward regulating them. Self-regulation is the process by which a person manages and adjusts his or her emotional and physiological responses to stimuli. Using substances such as drugs or alcohol is often a deliberate attempt to regulate unpleasant or undesired responses quickly and effectively. It is not uncommon to hear service members talk about the excessive use of drugs or alcohol as a way of "dealing with" emotions. "Dealing with" emotions through substance use is expressed in a variety of reactions, from drinking or using in an attempt to blunt or reduce the intensity of emotions (for example, taking opiates to avoid or escape distressing flashbacks) to drinking or using in order to be able to access and more easily experience a variety of emotions (for example, only being able to mourn the loss of a comrade and feel sadness or grief when intoxicated). Substance abuse treatment therefore involves the crucial aspect of connecting individuals with their emotions and building their skills to identify, express, and manage feelings successfully without the use of drugs or alcohol. When a co-occurring diagnosis is present, building those skills is even more crucial to sustained recovery. It is important and empowering, for example, for a patient to be able to tell the difference between situationally appropriate sadness and a depressive episode, and to respond accordingly.

Art therapy is an effective and expedient tool for connecting to and managing strong emotions while providing a measure of autonomy and flexibility. In an inpatient or residential setting, art therapy is often the first opportunity many service members have to explore their emotional experiences in a controlled and sober environment. Due to the perceived threat of judgment for expressing or even acknowledging difficult emotions such as sadness, anxiety, or shame, patients may require support when beginning the process of this exploration in a group art therapy setting. Providing a structured directive around identifying a specific emotion allows each individual to follow guidelines and maintain a sense of order in unfamiliar territory.

Setting a session or series of sessions to explore emotions through art making integrates easily into other modalities of treatment, including the aforementioned psycho-education and skill building, 12-step approaches, and insight-oriented verbal psychotherapy. Using a formal elements-based directive, where patients are educated on elements such as line, shape, space, and color and then invited to create images of a specific emotion using those elements, gently introduces the concept that each individual will experience and express emotions differently. Not only does this provide patients with an outlet to express emotions with clear instructions and limits, it also creates reflective distance that allows these expressions to be discussed, questioned, and processed in a non-threatening setting. Placing limitations on expression by encouraging patients to use only formal elements, rather than pictorial image representations or stereotyped symbols, further reduces the threat of judgment and the tendency to label artwork as "good" or "bad."

Please refer to Plate 8 in the color plate section.

Plate 8 and Figure 11.1 are examples of artwork made by two different patients in a structured session as described above exploring "anger." Anger management is often a component of substance abuse treatment, and service members frequently relate to anger as an easily identified and/or easily expressed emotion. As the above images show, patients may have very different experiences and expressions of anger, despite the expectation that all patients have the same foundational understanding of what anger is and how it manifests. In "Inner Demons" (Plate 8), the service member used a variety of strong colors and elements of containment, evident in the inward-focused directional line quality and increasingly smaller and more focused shapes nestled inside one another, with a tiny circle marked with an "X" at the center. He described his response to anger as "burying" it through humor, ignoring it, or otherwise trying not to acknowledge it. However, the explosive nature of his anger when he finally allowed himself to express it while intoxicated frightened him. That explosiveness and uncontrollability is evident in the image's strong sense of movement behind the static circles and square lines of the containing elements.

In contrast, "Twisted" (Figure 11.1) shows us an anger experience entirely in shades of black, gray, and white. Smooth, flowing lines in varying thicknesses move through the entire field, never finding a center or focal point, and indeed going off the edges of the page, giving the viewer a sense that the lines continue to wander indefinitely. This service member reported a great deal of difficulty expressing anger, and shared that he simply avoided it as much as possible. When conflict arose, or when something happened that might provoke an anger response, he became anxious, unable to focus, and his first impulse was to run away. As a result, he had trouble differentiating between anger and anxiety, and tried very hard to avoid both emotions as much as possible. The sweeping, softly blended lines in his drawing of anger invite exploration into how this confusion of feelings may have resulted in a deliberate attempt to deny or "smooth over" the discomfort of strong emotions.

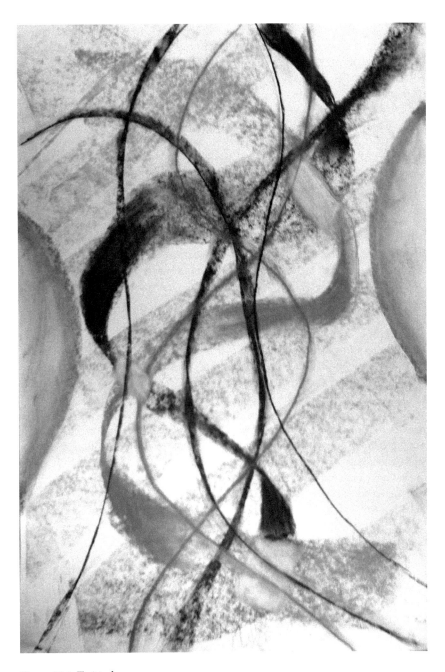

Figure 11.1 Twisted.

Sharing and discussing these differences in a group setting through structured art making not only allows patients to witness the wide variety of emotional expressions among themselves, it also provides a language for recognizing and adjusting to a more nuanced emotional landscape. In addition, clinical and diagnostic information gleaned from artwork and art processes can be a valuable asset to a multidisciplinary treatment team, providing insight into subtleties not otherwise available through verbal, educational, or manualized interventions.

Taking this directive a step further, an art therapist could easily expand upon this form of emotional exploration by inviting patients to create images of emotions experienced in relationship to drinking or using, and assisting patients in making connections to their emotions and their patterns of use. Providing patients with group and individual art therapy interventions to build on self-regulating skills individualizes treatment and increases patient confidence in their own abilities to identify and manage emotional triggers as they arise, setting the stage to form new patterns of proactive emotion regulation rather than reacting through substance use or other destructive behaviors.

Expressing and Exploring Resistance or Ambivalence

Military culture emphasizes consistency and observance of established guidelines and rules. Standards and practices are respected as cornerstones of efficiency, and adherence to these standards is necessary for the smooth management of the vast and diverse organization that is the United States military, and the dangerous or ambiguous situations the military is called to address. For these crucial reasons, military service members are trained to respect authority, comply with orders, and maintain discipline within their ranks. While this is certainly important in operational contexts, it can sometimes pose an interesting challenge therapeutically. As discussed earlier, individuals receiving treatment for substance abuse or addiction may have varying levels of resistance to treatment, or even to their presence in treatment. Whether or not a patient self-refers, is referred by their command, or is referred as the result of administrative or legal action has a strong effect on his or her personal interpretations and experiences in treatment. A patient who does not believe they have an issue with drugs or alcohol, but is nonetheless ordered to comply with treatment or else risk being labeled a "treatment failure" and potentially negatively impacting their military career, is fundamentally in conflict.

How does a therapist and treatment team address this tension between self and organization? The military service member who participates superficially in treatment, completing assignments and engaging in groups and meetings politely when prompted, is "complying" with treatment but is receiving minimal therapeutic benefit, because he or she is reluctant to share and acknowledge the authentic, difficult, and sometimes problematic thoughts and feelings of ambivalence. The key to addressing this conflict is creating space for these feelings and reactions to be expressed.

There is a wealth of information in substance abuse literature and research addressing patient ambivalence about treatment. Therapeutic orientations and techniques such as harm reduction psychotherapy, motivational interviewing, and acceptance and commitment therapy all have at their roots an acknowledgment of patient ambivalence and resistance (Horay, 2006). Effective substance abuse and co-occurring disorder treatment takes into account an individual's unique perspectives on their situation, allows that individual to explore those perspectives, and provides a context to challenge and adjust them when necessary.

The principle of remaining open and accepting of patient's expressions, without judgment of right or wrong, is an especially strong opportunity to engage in art making and creative work. A patient's feelings about substance abuse treatment, including whether or not it is necessary for them, or if it is effectively addressing their underlying mental health needs, may be a starting point to explore feelings about other areas of their life which may need attention. Service members may have strong or conflicted feelings about their diagnoses, their military career, incidents during deployments, or any number of other sensitive topics related to the unique experience of serving in the armed forces. Depending on the nature of these feelings, patients may be reluctant to acknowledge or express them, for fear of judgment, negative consequences (real or perceived), or because confronting them may be painful or uncomfortable, and potentially at odds with their military identity. This may manifest as a strong resistance to treatment, but the therapist should be aware of the power of simply allowing the expression of this resistance as an entry point into further exploration.

Art making provides a safe container for these complicated, imprecise, or unarticulated feelings. Reflective distance—being able to separate enough from a painful or difficult experience in order to explore it safely and productively—is once again invoked as a key component of art therapy with substance abuse and co-occurring disorder populations.

"Closet of Choices" (Figure 11.2) was a drawing completed early in residential treatment by an active duty service member who believed, very strongly, that he had been unfairly coerced into substance abuse treatment by his command. He was unhappy with his diagnosis of alcohol use disorder, and did not consider his drinking to be a primary problem. In addition to his substance abuse diagnosis, he also presented with significant combat-related post-traumatic stress disorder, for which he had received previous outpatient treatment. Outpatient treatment was minimally effective, however, due to the service member's uncontrolled alcohol consumption, for which he was referred to inpatient residential substance abuse treatment.

Frustrated with this referral, feeling betrayed by his command, and with lack of improvement in his PTSD symptoms, the service member was minimally engaged in verbal therapy and psycho-education groups, which he interpreted as confrontational and failing to meet his underlying mental health needs. He remained polite but superficial in sessions, and was guarded with providers. He had no previous art therapy experience, and spent the first few art therapy

144   E.A. McKee

Figure 11.2 Closet of choices.

group sessions sitting silently at the table, observing but not participating. "Closet of Choices" was a drawing he completed during an art therapy session exploring personal boundaries with others. He explained that each day, in each situation, he had to make choices about what part of himself would respond based on the needs of the military, the needs of those he commanded, or the best way to avoid conflict. The "closet" pictured represented this array of selves he had cultivated over the years—and, perhaps most significantly, he was unable to conceive of a true "self" which was choosing the masks, echoing Winnicott's (1960) understanding of the suffering that arises when the self fractures to defend its integrity. In the image, the viewer is only afforded a glimpse of one row of masks, while others remain half-hidden behind a closed door. The implication of another row of masks, unseen by the viewer and unacknowledged by the artist behind the closed door, raises questions about denial, protection, and hiding places. That this service member only chose minimally expressive but familiar tools (number 2 pencil on paper) to depict such a poignant experience of inauthenticity is also significant. Self-exploration was new and uncomfortable for this service member, and was evident in his cautious artwork.

This image began an exploration of identity, and how the lack of sincerity in his expressions with others had led to painful intrapsychic conflict. The feelings of betrayal by his command, of inauthenticity from providers, and the resistance to admitting the severity of his drinking may be seen as projections of his own struggles to be honest with himself. By accepting this resistance and creating space for this service member to admit this confusion within himself through image and metaphor, the foundation was laid for more fruitful therapeutic work around self-concept and his relationships with others. Utilizing reflective distance and staying within the metaphor of the closet of masks, the service member was able to claim some ownership of his emotions—the "Closet of Choices" meant that, in actuality, the choice of what self to portray was ultimately his alone, not that of his command or the treatment staff, or any other group or individual. Only by allowing and inviting exploration of resistance could he begin to tolerate the difficult work of confronting himself and start to heal. Following the creation and processing of this image, the service member grew more comfortable in art therapy sessions, and this eventually generalized to verbal sessions as well. He still struggled with feelings of resistance, but was able to expand his artistic expression through various media and accept feedback from others on his work. Expressing resistance provides a sense of agency in treatment, and a chance to create personalized experiences of recovery based on an individual's unique needs.

Recovery as a Creative Act

The therapeutic goals of building group cohesion, connecting with emotions, and addressing resistance are all uniquely engaged through the arts therapies, because of the open-ended possibilities inherent in creating. In many ways, treatment of substance abuse and co-occurring disorders is a search for definitive solutions—symptoms managed, substance use discontinued, traumas resolved. This clarity is a noble goal, but in our desire to solve the problem of addiction and mental health conditions that occur hand in hand, the true answer is in the murky, messy middle. When we expand the possibilities of treatment to explore each service member's unique experience, including the subtle interactions of their military identity, emotional landscape, and relational interactions, we empower both the individual and the collective community of which they are a part to strive for wholeness and healing. The camaraderie, sense of purpose, and ideals of service are an indelible part of military identity. Art therapy offers an opportunity for individual expression and uniform group identity to exist side by side rather than in opposition. Addressing addiction and co-occurring disorders involves uncovering and exploring layers of meaning, both for individual service members and for military culture as a whole. Addiction and co-occurring disorders frequently leave people feeling powerless, at the mercy of their diagnosis. What better metaphor for empowerment than the creation of new images and new understanding? Recovery itself is a creative act, involving inspiration, planning, execution, and examination. If we are sensitive to the complex connections and interactions of military service, substance use, and mental health diagnoses, we can find space to create recovery that is full of possibility.

References

American Psychiatric Association. (2013). *Diagnostic and Statistical Manual of Mental Disorders: DSM-5*. Washington, DC: American Psychiatric Association.

Department of Defense/Military OneSource. (2015). Substance abuse policy and treatment. Retrieved April 24, 2015, from http://www.militaryonesource.mil/crisis-prevention?content_id=268706.

Feen-Calligan, H. (1995). The use of art therapy in treatment programs to promote spiritual recovery from addiction. *Art Therapy: Journal of the American Art Therapy Association 12*(1), 46–50.

Gulliver, S.B. & Steffen, L.E. (2010). Towards integrated treatments for PTSD and substance use disorders. *PTSD Research Quarterly, 21*(2), 1–7.

Horay, B.J. (2006). Moving towards gray: Art therapy and ambivalence in substance abuse treatment. *Art Therapy: Journal of the American Art Therapy Association, 23*(1), 14–22.

Institute of Medicine. (2012). *Substance Use Disorders in the U.S. Armed Forces*. Washington, DC: The National Academies Press.

Schumm, J.A. & Chard, K.M. (2012). Alcohol and stress in the military. Alcohol research. *Current Reviews, 34*(4), 401–407.

Sturkey, M.F. (2002). *Warrior Culture of the U.S. Marines*. Plum Branch, SC: Heritage Press International, pp. 77–79.

Substance Abuse and Mental Health Services Administration/Office of Applied Studies. (2007). The NSDUH Report: Serious Psychological Distress and Substance Use Disorder among Veterans. Rockville, MD: SAMHSA.

Substance Abuse and Mental Health Services Administration. (n.d.) Co-occurring disorders in veterans and military service members: Treatment models for veterans and service members with co-occurring disorders. Retrieved April 5, 2017, from http://media.samhsa.gov/co-occurring/topics/military/treatment-models.aspx.

Winnicott, D.W. (1960). Ego distortion in terms of true and false self. In D.W. Winnicott (Ed.), *The Maturational Processes and the Facilitating Environment: Studies in the Theory of Emotional Development* (pp. 140–152). London: Karnac Books.

CHAPTER **12**

Using the Instinctual Trauma Response Model in a Military Setting

Linda Gantt and Mary Ellen Vesprini

Throughout the twentieth century, artists, writers, composers, and poets who witnessed war first-hand provided powerful and heart-wrenching testimony to its effects (for a range of examples, see the e-resources section). Adrian Hill, who developed art therapy in England in the late 1930s and early 1940s, worked with soldiers as well as with tuberculosis patients (Hogan, 2001). Since Hill's time, artists and art therapists have created a variety of therapeutic programs in rehabilitation hospitals and community settings employing the visual arts and writing for returning soldiers (Golub, 1985; Howie, Prasad, & Kristel, 2013; Kopytin & Lebedev, 2013; Malchiodi, 2012; Wise & Nash, 2013). Our chapter builds on this history by providing an account of another type of art-based program for processing combat trauma.

The Co-occurring Disorders Program

This chapter draws upon material gathered from the application of graphic narrative processing using the Instinctual Trauma Response (ITR) model (Tinnin & Gantt, 2012) in a therapeutic group setting for combat-related post-traumatic stress disorder (PTSD). It was based in a co-occurring partial hospitalization program attached to the Behavioral Health Department of a major Military Treatment Facility. Participants in the combat trauma group were primarily active duty service members referred to the program by their outpatient provider or when discharged from inpatient services. The majority of participants had a dual diagnosis of PTSD and substance abuse. A significant number were assigned to the Wounded Warrior Battalion and a relatively high proportion of patient cases were under review with the Medical Examination Board. The average length of stay in the program ranged from four to six weeks. All participants received both group and individual therapy. In addition to treatment for PTSD, other treatment modalities in the co-occurring program included relapse prevention, recreational therapy, cognitive processing therapy (CPT), and mindfulness practice.

The Structure of the Combat Trauma Group

Following the basic principles of the ITR model (described below), the primary focus of the combat trauma group consisted of graphic narrative processing and re-presentation of adverse combat experiences. The group met on an average of four times a week for 90 minutes with an average of six to twelve participants and was an open format (with rolling admissions). Participants evaluated by staff clinicians were assigned to the combat trauma group based on their presentation on intake and for their suitability in the group. These clinicians also served as the primary therapist of those they assessed. In addition to a more general interview, the clinicians used the Trauma Recovery Scale (TRS) (Baranowsky & Gentry, 2014), a self-report assessment that can be given on a weekly basis to measure current symptoms.

The group leader was a social worker with training in the ITR model as well as having considerable experience using it in a civilian PTSD clinic. A psychiatric technician, assigned to each group session, provided support for the soldiers and handled the videotaping of the re-presentations. This videotaping made it possible for the therapist to review it later in individual sessions if needed. If a person dissociated during any part of his re-presentation, he could watch the video later to see and hear the entire story.

The group leader provided handouts outlining the components of the ITR and other psycho-educational material from film clips and books such as *The Post-Traumatic Stress Disorder Sourcebook* (Schiraldi, 2016). As the participants drew, the leader circulated throughout the room answering questions about the process, helping identify the components of the ITR, monitoring the participants for dissociation, and grounding them as needed. Making the graphic narrative often took more than one session. Group members put considerable effort into making detailed drawings, looking on the Internet for photographs of military vehicles, planes, weapons, and other equipment so that they could draw a faithful rendition of a particular scene.

Major Problems of PTSD

Some major problems for PTSD survivors include: having fragmented memories that cannot generate a linear narrative, lacking words to describe the experiences, and feeling that one's sense of time has been altered in some fundamental way. The ITR model addresses these issues.

Fragmented Memories Due to Problems with the Verbal Brain

Recounting his difficulty in selecting a trauma for a research protocol at a Veterans Administrative hospital, Morris (2015) gives a sense of how frustrating it is to have only fragments of memory. He could have given the researchers different types of his experiences in Iraq,

> (b)ut there are other, less easily described moments. Moments with no clear narrative line. Moments of moral chaos. Moments when anything

became possible. Moments where nothing was real. Moments that occurred over the course of months. Moments I am still waiting to end. Moments that have yet to be tamed by language.

(Morris, 2015, p. 170)

When the neocortex gives way to the limbic system at the height of a trauma, much of the experience is not coded in words (Gantt & Tripp, 2016). Later, when a person attempts to relate what had happened, the result is a disjointed and fragmented account. Under usual circumstances the verbal brain has an inhibiting effect on the non-verbal brain. This inhibition is especially problematic when traumatic material stored in the non-verbal brain presses for expression.

> The result is that material from the right nonverbal brain, particularly implicit processes and memory, is kept from being accessed. Yet the right brain has the capacity for communicating in ways other than words. Many art therapists have experienced a client saying, about an emerging image, "I don't know where *that* came from!"
>
> (Gantt & Tripp, 2016, p. 77)

Lack of words

Being "at a loss for words" is a common statement frequently uttered following a trauma. Even professional writers have remarked on the difficulty of finding words to describe overwhelming traumatic experiences. Kurt Vonnegut, author of the influential anti-war novel *Slaughterhouse-Five*, described his intention to write his account of witnessing the bombing of Dresden in World War II, "But not many words about Dresden came to my mind then—not enough of them to make a book, anyway. And not many words come now, either" (Vonnegut, 1969, ch.1).

Toni Morrison's novel *Sula* (1973) tells of a veteran who had lost the capacity for understanding language in a metaphoric way, as well as his sense of bodily integrity. In the hospital ward, the staff put him in a strait-jacket:

> He wanted desperately to see his own face and connect it with the word "private"—the word the nurse (and the others who had helped bind him) had called him. "Private" he thought was something secret, and he wondered why they had looked at him and called him a secret.
>
> (Morrison, 1973, p. 10)

Alteration in the Sense of Time

PTSD results in profound changes in one's sense of time. The next trauma seems to be just about to happen; therefore, relinquishing one's hyper-vigilance is impossible. Shay compares the "destruction of time" in combat veterans with that of prisoners in concentration camps (Shay, 1994, p. 176). The sense of continuity between past, present, and future is radically transformed. In *The Evil Hours: A Biography of Post-traumatic Stress Disorder*, David Morris recounts that a psychoanalyst told him:

> [T]rauma destroys the fabric of time. In normal time, you move from one moment to the next, sunrise to sunset, birth to death. After trauma, you move in circles, find yourself being sucked backwards into an eddy, or bouncing about like a rubber ball from now to then and back again.
> (Morris, 2015, p. xii)

Later in the same book, Morris states that trauma "breaks your internal clock in some way. But to describe it as simply destroying your sense of time doesn't quite do it justice. Post trauma, there are probably as many experiences of time as there are survivors" (p. 129).

Tim O'Brien, who wrote widely acclaimed novels of the Vietnam War, structured *In the Lake of the Woods* (1994) in such a way as to immerse the reader in the subjective experience of a veteran for whom time in the present is intertwined with the past. O'Brien used quotations from characters in the novel as well as historical personages, along with scholarly works on war and its effects in an attempt to explain the motivations of the veteran and his wife for apparently mysterious actions. There is no easy linear narrative to follow. The reader feels the struggle of having to put together bits and pieces in order to make sense of what happened and, even then, is left with many questions at the end of the book.

The Instinctual Trauma Response (ITR) Model

Much of the material that morphed into the Instinctual Trauma Response model (Tinnin & Gantt, 2013) had its origin in the clinical work of Louis Tinnin, MD, in a Veterans Administrative hospital in West Virginia in the 1990s. Building on ideas from art therapy groups he conducted with Linda Gantt in the mid-1970s in a psychiatric unit of a general hospital in Maryland, he had veterans use art as a means of telling their trauma stories. At the same time, he treated trauma survivors in outpatient and inpatient psychiatric programs connected to the Department of Behavioral Health in the School of Medicine at West Virginia University.

Tinnin and Gantt continued to refine the ITR model over the following two decades (Gantt & Tinnin, 2007; 2009) in two different private outpatient clinics with survivors of various traumas such as car accidents, medical traumas, natural disasters, childhood sexual and physical abuse, kidnapping and captivity, rape, and industrial accidents. Their work has similarities to both narrative therapy (Schauer, Neuner, & Elbert, 2011; White & Epston, 1990) and trauma treatments based on animal survival mechanisms of fight–flight–freeze (Levine, 1997).

Features of the Model

The ITR model is based on information from three main sources: modern brain research, clinical observations and published case material, and an understanding of evolutionary survival mechanisms. The core of the ITR model is making a series of specific drawings (the graphic narrative) and having the therapist tell the story back to the artist (the re-presentation). A key principle is that trauma processing does not require reliving the event in order to process it and make it truly recede into the past so that one no longer has intrusive, avoidant, or anxiety symptoms that are the defining characteristics of a PTSD diagnosis. This is the polar opposite of prolonged exposure therapy (PE) or flooding that focuses on having a person relive an event by telling the trauma story repeatedly, with the goal of extinguishing the stimulus/response connection and habituating to the traumatic memories and situations that one had avoided. In the ITR model, making art provides a means of distancing one's self from the event (which, after all, did happen in the past) and does not require repeated retelling of the story.

The Graphic Narrative: Using the ITR as the Scaffold for Stories

Since trauma stories are inherently fragmented and difficult to tell because they were not verbally coded, it is critical that art therapists give structure to trauma processing. Tinnin and Gantt maintain that the ITR is a universal response to traumas of all types. Therefore, it provides a scaffold upon which any trauma story can be placed. It is telling the story through doing specific drawings, arranging those drawings in a particular sequence, attaching words to the experience, and finally hearing the story told by the art therapist that reverses the peri-traumatic dissociation which occurs at the time of the trauma and may be predictive of PTSD.

The basic components of the ITR consist of the startle, a thwarted intention to fight or flee, the freeze, an altered state of consciousness, automatic obedience, and attempts at self-repair. Body sensations accompany each of these aspects. While this is a general outline, some traumas are more complicated and require further drawings to capture the full story. By asking for a separate picture for each component, art therapists can guide a person in creating a linear order to what was previously overwhelming and confusing (see Gantt & Greenstone (2016) for a case example using the ITR to structure a story along with illustrations of drawings from some graphic narratives).

In art therapy sessions, people often say they do not have words to express something; yet, when they are encouraged to draw, they invariably come up with specific words. In this way, the drawing process liberates non-verbal material that had been experienced as troubling symptoms. Any aspect of a traumatic event can become a trigger, resulting in a flashback or a disturbing, intrusive symptom. Just as physical shrapnel often works its way to the surface of a person's body, "memory shrapnel" (Tinnin & Gantt, 2013, p. 62) unexpectedly works its way to consciousness. A layperson intuitively understands why loud noises, blood, and sirens can be triggers but actually, anything a person experienced can be a trigger if the brain has not coded it in words. Taken on their own, these elements are not usually significant (such as the color of a person's clothing or the sound of an animal call). The graphic narrative puts these elements back into the context of the particular event and they cease to be triggers.

The Re-presentation

The ITR model may be used in individual sessions as well as in groups. In both types of sessions there is a "re-presentation" (Tinnin's term for the therapist telling the trauma story back to the person). In preparing to do the re-presentation the therapist goes over each picture, making sure to put them in order with a separate "Before" picture to set the scene and an "After" picture to end the story. The pictures are pinned or taped to a wall or easel. The re-presentation is not an interpretation of the art but a faithful repeating of the artist's words. Speaking about the art in this way is a radically different approach from the one used by most art therapists, who typically ask group members to tell each other about their own artwork.

In the combat trauma group of the co-occurring disorders program, the group leader would position the individual in the front of the room so that she could watch for any signs of dissociation. (If that did happen, she could stop the story, get the person grounded, and resume the story.) She would tell the story from start to finish, using past tense, focusing on the drawings, incorporating the components of the ITR, and emphasizing that the story was truly over.

Benefits of a Group Re-presentation

There were several benefits of doing a re-presentation in a group, not the least of which is validating an experience that was frequently suffered alone even in the context of a military operation. The group listened respectfully to the re-presentation, serving as compassionate witnesses who did not flinch at the difficult material or pass judgment on a person's behavior. The therapist tried to use as many of the artist's own words as possible, so that the artist felt that his story was really heard. The rest listened attentively until the re-presentation was over. Next, group members would express their collective support and would engage in a vigorous discussion, facilitated by the group leader. By witnessing the stories as a group, soldiers could see that experiences they thought were "crazy" were actually surprisingly common. Some examples of such strange occurrences were hearing voices telling of eminent danger, having an out-of-body experience during sudden and severe pain, seeing blood still visible on one's body after having showered for hours, or hearing persistent command hallucinations (Holmes & Tinnin, 1995). Some of these stories were those of the Warrior parts, usually formed during basic training that helped the soldiers survive combat but found no place for themselves when they returned home. This also helped people to see that, at times, suicidal thinking originated in the freeze and altered state of consciousness of the ITR. For example, a person might feel that since having come back from the near-death experience of the freeze, the same would happen after suicide.

The greatest therapeutic impact for the group members transpired in the feedback directly after the re-presentation in which group members showed their solidarity with each other. The sentiment "a band of brothers" was often invoked. (This harkens back to the famous rallying cry in Shakespeare's (2002, IV.iii) *Henry V*, known as the St. Crispin Day speech by which Henry inspired his troops before battle: "We few, we happy few, we band of brothers.")

A year after his experience in the combat trauma group, one man summarized his benefits from the graphic narrative:

> Completing the graphic narrative was very beneficial in my treatment for PTSD in two specific ways. First, completing a graphic narrative on one of my worst experiences in combat enabled me to capture that experience in a way that brought a new perspective on the event and my reaction to the event. [It] gave me a sense of control and ownership of the traumatic event in ways that other therapeutic approaches had not. Seeing the events and my role ... drawn out graphically helped me connect the separate elements of the bigger event into more of a story rather than just a segmented series of bad memories. I believe this enabled me to take more control and ownership of the traumatic event than other approaches used in my treatment previously, resulting in a better ability on my part to manage the symptoms associated with my PTSD.
>
> The most difficult aspects of combat-related PTSD I have confronted are the feelings of isolation I experience around people who have no frame of reference for the experiences of combat. This includes other military members who may have been deployed, but never really experienced combat first hand. As I worked in a group setting on my graphic narrative I connected with other service members who truly understood the nature of my experiences. I honestly felt for the first time since returning from combat that there were other people on the planet who understood what I had experienced and to at least some degree how I felt. This sense of identification with others was invaluable in helping regain a sense of belonging.
>
> (personal communication, May, 5, 2016)

Special Note on the Freeze and Automatic Obedience

Many group members took special pride in telling the group leader they did not go into the freeze because of their training. It is certainly the case that not everyone who is exposed to the same traumatic event will develop PTSD. Crucial variables include previous traumas, resilience, and proximity to the event. Instead of going into the freeze (which results in feeling helpless or about to die), a well-trained person is more likely to go into a particular type of automatic obedience that might be better termed "automatic pilot." This comes from the process in basic training that purposely engenders an altered state of consciousness, resulting in a "psychological restructuring" (Morris, 2015, p. 128). This is not unlike being traumatized. A graduate art therapy student who had served in Iraq commented:

> One purpose of boot camp/basic training is to break a person down, instill discipline, and overwrite instincts. The ego is broken down through prolonged mental and physical exhaustion, the goal of which is to remold the individual into a member of a team with more efficient, disciplined, and standardized ways of thinking. For some, the indoctrination and training requires adopting a different set of morals – an organizational set of morals which allows for doing what needs to be done in difficult times to protect one's comrades and the interests of one's nation.
> (personal communication, February 24, 2016)

The differences between automatic obedience and automatic pilot may be seen in the attacks on the World Trade Center on 9/11. The majority of people were running *out* of the burning buildings. However, certain small groups of people were running *into* the buildings. These were the police and firemen who, by virtue of their extensive training and repeated practice of emergency procedures, knew how to respond to the horrific situation. However, these special units were not making up their responses on the spot but were relying on well-rehearsed protocols.

Soldiers in a war zone are prepared for a firefight when on patrol. While such an event is distressing and difficult, it may not generate PTSD symptoms because the soldiers are well prepared and hyper-vigilant. However, encountering something that is totally unexpected and not covered in training is likely to elicit a reaction that throws a person into the ITR. In short, what happens is that the verbal brain goes offline (Gantt & Tripp, 2016) and the non-verbal brain with its lightning fast reactions goes into survival mode. Such was the situation in Afghanistan in 2003 when US troops encountered the first improvised explosive devices (IEDs) (news/nation/2013/12/18/ied-10-years-blast-wounds-amputations/3803017/). No one had been trained to handle such a situation because the IEDs were entirely new weapons of a kind never seen before. The most thorough training cannot prepare for every possibility.

Addressing Problems of Non-verbal Material and the Alteration of Time

Making art gives the non-verbal brain an opportunity for "output by motor and symbolic expression" (Tinnin, 1990, p. 11). Once colors, shapes, and images are produced, words can be attached. According to Shay,

> [W]hen the traumatic moment reoccurs as flashback or nightmare, the emotions of terror, grief, and rage may be merged with each other. Such emotion is relived, not remembered. The naming of these as separate emotions,

creating a *language* of emotion—which may be in plastic and musical arts, not only in words—is an important part of gaining mastery over the traumatic memory. Naming is one of the early stages of the communication of trauma by rendering it communicable, however imperfectly.

(Shay, 1994, p. 173, emphasis in original)

Daniel Siegel offers a related concept that is supported by brain studies: "naming an affect soothes limbic firing" (Siegel, 2010, p. 116), or, as he succinctly says, "name it to tame it."

A person could quite literally get a new perspective by seeing the drawings placed on the wall at a distance and by hearing his story told in detail by the group leader. He could see with his own eyes that the story was finally over. Through the re-presentation, distortions in one's sense of time were thereby corrected and the story was made past tense.

Conclusion

For Operation Enduring Freedom and for Operation Iraqi Freedom (Afghanistan and Iraq) the estimated prevalence for PTSD is 13.8 percent (http://www.ptsd.va.gov/professional/PTSD-overview/epidemiological-facts-ptsd.asp, retrieved May 22, 2016). Given these statistics, our country faces a huge challenge to develop effective treatments for PTSD. When art therapists reframe intrusive symptoms as attempts for the non-verbal brain to "finish the story" they make a strong case for using art in trauma processing. The ITR model with its focus on the graphic narrative and re-presentation is easily applied to groups whose members have had combat trauma and holds promise for the future.

References

Baranowsky, A., & Gentry, J.E. (2014). *Trauma Practice: Tools for Stabilization* (3rd edition). Boston, MA: Hogrefe.

Gantt, L., & Greenstone, L. (2016). Narrative art therapy in trauma treatment. In J. Rubin, *Approaches to Art Therapy: Theory and Technique* (3rd edition, pp. 353–370). New York: Routledge.

Gantt, L., & Tinnin, L. (2007). Intensive trauma therapy of PTSD and dissociation: An outcome study. *The Arts in Psychotherapy, 34,* 69–80.

Gantt, L., & Tinnin, L. (2009). Support for a neurobiological view of trauma with implications for art therapy. *The Arts in Psychotherapy, 36,* 148–153.

Gantt, L., & Tripp, T. (2016). The image comes first: Treating preverbal trauma with art therapy. In J. King (Ed.), *Art Therapy, Trauma, and Neuroscience: Theoretical and Practical Perspectives* (pp. 67–99). New York: Routledge.

Golub, D. (1985). Symbolic expression in post-traumatic stress disorder: Vietnam combat veterans in art therapy. *The Arts in Psychotherapy, 12,* 285–296.

Hogan, S. (2001). *Healing Arts: The History of Art Therapy.* London: Jessica Kingsley.

Holmes, D., & Tinnin, L. (1995). The problem of auditory hallucinations in combat PTSD. *Traumatology, 1*(2), 1–7.

Howie, P., Prasad, S., & Kristel, J. (2013). *Using Art Therapy with Diverse Populations: Crossing Cultures and Abilities*. London: Jessica Kingsley.

Kopytin, A., & Lebedev, A. (2013). Humor, self-attitude, emotions, and cognitions in group art therapy with war veterans. *Art Therapy: Journal of the American Art Therapy Association, 30*(1), 20–29.

Levine, P. (with Frederick, A.). (1997). *Waking the Tiger*. Berkeley, CA: North Atlantic Books.

Malchiodi, C. (2012). Art therapy with combat veterans and military personnel (ch. 22). In *Handbook of Art Therapy* (2nd edition). New York: Guilford Press.

Morris, D. (2015). *The Evil Hours: A Biography of Post-traumatic Stress Disorder*. New York: Houghton Mifflin Harcourt.

Morrison, T. (1973). *Sula*. New York: Plume/Penguin Books.

O'Brien, T. (1994). *In the Lake of the Woods*. New York: Penguin Books.

Schauer, M., Neuner, F., & Elbert, T. (2011). *Narrative Exposure Therapy* (2nd revised and expanded edition). Boston, MA: Hogrefe.

Schiraldi, G. (2016). *The Post-traumatic Stress Disorder Sourcebook, Revised and Expanded Second Edition: A Guide to Healing, Recovery, and Growth*. New York: McGraw-Hill Education.

Shakespeare, W., & Smith, E. (2002). *King Henry V* (6th edition). Cambridge: Cambridge University Press.

Shay, J. (1994). *Achilles in Vietnam: Combat Trauma and the Undoing of Character*. New York: Scribner.

Siegel, D. (2010). *Mindsight: The New Science of Personal Transformation*. New York: Bantam.

Tinnin, L. (1990). Biological processes in nonverbal communication and their role in the making and interpretation of art. *American Journal of Art Therapy, 29,* 9–13.

Tinnin, L., & Gantt, L. (2012). *Intensive Treatment of Combat Stress and Traumatic Brain Injury: A Treatment Manual*. Morgantown, WV: Gargoyle Press (Amazon Digital Services).

Tinnin, L., & Gantt, L. (2013). *The Instinctual Trauma Response and Dual Brain Dynamics*. Morgantown, WV: Gargoyle Press (Amazon Digital Services).

Vonnegut, K. (1969). *Slaughterhouse-Five*. New York: Delacorte.

White, M., & Epston, D. (1990). *Narrative Means to Therapeutic Ends*. New York: Norton.

Wise, S., & Nash, E. (2013). Metaphor as heroic mediator: Imagination, creative arts therapy, and group process as agents of healing with veterans. In R.M. Scurfield & K.T. Platoni (Eds.), *Healing War Trauma: A Handbook of Creative Approaches* (pp. 99–114). New York: Routledge.

CHAPTER **13**

The Sketch Project: Volunteers Giving Veterans a New Perspective

Doris Arrington and Nancy Parfitt Hondros

What follows is an account of one woman's passion for art making, service to others, and a gift that has given back many times over, as witnessed by the co-author, an art therapy student at the time of their encounter.

Doris's Story

One weekend each year, for over ten years, the church I attend on the Bay area peninsula cancels worship service in order to serve our neighbors and their communities. The communities have submitted proposals for some interactive care services or property restoration service often located in senior residential facilities and local Veteran Administration (VA) hospitals. Four thousand volunteers branch out as small teams in response to these communities' requests. Property rehabilitation assistance provided by volunteers includes clean-up, new paint and restoration of local elementary schools, private or public, their libraries, faculty lounges, landscaping, and playgrounds. Other help is offered for the homeless and handicapped services, senior safe-at-home repairs, rehabilitation opportunities to build playhouses for all children's services, Habitat for Humanity, Samaritan House Clinic, and AIDS health kits for caregivers in Africa. Many of the volunteers visit with the seniors or play cards and other games with the vets as service. Money for these services and maintenance come from donations and special offerings collected at our church throughout the year.

Personal History

Like most Americans, I have a deep respect and affection for our veterans who have given so much in service to their country, so I was excited when I had an opportunity with a small team of volunteers to visit a VA hospital and interact with hospital patients in conversations or games. Games were not my interest, so after watching and visiting with individual vets in the recreation room, I asked a young vet in a wheelchair with multiple tubes strategically placed in his face and body if I could sketch him. With a solemn face and a twinkle in his eye he agreed, and then sat very still while I opened my sketch-book and with a pencil and an eraser began drawing him. Other vets rolled up in their wheelchairs to see what was happening and sat calmly watching. When I had finished the drawing I tore it out of my sketch-book and handed it to the vet whom I had sketched. He showed it to three or four other patients who had been watching. When I started sketching the next patient, the group lined up in their wheelchairs to wait patiently for their turn. Even though I am not greatly experienced working with service members, the trauma work I have done as an art therapist at home and abroad and my own personal research into cultural aspects of the Military made me comfortable in offering this approach. Prior to this event I had sketched people's faces with pencil and eraser whenever and wherever I could sit quietly. To capture a likeness in a look-alike portrait takes me about ten minutes and another ten minutes to refine the picture. Out of joy, I sketch a lot. I will often sketch when my husband and I travel on a train or a bus somewhere in the world. When appropriate, I ask permission or sometimes I am just able to sketch the people around me.

That morning at the VA I quickly finished six pencil sketches, maybe taking about an hour and a half. As artists would know, I had a grand time and the vets appeared to be as happy as I was. They interacted, chatting with each other about their newly acquired self-portraits gifts. The vets' simple act of altruism, sharing their portraits with each other, appeared to coalesce the group. I witnessed an instillation of hope, as described by Yalom and Leszcz (2005), to provide hope, comfort, and a connection with others. The element of hope may be the most precious gift from the portraits. The portraits offered the vets an opportunity to be treated with dignity, made a connection as they interacted with each other, and through these interactions appeared to be able to begin the process of "co-construct meaning in [their] lives, and moreover, co-construct [their] identity" (Henson, 2015, p. 43). I am not the first artist to create portraits of veterans or hospitalized patients.

A group of artists, participating in the Joe Bonham Project, created portraits of service members recovering at Walter Reed National Military Medical Center. Carol Kino (2012) discovered that both the artists and the service members found the experience to be cathartic. The illustrators formed bonds with the patients as they got to know them, their stories, and spent time working on the illustrations. Brandon Fortune, chief curator at the Smithsonian's National Portrait Gallery, commented that these portraits are a "way of exploring identity, and even group identity" (Kino, 2012).

Costello-Dubois (1989) noticed that her portraits of hospitalized patients "seemed to be a way of giving quiet affirmation" (p. 66), a reflection that mirrors my experience. Her patients expressed similar reactions to the veterans for whom I sketched portraits—pleased to have individual attention and a surprised, positive reaction to their images. By talking to the veterans as we, the artists, sketched, we seemed to create a unique space between us and were able to catch their spirit in the portrait, just as Costello-Dubois found during her portraiture experiences.

Why a one-day event of doing something I love, namely portrait sketches, has turned into a multi-day event with a team of artists and other volunteers can perhaps best be answered by a quote in my 2001 article in *Art Therapy* entitled "Why do we make art?" – "Art not only reflects the attitude of the times in which we live, but instills in us the courage to defeat our enemies, motivates us and others toward success in life tasks, and repairs broken hearts and minds" (Arrington, 2001, p. 106). This resonates with the portrait subjects, their families, and the volunteers.

Recruiting Artists, Photographers, and Models

As time passed, I told other artists about my success with the veteran portrait experience and asked if they would like to join me the following year. Five other artists agreed to join me the following spring. Concerned that we might have more vets than artists, I also recruited four or five photographers to help fill in any time gaps we might have. Success bred more success as we went back for another year.

Process

The subsequent year I contacted hospital nurses and administrators for permission to return to the VA again and sketch the vets. I also submitted a proposal to the appropriate church organization committee for an expansion of the "Veteran Portraits" program. The proposal requested support for one day at the Poly-Trauma Unit and one day at the Post-traumatic Stress Disorder (PTSD) Unit, the cost of 50 frames for the portraits, and scrumptious lunches for the vets, staff, and artists. These units are located in separate buildings. The Poly-Trauma Unit provides services to veterans diagnosed with co-morbid severe traumatic brain injury and psychiatric disorders. Offering two different days for the events reduces the logistic complexity and offers the volunteers an option to work for one or two days.

I call three months in advance of our planned visit to notify the two units' service people of our plans. These hospital employees work with the volunteers, and help with the schedule and details of the event. I get a head count to order food, though some years we have enjoyed a potluck lunch. About a week before the event, the nursing staff and/or the art therapists will create posters advertising the event. Some of the church volunteers begin to set up about an hour before other artists and the photographers arrive, moving through the VA campus to put up signs advertising the event and indicating where to find the veteran portrait event. Even with the large signs, volunteers miss the signs and the locations at this large hospital complex, so cell phones are helpful to bring them to the event.

The Poly-Trauma and PTSD units have different initial reactions to our arrival. The Poly-Trauma patients are more subdued and reluctant to be involved in the portrait, and usually join the event only after some prodding from family members or staff. The patient responses run the gamut from interest or excitement to resistance, many times based on how much autonomy the patient had in the participation decision. Cohesiveness in the Poly-Trauma Unit appears to be slow to develop; thus the interactions between the patients after the portraits are more restrained than in the PTSD Unit.

Each time we arrive at the PTSD Unit we are met by excited vets with big smiles and enthusiastic hellos. Those who are familiar with the portrait day event come early to get their place in line and urge other vets to become involved in the event. We, the volunteers, witness what Yalom and Leszcz (2005) describe as the universality of the group development. Many of the vets start off not wanting to do the portraits and pick it up when other patients become involved. Some vets watch how the pictures develop, other vets share with another patient and get them interested, and others show their pictures in the privacy of their rooms. The PTSD Unit response is similar to what the illustrators found when they visited Walter Reed National Military Medical Center.

The volunteers' jobs on the Vet Portrait Experience Day include the coordinator who takes the names of waiting vets and ushers them to an artist using the vet's preferred materials, ten artists who use graphite or colored pencils, pastels, watercolors, and pen and ink for the portraits, approximately seven photographers, three software workers, four members of the frame team, and three food servers and general volunteers who provide additional key support for the event.

The PTSD vets know we are coming from the signs posted in the hospital, and several meet us in the parking lot to help carry our materials and to be the first in line. A half hour before the portraits begin, a volunteer begins setting out name tags, the art materials, boxes of frames, rolls of tape, scissors, paper towels, and containers of Windex. Generally, on the Poly-Trauma ward, three or four volunteers are met by nurses who help us set up in the recreational room. The portraits are scheduled to begin at 10:00 a.m. and end at 3:00 p.m. but frequently last longer. Informed consents are signed by all participants and the artists and volunteers sign releases indicating they will not exhibit facial pictures or use the pictures later.

Artists arrive by 9:45 a.m. and check in to look over the instructions for the day. The instructions, written based on "lessons learned" from prior events, include guidance on conversation points. We suggest that the artists stick to very broad, not in-depth, conversational questions to build a rapport with the vet. We want to be clear that while the portrait event may have a therapeutic value it is not therapy, and the volunteers are not at the event to provide therapeutic services. To keep the project manageable and affordable, we have a one-frame-per-veteran rule and include other details in the instructions to ease the process. In addition, they pick up a colored apron, silkscreened with our logo *You Gotta Have Art*.

When the vets start arriving, the program coordinator introduces a vet and an artist who get started with the sketching process. Since most of the artists are returnees, they introduce themselves and ask the vet what medium they want used for their portrait. The first vet to step up may have some experience with the project or knowledge of the portraits, and offers courage to others who are uncomfortable with the idea. Because the previous experiences were positive, the visual stimulation generates supportive comments such as "Wow, that's good," and provides positive reinforcement for getting a portrait. A vet may have to wait 20 minutes or so as the crowd grows through the day. We found it works best if we can get them involved in watching the sketching artists and sketched models so that they understand how the portrait process works and how the artists strive to keep a low-key tone to the day. During this waiting period, we also set up photographed portraits to sustain their interest. The vets are particularly attached to the photo portraits because of the immediacy of the photographs and the fact that they can request corrections through the software program ensures that they have control of the process.

Please refer to Plate 9 in the color plate section.

Waiting Periods

As interest in the project grew and knowing we needed additional team members, I gladly opened the event to other artists, including crafts- and software-savvy people who enthusiastically joined our group. The artists created the portraits, photographers filled the wait time with photographed portraits, and the crafts people made the portraits' frames. If a waiting period is necessary, a photographer moves vets and often their family members around the beautiful garden areas and takes their pictures. The photographers and vets work with the software people to clean up the portrait by removing unwanted blemishes or wrinkles. Once the photographs are acceptable, the software volunteer prints them for the vet to take home.

The patients can be picky and will wait in line for a specific artist because of their artistic style. When the artist is ready for a new model, the vet has had a positive experience and is ready to be sketched. The way we have worked it out, each vet can have all of their pictures but we give them only one framed picture. The software-savvy services were helpful for refining or cleaning up the photographs and allowed the vets to have a say in the final photograph.

The Therapeutic Process

After receiving the picture, veterans will make comments such as "I didn't know I looked so good," or "I need to take this to group tomorrow." Before the portraits we hear the veterans using a lot of negative, self-deprecating talk about themselves. Many of them, both men and women, never saw themselves as attractive. Confirmation from other vets about the trueness of the image seems to offer acceptance, and a new self-image. One vet was surprised when another vet told her that the portrait was an honest portrayal of herself in the moment. The vets appear to like what they see and make connections with their peers in this therapeutic environment. Some veterans have what Yalom and Leszcz (2005) suggest as a corrective emotional experience, that they "discovered the previously unknown part of the self and thus was enabled to relate to others in a new fashion" (p. 29).

For the most part, the portraits are completed in black and white but we have found that portraits created in pastels or oils were very powerful and had quite an emotional impact. The color evoked a stronger response and the artist found a hidden essence in the vets that resonated with them. The vets who have never seen the multi-colored portraits before are impressed by their beauty and power.

Watching the artists create the portraits is a source of entertainment for the vets. Some will stay for three hours, moving around the room to see the different artists at work. Ketch, Rubin, Baker, Sones, and Ames (2015) suggested that when veterans have an opportunity to appreciate and experience artwork as well as learn about the lives of artists, the veterans can improve "mood, self-esteem, socialization and community participation" and this association with the art and artists may protect their mental health status (Ketch et al., 2015, p. 173). The veterans at our sites, by sharing their interest in the artistic process, provide the artists with validation of their craft as well as improved self-image and socialization.

The artists, during this portrait experience, get affirmation of their talents, though they work so fast that they become oblivious to the attention they are receiving from the vets. This volunteer opportunity provides the optimal experience or "flow," as Csikszentmihalyi and LeFevre (1989) characterized it. Flow is a complete enjoyment, when creativity comes easily, and the person has a kind of laser focus on the creative act. At these events the volunteers and artists are in an ideal space for a confluence of their altruistic yearnings with their artistic experiences mixing fast-paced action with their skills to let the portraits come into their own. Both the artists, the volunteers, and the veterans are energized by the experience.

Many of the artists return to do the portraits for more than one event because they find themselves energized by the experience. They are surprised that they feel as good about making the portrait as the person for whom they made the portrait. At the end of the volunteers' time, both the volunteers and the participants share reciprocal gratitude for the experience (Figure 13.1).

Debriefing

After a very busy day, by 3:00 p.m. team members and vets are beginning to slow down. The volunteers keep going until each vet has a portrait and is satisfied with the work. Most veterans either sit with new friends, using the portrait as an easy entry into conversation, or go to their rooms with their new treasures. The volunteer team gathers materials and begins our goodbyes, looking forward to meeting in a few weeks for a debriefing.

The team debriefing is a potluck dinner occurring sometime in the near future. We gather to look at what worked well and what we need to do to improve and review the instructions to see what updates should be made for future groups. We reminisce about our experiences but each year the vets tell us that the only way we could improve is to come and sketch them more often.

The Sketch Project: A New Perspective 163

Figure 13.1 The artists.
Source: Photograph by Belinda Carr of Arts of the Covenant, California, printed with permission.

Conclusion

Over a two-day event, this talented group works collectively for about 190 hours setting up the space, the portraits and framing, mealtime, and the take-down. Each vet receives several sketches, photographs, and a framed portrait. They are known to take them to their group sessions during the following week to show them to group members or to hang them in their room. We notice that something has changed about the patient, and he or she wants to share about themselves.

While the days have defined time limits, the artists often work overtime to make sure all of the vets get the portrait they wished for. At the request of the vets, the vet portrait teams now come twice a year. Our portraits are love gifts to the vets, not directives or assignments. Our team works very hard to make the portraits and their presentation exceptional, so sharing this event is not about the artists but about sharing a heartfelt event with our veterans in both the Poly Psy and PTSD departments at our local VA hospitals. I share this event in this book because artists, photographers, and other volunteers who love vets might be able to organize their own veteran portrait event holidays. This would give the vets something they are very proud of and a gift for their family members. The vets are not the only ones to get a gift from this event. The volunteers come away from each event with great big emotional muscles. For such a big payoff, the event runs on a small budget: under $1,000 or less depending on the donations of supplies and food.

These events with the vets could easily be done three or four times a year. Once the group has met, many of the volunteers keep coming back. They feel that they are working as a team and have developed a sense of rhythm and comradery in their work that keeps them committed to the vets. As discussed earlier in this chapter, we are one group of many who are doing this work. We can easily see it expand into hospice or extended care and nursing homes where the patients may feel they have lost their identity. It might also serve as a powerful service project for teenage artists to build generational bridges. Veterans Affairs (2016) has over 1,700 healthcare facilities, many of which have opportunities to spread the positive experience of these artists, volunteers, and veterans.

References

Arrington, D. (2001). Why do we make art? A reflective paper. *Art Therapy, 18*(2), 105–107.

Costello-Du Bois, J. (1989). Drawing out the unique beauty: Portraits. *Art Therapy, 6*(2), 67–70. doi: 10.1080/07421656.1989.10758868.

Csikszentmihalyi, M., & LeFevre, J. (1989). Optimal experience in work and leisure. *Journal of Personality and Social Psychology, 56*(5), 815–822. doi: 10.1037/0022-3514.56.5.815.

Henson, D.F. (2015). Finding a happier ending: The role of narrative in posttraumatic meaning-making. In M.C. Patron & S.S. Holden (Eds.), *Victim Victorious* (pp. 35–51). Hauppauge, NY: Nova Science Publishers.

Ketch, R.A., Rubin, R.T., Baker, M.R., Sones, A.C., & Ames, D. (2015). Art appreciation for veterans with severe mental illness in a VA Psychosocial Rehabilitation and Recovery Center. *Arts & Health: An International Journal of Research, Policy and Practice, 7*(2), 172–181. doi:10.1080/17533015.2015.1019700.

Kino, C. (2012), Portraits of war, arts & leisure, *New York Times*, May 25.

United States Department of Veterans Affairs (2016). *Veterans Health Administration*. Retrieved from https://www.va.gov/health/

Yalom, I.D. & Leszcz, M. (2005). *The Theory and Practice of Group Psychotherapy* (5th edition). New York: Basic Books.

CHAPTER 14

Group Therapy and PTSD: Acceptance and Commitment Art Therapy Groups with Vietnam Veterans with PTSD

Amy Backos and Corrie Mazzeo

Acceptance and commitment therapy (ACT) combined with art therapy is a promising modification of treatment that offers both verbal and non-verbal approaches to healing from PTSD. Art therapy affords veterans the opportunity to address their trauma in the visual and sensate ways in which it was experienced. ACT proposes that patients can build a new relationship with their long-standing thoughts and feelings, and focuses on creating a full, meaningful life while accepting the pain that inevitably accompanies it.

This chapter reviews an art therapy group we created utilizing ACT to treat veterans of all eras diagnosed with PTSD, most from the Vietnam era. Using ACT as the framework for group art therapy emerged from our previous clinical experiences, finding success in our individual and group work with veterans diagnosed with PTSD. The rationale behind this type of group is presented, as well as a brief overview of eight ACT core principles and the art interventions we used to make the cognitive strategies of ACT come alive in the creative therapeutic process.

Some veterans are unwilling to participate in recommended treatments for PTSD (prolonged exposure therapy and cognitive processing therapy) due to the trauma-processing focus of these treatments (U.S. Department of Veterans Affairs, 2008). When veterans engage in these treatments, they are asked to overcome the most influential and rigid symptom of PTSD, namely avoidance, by directly revisiting and often re-experiencing their traumas through talking and writing. This may seem like an overwhelming or insurmountable task for veterans with PTSD (Walser & Hayes, 2006). Veterans are trained to exert hyper-focus on combat missions and to block out thoughts or feelings that could affect their performance. This adaptive skill is no longer useful upon discharge and, in fact, makes managing painful memories more difficult. Veterans may also experience stigma related specifically to talking about internal struggles or seeking mental health treatment, as historically these led to being ostracized by peers and superiors or were even used as grounds for discharge from the military (Acosta et al., 2014).

ACT may be a better tolerated approach to addressing PTSD with veterans than exposure therapies. Through the primary goal of creating psychological flexibility, ACT emphasizes acceptance of unwanted private events, such as trauma memories and painful feelings of guilt and shame. Furthermore, ACT teaches veterans to identify personal values and commit to daily actions that construct a meaningful life, in spite of intrusive thoughts or uncomfortable feelings. Through this approach of acceptance and commitment, ACT targets the underlying processes that support and maintain PTSD symptoms. While art therapy may be used in many ways to address all the symptoms of PTSD, the art here was used to illustrate the core concepts of ACT for veterans and to reduce their symptom of avoidance so as to engage more fully in their lives.

Vietnam Veterans

Multiple factors negatively impacted veterans and their recovery from traumatic experiences when they returned from Vietnam: the socio-political climate in the United States, the unsupportive/antagonistic tension created by lack of public support for the war, and the lack of formal recognition of PTSD. Many veterans hoped to return to their previous lives, hiding their war experiences and avoiding the VA because of its association with the government. Upon their return, these veterans were not able to or were not afforded the opportunity to address and treat their traumas or to normalize their symptoms.

While the lifetime prevalence for PTSD in the general population is 8 percent (American Psychiatric Association, 2013), it is estimated that up to 30 percent of Vietnam veterans have PTSD, with similar estimates for OEF/OIF veterans (Spiegel, Malchiodi, Backos, & Collie, 2006). It has been theorized that PTSD is a disorder of recovery and PTSD results when veterans are not able to process and integrate the event into their overall life perspective (Resick, Monson, & Chard, 2008). This may be one reason why rates of PTSD are higher for Vietnam veterans; soldiers in combat do not have the resources available (i.e., time, safety, emotional capacity) to process events immediately, and many Vietnam veterans lacked the opportunity to do so upon discharge.

From these isolating and painful struggles following their return, Vietnam veterans developed peer-led rap groups, with the goal of creating a climate of acceptance, support, and recovery. These informal groups represent a historically important aspect of the group experience for veterans especially when they were ostracized and alienated. Mental health professionals, including many Vietnam veterans, built on this veteran-initiated, community-led treatment. The use of group therapy for mental health treatment with veterans has remained relevant throughout VA Medical Centers, and group psychotherapy theories and approaches continue to evolve.

Group Therapy for Veterans

A variety of group approaches are used in the treatment for PTSD: supportive, psychodynamic, and cognitive-behavioral. While scientific research on group treatment for PTSD has traditionally lagged behind research on individual treatments (Foa, Keane, & Friedman, 2000), the general consensus finds group therapy a favorable treatment component for many, and the VA/Department of Defense Clinical Practice Guidelines (2010) recommends consideration of group treatment for PTSD. Furthermore, cognitive-behavioral approaches are considered best practices for treating individuals with PTSD, and increasing evidence also suggests high efficacy in groups (Chard, 2005; Mendes, Mello, Ventura, Passarella, & Mari, 2008; Morland et al., 2014; Powers, Halpern, Ferenschak, Gillihan, & Foa, 2010; Resick et al., 2015).

Benefits of group therapy for veterans with PTSD include many of the therapeutic factors described by Yalom (1995): universality, social components, and catharsis. These factors may have particular significance for Vietnam veterans with PTSD, both because of the familiar group experience in the military and because of the isolating nature of their experiences upon returning home from a war, which lacked support from the American public. Through group therapy, veterans experience supportive social relationships and recognize that their PTSD symptoms are not unique to themselves, thus de-stigmatizing their experience and creating a sense of relief, hope, and solidarity.

At the time that we chose to run a group for veterans diagnosed with PTSD at the Cleveland VA, most of the outpatient groups that were available focused on support or psycho-education. Many of the veterans in the PTSD clinic had multiple diagnoses with pervasive dysfunctional patterns of avoidance, and had received treatment for an extended number of years without a successful resolution of PTSD symptoms. Our intent was to disrupt these patterns of avoidance and unresolved PTSD by providing a novel, trauma-focused treatment utilizing verbal and non-verbal modalities.

PTSD as a Non-verbal Experience

The experience of trauma is largely non-verbal, felt in one's body or experienced through witnessing. The psychological wounds of PTSD, which lead to emotional and cognitive disruption, stem from pre-verbal and somatic experiences (Kass & Trantham, 2014). PTSD can result from direct or indirect exposure to death or threatened death; actual or threatened serious injury; sexual violence; and/or repeated or extreme indirect exposure during the course of professional duties (American Psychiatric Association, 2013)

There are several lines of research demonstrating that PTSD is a non-verbal problem, suggesting the need for non-verbal treatment. First, PTSD symptoms reflect an evolutionary survival strategy (Valent, 2007; Van her Hart, Nijenhuis, & Steele, 2006). Along with flight or fight, the trauma reaction of freezing includes the loss of proprioception, numbness to pain, submissive behavior, and failure of usual verbal consciousness. These non-verbal survival patterns provide clues to understanding dissociation. Second, neuroimaging studies have indicated that the anterior cingulate cortex is relatively inactive in PTSD participants when recalling trauma as compared to those without PTSD (Gantt & Tinnin, 2009). The anterior cingulate cortex is associated with verbal control of attention for regulating emotional, cognitive, and autonomic responses. Third, studies of alexithymia (difficulty labeling and identifying emotional states) and PTSD found an association between the increased activation of posterior cingulate cortex activity and alexithymia. There is also an association between deficits in inter-hemispheric communication and alexithymia (Gantt & Tinnin, 2009). These lines of research point to the non-verbal aspects of encoding and recalling trauma. We hypothesized that the use of a non-verbal treatment modality, namely art making, to address emotional and behavioral avoidance of trauma-memories could disrupt dysfunctional patterns that maintained chronic symptoms of PTSD.

Acceptance and Commitment Therapy (ACT)

Acceptance and commitment therapy (ACT), is a transdiagnostic therapeutic approach focusing on the creation of a full, meaningful life while accepting inevitable pain. Based on rational frame theory, Zen Buddhism, and the Human Potential Movement, ACT is part of the third wave of cognitive therapies. This approach differs from most Western psychotherapy because symptom reduction is not the goal; it works to change the relationship we have with our thoughts and feelings (Harris, 2009). ACT demonstrates broad applicability in various modalities, including individual, couples and group as well as in brief or long-term treatment. ACT demonstrates efficacy with a variety of diagnoses: depression, OCD, pain, anxiety, PTSD, eating disorders, substance abuse, and schizophrenia (Harris, 2006). It lacks rigid protocols or prescribed manuals, allowing for flexible utilization of the concepts in a patient-centered way, thus allowing for a combination with art therapy. ACT utilizes a wide variety of techniques that emphasize the importance of experiential exercises, metaphor, paradox, stories, exercises, and behavior tasks (Luoma, Hayes, & Walser, 2007).

Created by Steven Hayes, ACT is based on rational frame theory (RFT), a basic theory of language and cognition (Hayes, Barnes-Homes, & Roche 2001; Hayes & Strosahl, 2004). This theory suggests that while human language is an essential aid to communication, it can also lead to unnecessary suffering. For example, language is utilized to plan, problem solve, and communicate. Conversely, it is used to manipulate others, judge, and ruminate about the past. ACT assumes that the suffering created by our use of language is a universal human experience.

In 2007, the VA initiated nationwide ACT training for mental health professionals to treat depressive disorders (R. Walser, personal communication, July 2015) as part of a wider roll-out of training to increase access to evidence-based treatments (EBT) for veterans. ACT has not yet garnered status as an EBT for PTSD, by demonstrating efficacy in two or more randomized controlled studies (Management of Post-Traumatic Stress Working Group, 2010; U.S. Department of Veterans Affairs, 2008). Currently, ACT is deemed an EBT for depression and substance-use disorders, both common co-morbidities of PTSD. The VA's National Center for PTSD recommends that ACT may be considered for veterans unwilling to participate in exposure therapies (Walser & Batten, 2012).

Art Therapy for PTSD

Art therapy accesses trauma memories via visual experiences. Compared to only utilizing linguistics, art serves to express trauma based on visuals and sensations, closer to the original encoding. Literature suggests that art therapy can address PTSD symptoms in veterans as well as the underlying processes that maintain PTSD (Spiegel et al., 2006). The International Society for the Study of Traumatic Stress adopted guidelines in 2000 (Foa et al., 2000), including art therapy as a helpful ancillary treatment for trauma disorders.

There are several models describing the hypothesized mechanisms of art therapy. Sarid and Huss (2010) proposed that art (1) engages the senses via observing, touching, and manipulation of material; (2) stimulates trauma memories through personal symbolic meanings; and (3) includes a cognitive component via reflection, contemplation, and reframing with the goal of creating a coherent trauma narrative. Gantt and Tinnin (2009) recommend that trauma-focused art therapy include exposure-based art interventions and less reliance on non-directive, psychodynamic-influenced approaches.

Art therapy for PTSD reduces avoidance symptoms because the art allows veterans to access and depict uncomfortable feelings and trauma memories. The artwork can serve as sufficient expression or it can stimulate verbal expression and the development of a trauma narrative. Somatic experiences of safety are provided by using art to express trauma, while exploring these memories can be processed without dissociative regression (Kass & Trantham, 2014). Through art making, the veteran remains in control of the verbal component. Our own observations suggest that using the art for expression also allows veterans to control the relational context of the trauma processing: the veteran can vacillate between relating to the art or to the therapist. This is particularly important if the relational context of therapy is a barrier for a veteran engaging in treatment.

Interventions

The ACT art therapy curriculum we created is a cohort-based, eight-week group. Each module included: a mindfulness art intervention, psycho-education, an ACT art therapy experiential, discussion, and art homework. ACT interventions were based on Walser and Westrup's (2007) treatment recommendations for PTSD. We utilized mostly controllable media such as markers, pencils, oil pastels, and watercolors to allow for greater familiarity, control, and mastery of the materials. Because ACT interventions are cognitive in nature, and because of the trauma-focused content of the art, the more structured art material was appropriate. Six ACT modules are summarized below with examples of the art interventions utilized.

Mindfulness

The ACT core concept of contact with the present moment, a mindfulness concept, allows veterans to remain grounded and conceptualize PTSD symptoms as primarily thoughts, emotions, bodily sensations, and memories of past events. It encourages being present with the symptoms without trying to avoid or dwell on them. Veterans were asked to practice mindfulness at the start of each group by creating mandalas using pencils and markers on pre-drawn paper circles. Each veteran verbally reported thoughts, feelings, or body sensations present during the practice to reinforce their conscious awareness of these internal experiences. Mindfulness practice was also integrated into every art intervention throughout the group, as veterans were challenged to stay in contact with not only their thoughts and feelings, but also their experience of making art.

Control as the Problem

Once a veteran identifies his previous coping strategies as hopeless and unlikely to help him resolve the trauma, he is ready to shift his perspectives on and relationships to his pain. Using experiential avoidance (abusing substances, overworking, overeating, etc.) to control the problem of negative feelings related to the trauma not only creates more problems, but may actually be the problem (Walser & Westrup, 2007). Essentially, the coping strategies control the veteran's life, limiting where he can go, whom he sees, and what he can do. This concept was illustrated in two drawings designed to compare (1) art when given freedom over intent, strategy, and media choice as compared to art when given constrained media and choice. Veterans were asked to make a ten-minute free drawing with many media choices. They were then asked to begin a second drawing in the same way, but were given increasing constraints. Each minute they were asked to eliminate something else from their choices—particular colors, a quadrant of the paper on which they were drawing, use of their dominant hand, curving lines, straight lines, etc. At the point when all the veterans gave up drawing because they could not think of any more options, they were asked to connect the drawing experience to their own self-imposed limitations for coping with trauma and many shared significant insights about how their coping became their biggest problem. From this point, veterans were asked to re-engage with their traumatic memories without the avoidance strategies, shifting their attention to the original problem/trauma now that they were willing to stop avoiding it.

Willingness

Willingness is an active stance of accepting the inner experiences (negative feelings) and dropping the struggle/avoidance with them. This session was trauma-focused and veterans were asked to depict the painful feelings they were most trying to avoid. Creating willingness is essential from an ACT perspective in addressing the avoidance symptoms of PTSD. Veterans were asked to adopt this stance of willingness to experience pain, without using their avoidance strategies, by creating a drawing related to a painful memory. While they were not directly asked to depict military trauma, most focused on these traumas, using controlled media to creating concrete and abstract images, and sharing certain details of their traumas with the group. These trauma-focused sessions, while painful for the veterans, were possible only after the successful processing the previous weeks related to creative hopelessness and control as the problem.

Cognitive Defusion

The inability to recognize thoughts as internal phenomena rather than the literal truth is called cognitive fusion (Walser & Westrup, 2007). Learning to defuse or curiously observe the inner experiences and thoughts fosters a more objective stance, allowing the veteran to decide whether the thought is something useful to attend to or whether it creates increased distance between the individual and so his/her goals. Cognitive defusion was introduced using the metaphor of Monsters on a Bus, adapted from Hayes, Stroshal, and Wilson (1999). In this cognitive and creative exercise, each veteran imagines himself as a bus driver and thoughts were described as passengers on a bus with unhelpful passengers/ thoughts attempting to derail the bus driver's route. Veterans created three drawings of "monsters" that represent their commonly fused thoughts, as well as externalizing the details of these distorted thoughts via written descriptions, including the age of the monster, what the monster says, other related monsters, and what situations bring out each monster (Figures 14.1 and 14.2, and Plate 10).

Figure 14.1 Monsters on the Bus—Brickhead.

172 A. Backos and C. Mazzeo

Figure 14.2 Monsters on the Bus—Dipshit.

Please refer to Plate 10 in the color plate section.

These drawings are examples of the monsters on the bus created by a veteran in the group. By the veteran identifying the "tiny" monster, he allowed himself to become mindfully aware of thoughts such as "I'm not good enough" or "I don't matter" which led him to choices that took him away from his values, such as not enrolling in school or avoiding people. Defusing allowed the veteran to see the thoughts/monsters as they are, just thoughts, and to be able to make choices led by his life goals, rather than by distorted thoughts.

Values

Values as principles and standards to guide behavior were introduced as a foundation to help veterans make choices consistent with their aspirations in life, even in the presence of painful inner/outer experiences.

In order for the veterans to become more aware of their values, they were asked to write about the person they yearned to be in ten domains: marriage/intimate partner, parenting, family, friendships, career, education/personal growth, recreation/leisure, spirituality, citizenship, and health. Examples of values included being a dependable, supportive partner or having an active, healthy lifestyle. They decorated small paper shapes with symbols to represent values in each domain and then the shapes were crafted into mobiles using yarn and wire. The mobile served as a metaphor, reminding them that positive changes in one area impact all the other areas.

Committed Action

Successful ACT treatment involves daily commitment toward engaging in behavior that is value-driven. This involved veterans making behavioral commitments consistent with their specific values (parenting, family, school, etc.), taking action on those values, and reflecting upon the experience of engaging in value-based behavior. Each veteran made written commitments and art specific to each of the value domains they had previously identified. These were shared verbally and visually and, using a relapse-prevention technique, veterans reflected upon strategies to address barriers that may arise. To provide an opportunity for veterans to engage in value-based behavior with friends and family, the veterans and facilitators curated an art show at the VA and attendees were invited guests of the veterans, including family, peers, and VA staff. This opportunity for community engagement provided a seminal activity upon which veterans could reflect with pride on their work as well as share their commitments toward value-based behavior with their friends and family.

Discussion

Mindfulness and art therapy continue to gain popularity and research support (Rappaport, 2014). We endorse the continued use and research of the combination of ACT and art therapy as a treatment modality for PTSD. The greatest strength of ACT art therapy was how well tolerated it was; there was no attrition. Exposure-based therapies can be poorly tolerated by veterans with PTSD who have been using avoidance to cope. ACT art therapy afforded the veterans a chance to engage in a trauma-focused treatment. By targeting experiential avoidance, ACT art therapy created increased willingness for veterans to engage with thoughts, emotions, and memories of their traumatic experiences. Because the ACT art therapy group was conducted in a clinical setting and was so well tolerated, the work holds good generalizability to other veterans.

We believe that the lack of attrition of this group was related to the use of ACT in addressing experiential avoidance and trauma in a more tolerable way. We suggest that the combination of ACT with art therapy created another layer of willingness and increased feelings of safety for veterans to approach their trauma experiences. The use of art allowed for the veterans to make contact with their unwanted private experiences through non-verbal expression and to have more control over the relational aspect of trauma processing. The artwork served as sufficient expression and it also stimulated the verbal expression of emotional pain and the development of a trauma narrative.

A strength of ACT art therapy includes a grounding of the cerebral and scholarly concepts of ACT, thus making it more accessible to those who have less developed verbal capacities. Furthermore, it appears ideal for veterans who experienced traumas, which are generally considered somatically encoded and pre-verbal (Kass & Trantham, 2014). ACT involves the use of metaphor to facilitate the learning of core concepts, and art provided ample use of metaphor. ACT manuals encourage the therapist to create new metaphors, and art therapists and their patients can easily develop a plethora of ACT art interventions. This approach could also be used to increase willingness to engage in the recommended EBTs. Perhaps veterans who tolerated and accepted previously avoided internal events in this setting would be willing to participate in EBT in the future.

Another consideration in using an ACT art therapy with veterans with PTSD is the applicability of this transdiagnostic approach, since PTSD has a high co-morbidity rate. The DSM-IV (2013) reports that individuals with PTSD are 80 percent more likely than those without PTSD to meet diagnostic criteria for at least one other mental disorder. In our groups, 81 percent had a co-occurring substance use disorder. The issue of co-morbidity often presents providers with a difficult decision about the order in which to treat diagnoses, as many programs do not offer concurrent treatment strategies for multiple disorders. ACT offers a treatment that is applicable for co-occurring disorders, has shown promising results with a wide range of diagnoses, and is considered an EBT for both depression and substance use disorders, common co-morbid disorders with PTSD.

One limitation of using ACT is the need for clinician training: the concepts are scholarly and often involve challenging other, more traditional approaches to the treatment of PTSD. For example, one of our patients worked continually at challenging his thoughts, a typical approach in cognitive therapies. However, ACT teaches mindfulness and acceptance, which does not involve challenging the thoughts, but rather accepting them as one component of a private experience that may or may not be the literal truth. This type of unlearning old models and learning the ACT model can present challenges for both patient and therapist.

Advances in neuropsychology have given new directions for understanding how art therapy impacts brain functioning (Hass-Cohen & Carr, 2008; Kass & Trantham, 2014) and we hope to continue developing our manual based on emerging evidence. The application of mindfulness and trauma-focused art therapy will benefit from these continued studies and we look forward to more research using ACT and art therapy to treat PTSD. Future areas of exploration include the use of more fluid media to deepen trauma processing, linking ACT to long-term art studio groups for veterans, and comparison of ACT art therapy to typical PTSD treatments.

References

Acosta, J.D., Becker, A., Cerully, J.L., Fisher, M.P., Martin, L.T., Vardavas, R., & Schell, T.L. (2014). *Mental Health Stigma in the Military*. Santa Monica, CA: RAND Corporation.

American Psychiatric Association. (2013). *Diagnostic and Statistical Manual of Mental Disorders* (5th edn). Washington, DC: Author.

Chard, K.M. (2005). An evaluation of cognitive processing therapy for the treatment of posttraumatic stress disorder related to childhood sexual abuse. *Journal of Consulting and Clinical Psychology*, 73(5), 965–971.

Collie, K., Backos, A., Malchiodi, C., & Spiegel, D. (2006). Art therapy for combat-related PTSD: Recommendations for research and practice. *Art Therapy: Journal of the American Art Therapy Association*, 23(4), 157–164.

Foa, E.B., Keane, T.M., & Friedman, M.J. (Eds.). (2000). *Effective Treatments for PTSD*. New York: The Guilford Press.

Galloucis, M., & Kaufman, M.E. (1988). Group therapy with Vietnam veterans: A brief review. *Group*, 12(2), 85–102.

Gantt, L., & Tinnin, L. (2009). Support for a neurobiological view of trauma with implications for art therapy. *The Arts in Psychotherapy*, 36(3), 148–153.

Harris, R. (2006). Embracing your demons: An overview of acceptance and commitment therapy. *Psychotherapy in Australia*, 12(4), 2–8.

Harris, R. (2009). *ACT Made Simple: An Easy to Read Primer on Acceptance and Commitment Therapy*. Oakland, CA: New Harbinger Publications.

Hass-Cohen, N. & Carr, R. (Eds.). (2008). *Art Therapy and Clinical Neuroscience*. London; Philadelphia, PA: Jessica Kingsley.

Hayes, S.C., & Smith, S. (2005). *Get Out of Your Mind and Into Your Life: The New Acceptance and Commitment Therapy*. Oakland, CA: New Harbinger Publications.

Hayes, S.C., & Strosahl, K.D. (Eds.). (2004). *A Practical Guide to Acceptance and Commitment Therapy*. New York: Springer.

Hayes, S.C., Barnes-Holmes, D., & Roche, B. (Eds.). (2001). *Relational Frame Theory: A Post-Skinnerian Account of Human Language and Cognition*. New York: Kluwer Academic/Plenum/Springer.

Hayes, S.C., Strosahl, K.D., & Wilson, K.G. (1999). *Acceptance and Commitment Therapy: An Experiential Approach to Behavior Change*. New York: The Guilford Press.

Kass, J.D., & Trantham, S.M. (2014). Perspectives from clinical neuroscience: Mindfulness and the therapeutic use of the arts. In L. Rappaport (Ed.), Mindfulness and the Arts Therapies: Theory and Practice (pp. 288–315). London: Jessica Kingsley.

Luoma, J.B., Hayes, S.C., & Walser, R.D. (2007). *Learning ACT: An Acceptance and Commitment Therapy Skills-training Manual for Therapists*. Oakland, CA: New Harbinger Publications.

Management of Post-Traumatic Stress Working Group (Internet). (2010) VA/DOD Clinical Practice Guideline for Management of Post-traumatic Stress. Washington, DC: Department of Veterans Affairs, Department of Defense. Retrieved May, 15, 2015 from: http://www.healthquality.va.gov/guidelines/MH/ptsd/cpgPTSDFULL201011612c.pdf

Mendes, D.D., Mello, M.F., Ventura, P., Passarella, C.M., & Mari, J.J. (2008). A systematic review on the effectiveness of cognitive behavioral therapy for posttraumatic stress disorder. *The International Journal of Psychiatry in Medicine*, 38(3), 241–259.

Morland, L.A., Mackintosh, M.A., Greene, C.J., Rosen, C.S., Chard, K.M., Resick, P., & Frueh, B.C. (2014). Cognitive processing therapy for posttraumatic stress disorder delivered to rural veterans via telemental health: A randomized noninferiority clinical trial. *The Journal of Clinical Psychiatry*, 75(5), 470–476.

Powers, M.B., Halpern, J.M., Ferenschak, M.P., Gillihan, S.G., & Foa, E.B. (2010). A meta-analytic review of prolonged exposure for posttraumatic stress disorder. *Clinical Psychology Review*, 30(6), 635–641.

Rappaport, L. (Ed.). (2014). *Mindfulness and the Arts Therapies: Theory and Practice*. London; Philadelphia, PA: Jessica Kingsley.

Resick, P.A., Monson, C.M., & Chard, K.M. (2008). *Cognitive Processing Therapy Veteran/Military Version: Therapist and Patient Materials Manual*. Washington, DC: Department of Veterans' Affairs.

Resick, P.A., Wachen, J.S., Mintz, J., Young-McCaughan, S., Roache, J.D., Borah, E.V., Dondanville, K.A., Hembree, E.A., Litz, B. T., & Peterson, A.L. (2015). A randomized clinical trial of group cognitive processing therapy compared with group present-centered therapy for PTSD among active duty military personnel. *Journal of Consulting and Clinical Psychology, 83*(6), 1058–1068.

Sarid, O., & Huss, E. (2010). Trauma and acute stress disorder: A comparison between cognitive behavioral intervention and art therapy. *Arts in Psychotherapy, 37*(1), 8–12.

Sloan, D.M., Bovin, M.J., & Schnurr, P.P. (2012). Review of group treatment for PTSD. *Journal of Rehabilitation Research & Development, 49*(5), 689–702.

Spiegel, D., Malchiodi, C., Backos, A., & Collie, K. (2006). Art therapy for combat-related PTSD: Recommendations for research and practice. *Art Therapy: Journal of the American Art Therapy Association, 23*(4), 157–164.

U.S. Department of Veterans Affairs (2008). *Uniform Mental Health Services in VA Medical Centers and Clinics* (VHA Handbook 1160.01). Washington, DC: Author.

Valent, P. (2007). Eight survival strategies in traumatic stress. *Traumatology, 13*(2), 4–14.

Van der Hart, O., Nijenhuis, E.R.S., & Steele, K. (2006). *The Haunted Self: Structural Dissociation and the Treatment of Chronic Traumatization*. New York: W.W. Norton.

Walser, R., & Batten, S. (2012). Acceptance and commitment therapy (ACT): What do we know about ACT for traumatic stress. [PowerPoint slides.] Retrieved April 5, 2017, from http://www.ptsd.va.gov/professional/continuing_ed/actherapy.asp.

Walser, R.D., & Hayes, S.C. (2006). Acceptance and commitment therapy in the treatment of posttraumatic stress disorder: Theoretical and applied issues. In V.M. Follette & J.I. Ruzek (Eds.). Cognitive-behavioral Therapies for Trauma (2nd edn; pp. 146–172). New York: Guilford Press.

Walser, R.D., & Westrup, D. (2007). *Acceptance and Commitment Therapy for the Treatment of Post-traumatic Stress Disorder and Trauma-related Problems*. Oakland, CA: New Harbinger Publications.

Yalom, I.D. (1995). The Theory and Practice of Group Psychotherapy (4th edn). New York: Basic Books.

CHAPTER **15**

Art Therapy and the Treatment of Military Sexual Trauma

Jeff Stadler

Sexual trauma can change a person's life forever. Emotionally laden images of the traumatic experience erupt in nightmares or flashbacks, with a horrifying feeling that the trauma is happening all over again. Sensory triggers related to the trauma are a constant reminder that something really bad happened, and feels like it is again happening or may happen again if action isn't taken. One's nervous system is sensitized to quickly go into fight-or-flight mode, and intrusive images and emotions of the experience invade both waking and sleeping hours (van der Kolk, 1995). Trust in humanity is shattered, self-concept becomes distorted, and lives become more constrained, as avoidance feels like the safest manner of living. Fear, anger, depression, and anxiety overshadow happiness and tranquility. Being able to live a life of contentment becomes a fantasy that seems unattainable.

Military Sexual Trauma (MST)

Sexual trauma is an unfortunate reality in the US Military. For traumatic sexual experiences occurring during times of military service, the Department of Veteran Affairs (VA) and the Department of Defense (DoD) have coined the acronym MST (for *military sexual trauma*). The VA defines sexual trauma as a "physical assault of a sexual nature, battery of a sexual nature, or sexual harassment (repeated unsolicited verbal or physical contact of a sexual nature which is threatening in character), which occurred while a Veteran was serving on active duty or active duty for training" (Department of Veteran Affairs, 2010).

The VA has indicated that one in four female service members report having experienced MST, and for male service members the statistics are one in 100. Given the disparity between male and female service members, the prevalence of MST is only slightly greater for female service members (Department of Veteran Affairs, 2010).

Sexual trauma may manifest differently than other types of trauma, as the perpetrator uses power, control, and violence with flagrant disregard for the survivor. Compared with other types of trauma (accidents, natural disasters, combat, etc.), sexual trauma may result in a deeper distrust of others, issues related to intimacy, as well as increased hyper-vigilance and the need to feel safe (Department of Veteran Affairs, 2010).

Further, sexual trauma occurring during military service manifests somewhat differently from traumatic sexual experiences experienced outside the military. Distrust and fear of others can be more severe from sexual assault experienced during military service, especially since perpetration is often by fellow service members who are understood to "have your back." Power dynamics within the ranks may be used to keep survivors silent. If the survivor reports the MST, and if measures are not taken to institute a safe environment or prosecute the perpetrator, survivors feel even more powerless. Often, those who have sexually harassed or even sexually assaulted are those who have to be seen or worked with, which may trigger and perpetuate ongoing traumatic stress reactions (Department of Veteran Affairs, 2010).

Although survivors of MST generally experience many of the symptoms, men and women often have different reactions to sexual trauma. Male service members may not consider themselves vulnerable to sexual assault, and an unfathomable experience of MST may result in changes in a male survivor's self-concept as a "man," affecting his sexuality, sexual functioning, or masculinity. For women, sexual assault may validate and potentiate existing fears of vulnerability and personal safety, and in a male-dominated military culture this often results in having to suppress memories and feelings and put up a tough façade to be able to function alongside their fellow service members (Department of Veteran Affairs, 2010).

The VA and DoD have recognized the epidemic prevalence of MST, and have made significant efforts to address this issue. They have instituted preventive measures, changed policy regarding reporting MST, worked to raise awareness of the prevalence of MST, and offer free treatment to anyone who has experienced MST.

Sexual trauma is more likely to result in diagnosis of post-traumatic stress disorder (PTSD) than other types of trauma, including combat-related traumas (Department of Veteran Affairs, 2010). Symptoms are clustered into four general categories: intrusions (of memories or images of the trauma); avoidance (of people, places, things, and thoughts or feelings associated with the trauma); negative alterations in cognitions and mood (including increased anger, fear, and guilt, and changes in one's self-concept); and alterations in arousal and reactivity (heightened response to external stimuli, from the activated fight-or-flight reaction) (American Psychiatric Association, 2013).

Art Therapy and the Treatment of MST

During traumatic experiences, the brain activates the "fight-or-flight" reaction, mobilizing the brain and body to gear up to handle a potentially life-threatening event. Senses sharpen, actions become instinctual, with survival the sole focus. In this heightened emotional and physiological state, memories of a traumatic event are encoded differently than non-traumatic events. Parts of the experience may not be able to be recalled, whereas other memories may intrude into consciousness (van der Kolk, 1995). Traumatic memories are often encoded in the right brain as a series of fragmented visual clips of the experience- a series of distinct "snapshots" with rich sensory information, involving the sights, sounds, smells, and feel of the environment (Chapman, 2014).

Recent approaches in the field of art therapy for PTSD have developed protocols based on the understanding of the underlying neurobiology of trauma, and the psychological and physiological responses that have evolved to help ensure survival in life-threatening situations. Effective treatment of sexual trauma involves helping survivors create a coherent and cohesive narrative of the event, with a beginning, middle, and end (Gantt and Tinnin, in Arrington, 2007).

The instinctual trauma response (or ITR) involves having survivors create images symbolic of the stages that all people go through during traumatic experiences. The ITR has evolved as an automatic response to a potentially life-threatening threat, to more likely ensure survival, and is described as six distinct stages: the startle, thwarted intention, freeze, altered state of consciousness, body sensation, and automatic obedience (Tinnin and Gantt, in Arrington, 2007). Linda Chapman's (2014) approach is also based on the neurobiology of traumatic experiences, and how traumatic memories are often stored visually or associated with other senses, and may be retrieved most effectively through visual or other sensory means (Chapman, 2014). By accessing and expressing both visually (through the art) and verbally (as the art is processed), survivors can piece together fragmented memories to develop a more integrated narrative of the experience, which serves to help survivors develop a different relationship with that memory and experience.

For the treatment of MST in the VA, evidenced-based therapies of Prolonged Exposure (PE) and Cognitive Processing Therapy (CPT) are used as front-line treatments. Although these treatments have demonstrated effectiveness in relieving PTSD symptoms, some survivors do not respond to or engage well in these therapies, or have treatment-resistant symptoms that persist following treatment.

There is good rationale why art therapy can be an effective treatment for PTSD and sexual trauma, and why traditional verbal therapies are not always effective for certain symptoms or some survivors. The process of creating art and expressing one's feelings and experiences involves both left- and right-brain activation. Expressing experiences in imagery or symbols, and talking about those experiences and their symbolic expression, helps integrate the left (verbal) and the right (visual, expressive) hemispheres (Arrington, 2007). This integration can help facilitate creating a more cohesive and coherent narrative of the experience, which can provide a sense of resolution of a traumatic event (Arrington, 2007).

Oftentimes throughout the therapy process, unconscious or subconscious material is elicited, as the language of imagery is often less familiar and can bring forth material lying below the level of consciousness. Survivors are able to reflect upon and project onto a concrete piece of artwork that may allow further development of insight, perhaps seeing something in their artwork that is a representation of a feeling, belief, or a forgotten memory. Working with symbolism and metaphor in the artwork can offer survivors a new perspective, outlook, personal insight, and confidence that expressing a distressing internal experience will not reinjure them. Art can be a vehicle to allow survivors to own their thoughts, feelings, memories (and behaviors), to acknowledge them and be present with them (rather than avoid), and to develop a different relationship with those internal experiences.

Having an externalized, symbolic expression of a distressing memory or emotional state can make processing those thoughts and feelings easier. Survivors often express that their artwork more accurately conveys what they are feeling than their words can. This makes sense, given the visual manner in which traumatic memories are often stored in the right brain, lacking connection to the left-brain verbal centers. When the words simply aren't there (known to the psychiatric community as alexithymia), imagery and symbolism are the necessary language. Survivors find profound meaning and symbolism in color, line, brushstroke, images, and form, relating these elements to their innermost experiences.

Consideration of the survivor's sense of safety is necessary throughout the therapeutic process. Art therapists must choose materials and directives judiciously, so that clients are challenged to approach their feelings with a sense of curiosity, rather than of fear or avoidance. Clinical judgment informs therapists of survivors' readiness, and the decision to use less structured materials (like water-color or wet clay) or more structured materials (such as pencil or collage). Survivors who are highly activated, agitated, or angry should be offered more structured materials to help them express those feelings with a higher degree of containment. For those who are avoidant, disconnected from their emotions, or feeling stuck, less structured materials can facilitate more spontaneous and emotional expression (Hinz, 2009).

Art therapy has begun to be understood as an effective complementary or alternative modality, involving non-verbal creative expression, and verbal processing of the artwork and the trauma. The combination of these two very different processes, involving both left- and right-brain activation, serves to help process and reintegrate cognitively in a much more complex way than words alone can.

As in any therapy involving trauma survivors, an environment and therapeutic relationship that is perceived to be safe is essential. Survivors need to feel a sense of safety to be able to psychologically manage exploring disturbing memories and distressing emotions. Creating artwork in the context of art therapy is an intimate experience and, without feeling safe with the therapist, progress will be limited at best, and potentially re-traumatizing. The creative process can elicit psychological and emotional material that is below the level of consciousness, and when it arises in visual form it is imperative that there is a trusting relationship, so that the artwork, memories, and emotions can be processed and effectively managed without becoming overwhelming and avoided.

Intrusions: Nightmares

Nightmares are often reported as one of the most disturbing symptoms of PTSD, and may be considered an intrusion of the traumatic memory during times of sleep. Nightmares of trauma are qualitatively different than normal nightmares, in that they are often an exact recounting of the traumatic event, experienced repeatedly and with tremendous detail and distressing emotional tone. Survivors suffering from these nightmares often feel as if they are re-experiencing the trauma. Nightmares are especially challenging to treat, and in many cases are treatment-resistant to traditional verbal therapy. Due to the highly visual encoding of trauma, nightmares are difficult to treat with words alone.

The VA has instituted an evidence-based treatment specifically for nightmares called imagery rehearsal therapy (IRT). Survivors recount the sequence of the nightmare, and then create a new ending to the dream, one that is not distressing. The new dream sequence, with a less distressing ending, is mentally rehearsed during consciousness to change the dream experience during sleep.

Art can facilitate this process, perhaps even more robustly, as it is a visual and symbolic language, just as are dreams. One directive involves having the survivor create an image about the nightmare, and then change the image to represent a dream with a different ending, akin to IRT. Working with the images, physically altering them to a less distressing end-point, and being able to witness the transformation can be a powerful way to help change the dream process. Clients are able to regain a sense of psychological control, challenging fears of powerlessness, and helping to develop their self-concept as a survivor rather than as a victim.

One project involves representing the nightmare using highly-structured materials of cut shapes (or images) that are laid onto a piece of paper, and the client is given the opportunity to verbally share about the nightmare. The client is then asked to rearrange those shapes or images into a new image that is the antithetical to the first, and to process the new image. An example of a survivor of MST is given in Figure 15.1.

In the first part of the directive (left), the client represented the emotional turbulence of her nightmare, composed of colored, cut shapes that she assembled into the image, laying out the shapes onto her paper without using adhesive. Using those same colored, cut shapes, the survivor transformed the image to its final product (right), and glued the shapes into their final form. This process provided her with a sense of control, and even hopefulness, in spite of her ongoing life struggles. Rather than being overwhelmed by feelings of anger, anxiety, and depression, she re-conceptualized herself as being able to be happy and having some control over her life. It is significant that in the final image she represented herself as a more complete person, having a body, arms, and legs, to better navigate and control her world, constructed from pieces representing something negative in the first image. By taking all of the pieces and reconstructing herself with a new relationship with her world, this survivor acknowledged her challenges, and became empowered to live her life. At last

182 J. Stadler

Figure 15.1 Transformation of a nightmare into a pleasant dream.

contact, the survivor reported that she had decided to move to follow her dream to start a business of her own.

Avoidance

Those who have suffered sexual trauma have a tendency to avoid people, places, and things that evoke a memory or feeling of the trauma. Schema are developed involving certain characteristics of the perpetrator or the situation in which the trauma occurred, which often become generalized and create associations that serve as a reminder of the trauma (van der Kolk, 1995). Avoidance becomes the safest way to deal with internal or external stimuli that have the capacity to trigger flashbacks, intrusive thoughts, or distressing feelings. This is especially true for men and women who are serving, expected to do their job, and sometimes have to interact with their perpetrator, and work in a highly structured and male-dominated hierarchy, where power and authority are overtly administered. This can be challenging for survivors with a sensitized nervous system, requiring allocation of energy into containing reactions, exercising self-control, and keeping focus to stay within the ranks of the military structure.

Art therapy can be a way for the survivor to begin approaching, rather than avoiding, those thoughts and feelings. Some find it much easier to express their most intense and deeply guarded feelings through the art therapy process, for a variety of reasons. Giving form to something as nebulous and confusing as intense fear, anger, guilt, shame, and depression allows survivors to be able to talk about the symbolic representation of their feelings, rather than the feelings themselves. Using the artwork as a means to be grounded while talking about disturbing experiences can help survivors realize that the feelings and memories cannot reinjure them, and that they can feel safe processing those experiences with a therapist.

Please refer to Plate 11 in the color plate section.

The image shown in Plate 11 representing an MST survivor's representation of how he experienced and has been affected by sexual trauma is the final result of months of tenacious work, including over 50 iterations of designing, drawing, refining, destroying, remembering, feeling, and directly confronting and expressing memories and emotions that had long been buried. In the image, he wished to convey his initial patriotism serving in the military, and how he became disillusioned after being repeatedly and forcibly sexually assaulted by higher ranking military personnel. Expressing thoughts of suicide and feelings of homicide, the survivor worked compulsively, needing the image to accurately convey his experience of having suffered these sexual assaults. Common to other survivors of sexual assault, the survivor reported a sense of having been forever changed, feeling his soul was taken from him, represented by the sinister creature tearing his heart out of his chest. Rather than avoiding the memories and emotions of the repeated traumas he endured, the survivor was able to acknowledge and express the distressing imagery and emotion, connect with and release emotion and energy that fueled them, and resolve many inner conflicts and issues of self-concept. This image was drawn onto a T-shirt as part of the VA's annual Clothesline Project, a nationwide effort to give voice to survivors of MST and to raise awareness of sexual assault in the Military.

Negative Alterations in Mood and Cognitions

As symbolized in the previous image, survivors of MST frequently describe the consequence of their sexual trauma as "having lost my soul," "I'm not the same person I used to be," or "I can never be truly safe." Trauma survivors often experience significant shifts in their concept of self, their worldview (viewing others and the world as a dangerous place), and mood. It is common for survivors to question their own actions and blame themselves, and to harbor self-defeating thoughts (i.e., "It was my fault," "I should have done something different," "I'm not good enough," "I can never be happy"). This change in self-concept frequently results in depressed, anxious, fearful, or angry mood states. (van der Kolk, 1995). These distressing feelings are not pleasant to experience, and are consequently often avoided, through distraction, self-medication with alcohol and drugs, and suppression, which may ultimately result in emotional numbing. Often, the process of creating artwork can connect survivors with their feelings in an unexpected and powerful way. It is not uncommon for clients of art therapy to feel emotions from which they have been disconnected for a long period of time, facilitated by the creative process.

At times, this reconnection with emotion can be distressing, and clients may question the rationale for expressing, being present with, and processing the thoughts and feelings that they have put forth so much effort to avoid. Creating art provides a manner which may feel safer to give expression to these previously avoided and feared experiences.

Through creative and verbal expression, these internal experiences may be learned to no longer be feared and avoided, but rather acknowledged, accepted as a result of experiencing a horrifying situation, and redefined as "a normal reaction to an un-normal situation." By challenging and letting go of self-defeating beliefs, and creating a vision of possibility, survivors can redefine themselves and how they see the world.

Increased Arousal

With body and brain activated by the fight-or-flight response, the trauma survivor's nervous system is primed to respond instinctively to perceived threat. Constantly vigilant and prepared to react quickly, survivors frequently suffer from anxiety, insomnia, and depression. With so much energy devoted to attending to one's surroundings, possible threats, and means to escape or effectively manage a potentially threatening situation, survivors spend tremendous energy and awareness on assuring themselves of safety (Gantt & Tinnin, 2009).

Art therapy directives can serve as a means to express distress, using materials to symbolize survivors' experience, in a controllable and intentional process. Frequently, art therapy clients experience relief from expressing distressing feelings in symbolic form, and discussing the symbolism as it relates to their lives can provide catharsis of these feelings.

Creating art for art's sake can be therapeutic, but the prescriptive use of art therapy directives has the potential to be unintentionally re-traumatizing. It is important that art therapists are aware of the heightened state of their clients' nervous system, which can cause strong emotional reaction to unconscious material elicited through the creative process. It is important for therapists to be clients' sensitivities, and be prepared to respond in a compassionate and supportive manner, validating their clients' experience.

Figure 15.3 shows the image a female survivor created which culminated and synthesized months of art therapy in her recovery from numerous MSTs. It is symbolic of releasing painful emotion, allowing expansion of love through release of sadness, represented by tears symbolic of five separate sexual assaults. There is a flowing sense as the giraffe (representing the survivor) appears to be observing the process of emptying the (psychological and emotional) trash, with a detached sense of curiosity. This was symbolic of letting go of the sadness, anger, and despair, and allowing for reconnection with more positively experienced emotions, which had gone numb over the years as painful emotions were avoided and suppressed.

Figure 15.2 Image of recovery from MST.

The survivor represented and described her path in therapy, with black and white footsteps representing uncertainty and "black and white thinking," which led to engagement in art therapy, and provided her the opportunity to "empty the trash." In the footprints leading to the future, there is an expansion of the color palette, with flesh tone used for the first time in any of her artwork, previously avoided as a reminder of numerous sexual traumas and lost innocence. After learning to express herself, first artistically, and then verbally, she chose to use the flesh color, but now with a new meaning of renewed birth and self-determination. The survivor "took back" the color, and changed its meaning to be associated with reconnection with her innocence. Throughout her process using art therapy, she became fluent in the language of imagery, which became a vital outlet for her personal expression.

Rather than fearful, she became curious. Instead of solely defining herself as a victim, she developed an identity as an artist who uses her artistic expression to validate and communicate her experiences. She expressed that by letting go of the sadness from past experiences, she was able to feel more love, which was an unfamiliar experience after feeling numb for years following the traumas. This image was created with intentionality, clarity, and hope to manifest in her life what she created in her artwork.

Conclusion

Art therapy is a largely untapped resource that, when guided by clinicians who are able to develop a trusting relationship with the MST survivor, can provide treatment involving a very different process and approach than traditional psychotherapy and behavioral interventions. It is hoped that future research will involve more scientifically based randomized control studies to develop an evidence base, and to demonstrate how art therapy can be a viable treatment option for a variety of survivors of PTSD, as an alternative or complement to traditional psychotherapeutic practice. There are many commonalities in current treatment approaches for trauma, including expression of feelings rather than suppression, approaching rather than avoiding, challenging self-defeating beliefs, being presented with distressing thoughts and feelings, and processing them in a safe environment, With a variety of different treatment approaches for trauma, it is hoped that art therapy's right-brained, creative approaches will be valued as qualitatively different and intrinsically powerful therapies, well-suited for the treatment of trauma.

References

American Psychiatric Association. (2013). *Diagnostic and Statistical Manual of Mental Disorders* (5th edn). Washington, DC: Author.

Arrington, D. (2007). *Art, Angst, and Trauma.* New York: Charles C. Thomas Publishers.

Chapman, L. (2014). *Neurobiologically Informed Trauma Therapy with Children and Adolescents: Understanding Mechanisms of Change.* New York: W.W. Norton.

Department of Veteran Affairs. (2010). *A Primer on Military Sexual Trauma for Mental Health Clinicians.* New York: Department of Veteran Affairs.

Gantt, L. and Tinnin, L. (2009). Support for a neurobiological view of trauma with implications for art therapy. *The Arts in Psychotherapy.* doi: 10.10.16/j.aip.2008.12.005.

Hinz, L. (2009). *Expressive Therapies Continuum: A Framework for Using Art in Therapy.* Abingdon: Brunner-Routledge.

van der Kolk, B.A. (1995). Dissociation and the fragmentary nature of traumatic memories: Background and experimental evidence. *Journal of Traumatic Stress, 8,* 505–525.

CHAPTER **16**

How the Studio and Gallery Experience Benefits Military Members and their Families

Jennifer DeLucia

We need more brothers-and-sisters-in-understanding.
(Navy Combat Veteran and Art Therapy Participant)

Transitioning from military to civilian life is a complex process. Transition challenges can affect veterans and their families as veterans return home from military service and attempt to resume civilian life and responsibilities. The process of transition occurs within the context of interpersonal relationships and a community of civilian citizens—the people and places which veterans call "home." As such, it is important to consider the ability, willingness, and preparedness of friends, family, and civilian community members to take part in the transition process.

When civilian citizens are able to acknowledge the realities of war and understand the full veteran experience, they can begin to be involved in rituals that help veterans readjust and reintegrate into civilian life. These rituals will involve listening to and witnessing veterans' complete experiences of war and military service. These rituals will also normalize transition challenges and welcome stories of struggle and triumph. Art therapists can intervene by using the rituals of making and viewing artwork to address the unhealed wounds of war and set the stage for successful transition, for both veterans and their close civilian friends and family.

An art therapy program in Rochester, NY was established to do just that: to attend to the psychosocial concerns of transitioning veterans and their families by creating a program based on needs identified by the veterans it served. The program model incorporates three different services: individual art therapy sessions, drop-in art therapy studio groups, and art exhibitions in a veterans' art gallery. These components are designed to address specific aspects of the military-to-civilian transition.

This chapter will outline some key aspects of the military-to-civilian transition experience that were identified by participating veterans at the Veterans Outreach Center in Rochester, NY. It will then focus on how studio and gallery services at the Center addressed the concerns of participating veterans. Their words, shared herein, were documented in a focus group for veterans that identified the most effective art therapy interventions to support military-to-civilian transition (for details of the research study, see DeLucia, 2015).

Military to Civilian Transition

All returning veterans undergo some form of transition when they come home from service and re-enter civilian life. Transition, a term used by participating veterans at the Veterans Outreach Center, Inc. (VOC), refers to service members' passage from military life to civilian life, which often involves emotional, physical, and social changes (DeLucia, 2015). These veterans considered "transition" to be a more accurate representation of their experience than the current terms used in the literature and media, such as re-entry, reintegration, and readjustment. They explained how the term *transition* references a normal change that occurs between two distinct experiences. For them these two experiences were military life and civilian life. Further, they believed the words *readjustment* and *reintegration* had a negative connotation, implying that the emotional, physical, and social changes they experienced were not part of a normal and expected process. This chapter uses the term *transition* to describe the experience of shifting from military to civilian life.

Healthy and Successful Transition

The return home is a moment that many veterans look forward to with great anticipation. This is matched by the expectancy of family and friends at home eagerly awaiting the service member's return. Many returning veterans transition successfully back into family life, resuming the roles of father, mother, son, daughter, husband, or wife. Many veterans find meaningful and gainful employment or return to school. Social supports, including friends and some professional services, can serve as buffers to the contrast between military and civilian lifestyles and, with that help, some veterans are able successfully to adapt to the norms of civilian society.

A healthy veteran is a successful and contributing citizen. Veterans without mental health concerns or transition challenges are typically better educated than their civilian counterparts, more likely to be employed, earn a higher than average salary, and are more likely to vote and volunteer in their communities (Veterans Prevail, 2010). Every veteran likely strives for this kind of success; however, there can be many challenges that complicate the transition home. Veterans who lack the support and resources to overcome challenges will struggle with transition. This struggle can lead to adverse outcomes ranging from unemployment to homelessness and severe emotional distress.

Difficult and Unhealthy Transition

Although it is true that a majority of service members are able to return home and make a successful transition to civilian life, many veterans have great difficulty doing so. There are several concerns that veterans have identified as being pivotal to successful transition back into civilian life. A group of ten veterans at the Veterans Outreach Center served as co-researchers in a recent research study (DeLucia, 2015). They identified seven challenges they felt to be pivotal, based on their personal transition experiences. These seven concerns were: (1) fear of the unknown, (2) cultural dissonance, (3) survival guilt, (4) lack of adequate time for decompression after combat, (5) social disconnection from friends or family, (6) expectations from family and friends that transition can be completed in a certain time frame, and (7) a lack of personal direction or purpose. They also identified several factors that impact the transition process, including their original reasons for joining the service, their level of psychological functioning prior to enlistment, their combat exposure and related injuries, any military sexual trauma, and the particular circumstances surrounding their discharges.

For some veterans the difficulties with transition may include mental health conditions such as post-traumatic stress disorder (PTSD), depression, and traumatic brain injury (Committee on the Initial Assessment of Readjustment Needs of Military Personnel, Veterans, and Their Families, 2010; Hoge et al., 2004; Tanielian & Jaycox, 2008). In a 2008 study conducted by the RAND Corporation, it was estimated that 26 percent of returning veterans from the wars in Iraq and Afghanistan would potentially meet the criteria for a mental health condition, most commonly PTSD, major depression, and generalized anxiety (Tanielian & Jaycox, 2008).

Transition is further complicated when civilians surrounding a veteran lack a complete understanding of the veteran's experience and military culture. A nationally representative survey among veterans who had had combat experiences in Iraq and Afghanistan found that 55 percent of respondents felt disconnected from civilian life and that approximately seven in ten veterans felt that the average US citizen misunderstands their experiences (Chandrasekaran, 2014). When civilian citizens set veterans apart from others by idealizing or disparaging their military service, they reveal a lack of detailed knowledge about what veterans' service entailed (Herman, 1992). This reaction creates a social disconnection between veterans and the civilian communities they call "home."

The absence of support and understanding often comes at a high cost to the veteran: isolation (DeLucia, 2015). Veterans with whom I have worked report a common experience among them that feeling misunderstood resulted in social withdrawal. One veteran declared, "You have one or two opportunities. If a veteran is opening up to you and you shut him down, that's it. Chances are he is not going to try again." Research has demonstrated that the greatest concern of most US veterans transitioning from military to civilian life is a perceived lack of social support and understanding (Caplin & Lewis, 2011; Sayer et al., 2010). This finding is significant given that such social support is a key factor in successful transition (Caplin & Lewis, 2011; Furukawa, 1997; Larson & Norman, 2014; Mallow, Williams-Gray, Kelly, & Alex, 2011).

The sudden separation from military culture and immersion into civilian culture can be experienced as a cultural loss (DeLucia, 2015). Veterans depart from the values, rules, traditions, and supports to which they have become accustomed. Veterans lose the sense of camaraderie which comes from the knowledge that fellow service members are looking out for their safety and well-being (Coll & Weiss, 2013). This strong sense of group cohesion is not easily found in civilian society. In addition, the US military community has a strong built-in support network. Military families often seek support from one another because of shared experiences and a common understanding of military life (Coll & Weiss, 2013). When veterans return home they may lack proximity to their military support network at the same time that they lose the familiarity and structure of military culture.

Consequences Associated with Transition Difficulty

Failure to successfully transition back into civilian personal and professional roles can lead to more serious consequences. Adverse outcomes associated with failure to adjust include poorer social and family functioning (Khaylis, Polusny, Erbes, Gewirtz, & Rath, 2011; Vasterling et al., 2010), unemployment (Adler et al., 2011), financial issues (Vasterling et. al, 2010), and homelessness (Caplin & Lewis, 2011; Metraux, Clegg, Daigh, Culhane, & Kane, 2013). Further, veterans who struggle with the transition may be more prone to isolate themselves from potential social supports (Larson & Norman, 2014). All of these consequences put the veteran at greater risk for developing mental health issues (Furukawa, 1997; Lee et al., 2009), substance abuse problems (Seal et al., 2009), functional impairments across the lifespan (Larson & Norman, 2014), and in the very worse-case scenario, suicide (Mansfield, Bender, Hourani, & Larson, 2011; Pietrzak et al., 2010).

Housing and employment can be a significant source of stress for transitioning veterans. For example, an Afghanistan veteran and participant in the art therapy program described his flight home to the United States. He recalled being on the airplane and remembered his fears of coming home and not being able to find employment. He explained that the fear of losing his home and everything he had was significantly greater than his fear of dying in combat. Housing concerns may develop secondary to failed relationships, family rejection, and low income (Caplin & Lewis, 2011). In the absence of the stability that healthy relationships and steady income provide, veterans may become at risk for homelessness.

The Veterans Outreach Center, Inc.

The art therapy program at The Veterans Outreach Center, a community-based non-profit in Rochester, New York, was created to address the needs and concerns identified by the veterans and family members it serves. The program was founded in 2010 when individual art therapy sessions were offered for the first time. Now serving aroundе 75 veterans annually, the program has expanded to include three full-time art therapists on staff; these therapists provide individual art therapy sessions, drop-in art therapy studio group sessions, and opportunities for participating veterans to display their artwork in the center's own veterans' art gallery.

Individual and group art therapy sessions are offered in an art studio environment. The studio holds the promise of infinite creative potential and serves as the first point of engagement in the art therapy process (Henley, 1995). Veterans walk into a space that differs vastly from their expectations of a therapist's office. Entry to the studio is a multisensory experience. Where veterans expect to find the professional license and credentials of their therapist mounted on the wall, they see instead artwork made by their peers. Where they expect to find a couch or two chairs nestled near a dimly lit lamp, they see easels, stools and a large table for making art. Contrary to the emptiness of clinics with white walls and florescent lights, they experience "life" in the studio, a gently worn and used space. They see bits of dried paint in the sink and freshly rinsed brushes in the drying rack. Evidence that others have made art in the studio brings a sense of comfort; it communicates that other veterans have taken this same path.

Veterans experience the studio as a creative, supportive, and safe atmosphere, and may find comfort by visually connecting to certain aspects of the space (see also Fenner, 2012). For example, they may identify with the studio as a workspace, feeling drawn in and engaged by in-progress artwork evident on the walls and easels. Veterans may also experience the studio as a metaphoric holding space for painful emotions and memories. Having a designated place to store their artwork is one way in which the studio offers veterans a sense of containment. As one combat veteran described, "my workspace is my safety area." Conversely, veterans may experience vulnerability by choosing to display artwork on the walls. The studio offers veterans the ability to choose how and when they engage in the therapeutic potential of the space (McGraw, 1995). Participating veterans described the art studio as "a loving and caring environment" and "a place that lifts me up."

Individual Art Therapy Sessions

Participants in VOC's art therapy program identified that individual art therapy sessions address mental health symptoms and psychosocial stressors tied to difficult or unhealthy transitions, using an approach that builds on the veteran's strengths and operates from an understanding of how trauma impacts an individual's overall psychosocial functioning (DeLucia, 2015).

Veterans who engaged in individual art therapy sessions were drawn in by the idea of an active, hands-on approach to therapy. Often, this approach was more appealing to veterans than were traditional office-based therapies such as psychotherapy or cognitive behavioral therapy. Veterans also recognized that they were able to express thoughts and emotions through art making easier than they were able to through using words alone. Veterans identified how individual art therapy sessions helped them to heal from past traumas, to improve relationships, and to develop new ways to manage stress. As described by a Navy veteran,

> Art therapy has saved my life. There was an emptiness in my soul … [with art therapy] I was able to let out the secrets and not be afraid of judgment. I released years of poison through my paintings, making several a week for two years. Now that all that poison is out I can focus on the positive.

Art making helped this Navy veteran to express and release years of built-up negative thoughts and feelings and in the process he discovered that art making was a way for him to focus on his emotional health, by attending to his negative thoughts and feelings on a routine basis through art making. He used art to express inner conflicts as well as his personal and political beliefs.

Please refer to Plate 12 in the color plate section.

In the process of engaging in individual art therapy sessions, participating veterans started to define themselves with a new "creative" identity. In turn, art therapy supported success and achievement of the tasks related to the transition. An Army veteran described his experience in art therapy:

> You don't know [who you are], because most of your life you are told who you should be, by your parents, your teachers, and then the military. … Making art is a way of calming and I can concentrate, get into the good part of my brain. The part that was a kid once and thought anything was possible.

Engagement in the art therapy process was the first and most important step, particularly for veterans who were reluctant to work with mental health professionals.

Art Therapy Studio Group Sessions

The art therapy studio was developed as a place for veterans to connect to other veterans through activities such as drop-in art therapy studio group sessions. These sessions typically run two to three hours in length and are conducted by an art therapist. In this model, veterans may engage in these groups for an extended period of time (up to a year or longer) or may participate on a more time-limited basis (as few as five visits). The drop-in model helps engage veterans who may be reluctant to make a long-term commitment. The art therapist mitigates any potential therapeutic interference that may be caused by the lack of constancy and predictability in this type of model (Luzzatto, 1997) by screening new referrals and alerting regular group members when new participants are expected to join.

Veterans experienced art making in studio sessions among veteran peers as a psychologically safe way to connect with others. One Army veteran said, "I've never had a safe place before. … It's safe to share these things here because we all illustrate them." Seeing commonalities that were apparent between his

The Studio and Gallery Experience 193

artwork and the artwork of veteran peers encouraged a sense of emotional safety for this veteran and helped him open up and receive support from other veterans in the program.

One participating veteran created a mixed-media drawing (Figure 16.1) that represented his experience of military to civilian transition. He described that it was not the "black and white" moments that made transition difficult; it was the "gray," all the "space in between," and the "hurry up and wait" that made

Figure 16.1 Simple Solution, Endless Execution, mixed media on paper, 18 × 24 inches.

transition difficult. His description resonated with the other participating veterans who nodded in recognition.

Participating veterans talked about the skills they learned from each other through art making and discussion in the open studio sessions (DeLucia, 2015). One young veteran described how weekly participation in open studio sessions decreased his anxiety and helped him learn ways to deal with PTSD using artwork and conversations with other veterans. Several veterans noted that the therapy often occurred directly in their relationship to their images and in the process of creating art. "The imperfections that we create [in our artwork] are the things that allow us to grow and develop and change," an Afghanistan combat veteran declared. Learning to cope with these imperfections, practicing frustration tolerance, and persevering in the face of adversity were exercised in the process of making art. Many veterans took the therapeutic benefits of art making outside of the studio, finding it to be a helpful outlet to use at home (DeLucia, 2015).

In this model of art therapy group sessions, the environment can foster a welcome sense of camaraderie among veteran participants as they share workspace and materials with others while creating their own individual artwork. During this process veterans give attention to one another by witnessing and receiving artistic expressions both verbally and non-verbally. This exchange creates a healing environment within the studio as a culture of support develops among participants. The studio group becomes a place where veterans can normalize and honor each other's transition struggles and successes through symbolic and verbal sharing.

From my experience working in drop-in art therapy studio groups, the act of creating art in a shared physical space brings veterans together in a way that promotes honest interpersonal exchanges. Participating veterans have described the studio group as an anchor for them during intermittent struggles with substance abuse, post-traumatic stress disorder, transition to civilian life, and other psychosocial challenges. The format enables veterans to engage with art making and one another—a positive activity that increases social support among veterans who may otherwise feel isolated and alone in their experience of transition. Art making is the ritual that brings these veterans together.

A Veterans' Art Gallery

The veterans' art gallery serves as an extension of the studio and is a separate storefront property where monthly art exhibits are held. The addition of an art therapy gallery space embedded within the city where the program resides allowed veterans to connect to a larger audience through public display of their artwork. Participation in gallery exhibits helped connect veterans to the civilian citizens they often reported feeling disconnected from and misunderstood by.

There are a variety of opportunities for veterans to display their artwork in the gallery. An average of ten individual and group art shows are held throughout the year and are open to all veterans participating in the art therapy program. Art therapy staff members help veterans consider the various aspects of the exhibition experience by guiding them when they choose what to display in an exhibit. The art therapists may also help veterans consider what it will be like to put personal art expression on display, how it will feel to engage with people during public viewing times, and what it may feel like to have someone give them feedback about their artwork. Guidance may occur during individual art therapy sessions or separate meetings scheduled with an art therapist that focus on the art show experience. All gallery exhibits have a formal art show opening, including a modest reception, and are advertised through local art venues. In addition, the art gallery has weekly open gallery hours staffed by volunteers. Some veterans have chosen to be present during gallery hours so that they can be available to talk with visitors, although this is not required.

Gallery exhibitions are much more than simply a formal display of artwork; public exhibition raises awareness and understanding among the general population. As exhibiting artists, veterans self-advocate and inform the public of their experiences, externalizing and taking ownership of their own perspective (see also Block, Harris, & Laing, 2005; Spaniol, 1990; Thomas, Gray, McGinty, & Ebringer, 2011). Participating veterans emphasized that art exhibitions contribute to a positive veteran narrative, one that counters the focus on disorder and dysfunction that is often portrayed in the news media. Thus, the gallery becomes another intervention for decreasing their isolation and reducing disconnection between veterans and the civilian community they call "home" by educating civilians while combatting stigmas that contribute to marginalization (see also Cutler, Harding, Hutner, Cortland, & Graham, 2012; Potash, Ho, Chick, & Au Yeung, 2013).

Research has demonstrated the importance of emotional support from significant others, family, friends, co-workers, and academic peers to create an environment that will encourage successful transition (Caplin & Lewis, 2011). Veterans who participated in the art therapy program emphasized the social, emotional, and psychological damage that is caused when that emotional support is lacking. Several veterans admitted that they had withdrawn from these unsupportive relationships. They stressed the need for more "brothers-and-sisters-in-understanding," an expression they developed to describe people who were able to know, appreciate, and deeply comprehend their military experiences, from enlistment to combat to the return home.

Developing rituals of return for veterans creates opportunities for healing in the context of a supportive civilian community, which can offer rituals of return by witnessing (Junge, 1999; Learmonth, 1994) veterans' stories within a participatory public space designed to invite dialogue and reflection (Timm-Bottos, 2006; Watkins & Shulman, 2008). A veterans' art gallery can be such a space where civilian community members listen to and observe veterans' stories as told symbolically through images and words. These opportunities for recollection are underscored with the caveat that civilians can never fully understand the veterans' experiences. Instead, these spaces offer an opening where iconic images can be displayed (Watkins & Shulman, 2008). A combat veteran who recently returned from deployment described it as follows:

What most people know about the wars and the conflicts comes from the news media but to have a group of veterans that put together some art that speaks to their experiences when they are deployed, the problems they have had transitioning, the emotions they were going through … to get people out to see it because this is information goes beyond what they are learning from the newspapers, because this information comes from the soldiers. It is what they [the veterans] are thinking, their emotions, and their experiences transitioning. And at the same time it also helps those veterans to get it out.

Participating veterans emphasized that, by sharing their personal experiences in this venue, they may help normalize the challenges associated with transition and provide hope to other veterans. The metaphors and images of pain, sorrow, hope, and healing create a bridge between the veteran artist and the viewer, a bridge which connects veterans to the social support and understanding that will help them have a healthy and successful transition.

Self-esteem seems to have increased for many veterans who witnessed their artwork being seen and valued by their families as well as the general public. Further, elevating completed artwork to professional status through formal display can build self-confidence (Alter-Muri, 1994). The therapeutic value of gallery exhibitions starts with the veteran and extends to people who view the

Figure 16.2 Opening reception for veterans' art exhibition in Our House Gallery.

artwork, veteran and civilian alike. Viewing artwork generates empathy, support, and a sense social connection for veterans who are transitioning from military to civilian life.

Conclusion

When art therapy programming incorporates these three services, participants receive unique benefits that can address the multiple levels of need starting with veterans and reaching out into the context of the community or "home" where they return. These program elements provide a range of options for recipients who can elect to participate in one or all three services. Veterans may initiate treatment in one service (e.g., individual sessions) and progress toward involvement in other activities (e.g., studio groups and/or gallery exhibitions). The variety of options and the flexibility inherent in this model are part of the success. Veterans find what they need in one or several services designed to help them start a healthy transition home.

Acknowledgment

This chapter is a revised version of the following article accepted for publication by the American Art Therapy Association (http://www.arttherapy.org): DeLucia, J.M. (2016). Art therapy services to support veterans' transition to civilian life: The studio and the gallery. *Art Therapy: Journal of the American Art Therapy Association, 33*(1), 4–12.

References

Adler, D.A., Possemato, K., Mavandadi, S., Lerner, D., Chang, H., Klaus, J., … Oslin, D.W. (2011). Psychiatric status and work performance of veterans of Operation Enduring Freedom and Iraqi Freedom. *Psychiatric Services, 62*(1), 39–46.

Alter-Muri, S.B. (1994). Psychopathology of expression and the therapeutic value of exhibiting chronic client's art: A case study. *Art Therapy: Journal of the American Art Therapy Association, 11*(3), 219–224.

Block, D., Harris, T., & Laing, S. (2005). Open studio process as a model of social action: A program for at-risk youth. *Art Therapy: Journal of the American Art Therapy Association, 22*(1), 32–28.

Caplin, D., & Lewis, K.K. (2011). Coming home: Examining the homecoming experiences of young veterans. In D.C. Kelly, S. Howe-Barksdale, & D. Gitelson (Eds.), *Treating Young Veterans: Promoting Resilience through Practice and Advocacy* (pp. 101–124). New York: Springer.

Chandrasekaran, R. (2014, March 29). A legacy of pain and pride. *The Washington Post*. Retrieved April 5, 2017, from http://www.washingtonpost.com/sf/national/2014/03/29/a-legacy-of-pride-and-pain/.

Coll, J.E., & Weiss, E.L. (2013). Transitioning veterans into civilian life. In A. Rubin, E.L. Weiss, & J.E. Coll (Eds.), *Handbook of Military Social Work* (pp. 281–297). Hoboken, NJ: Wiley.

Committee on the Initial Assessment of Readjustment Needs of Military Personnel, Veterans, and Their Families, Board on the Health of Select Populations, Institute of Medicine. (2010). Returning home from Iraq and Afghanistan: Preliminary assessment of readjustment needs of veterans, service members, and their families. Retrieved April 5, 2017, from http://www.nap.edu/catalog/12812.html.

Cutler, J.L., Harding, K.J., Hutner, L.A., Cortland, M.A., & Graham, M.J. (2012). Reducing medical students' stigmatization of people with chronic mental illness: A field intervention at the "Living Museum" state hospital art studio. *Academic Psychiatry, 36*(3), 191–196.

DeLucia, J.M. (2015). Creating home in an art therapy program for transitioning veterans (Doctoral Dissertation). Mount Mary University, Milwaukee, WI.

DeLucia, J.M. (2016). Art therapy services to support veterans' transition to civilian life: The studio and the gallery. *Art Therapy: Journal of the American Art Therapy Association, 33*(1), 4–12.

Fenner, P. (2012). What do we see? Extending understanding of visual experience in the art therapy encounter. *Art Therapy: Journal of the American Art Therapy Association, 29*(1), 11–18.

Furukawa, T. (1997). Sojourner adjustment: Mental health of international students after one year's foreign sojourn and its psychosocial correlates. *Journal of Nervous and Mental Disease, 185*(4), 263–268.

Henley, D. (1995). A consideration of the studio as a therapeutic intervention. *Art Therapy: Journal of the American Art Therapy Association, 12*(3), 188–190.

Herman, J. (1992). *Trauma and Recovery: The Aftermath of Violence – From Domestic Abuse to Political Terror*. New York: Basic Books.

Hoge, C.W., Castro, C.A., Messer, S.C., McGurk, D., Cotting, D.I., & Koffman, R.L. (2004). Combat duty in Iraq and Afghanistan, mental health problems, and barriers to care. *The New England Journal of Medicine, 351*(1), 13–22.

Junge, M.B. (1999). Mourning, memory and life itself: The AIDS quilt and the Vietnam veterans' memorial wall. *The Arts in Psychotherapy, 26*(3), 195–203.

Khaylis, A., Polusny, M.A., Erbes, C.R., Gewirtz, A., & Rath, M. (2011). Posttraumatic stress, family adjustment, and treatment preferences among National Guard soldiers deployed to OEF/OIF. *Military Medicine, 176*(2), 126–131.

Larson, G.E., & Norman, S.B. (2014). Prospective prediction of functional difficulties among recently separated veterans. *Journal of Rehabilitation Research and Development, 51*(3), 415–428.

Learmonth, M. (1994). Witness and witnessing in art therapy. *Inscape: Journal of the British Art Therapy Association, 1*, 19–22.

Lee, C-S., Chang, J-C., Liu, C-Y., Chang, C-J., Chen, T.H.H., Chen, C-H., & Cheng, A.T.A. (2009). Acculturation, psychiatric comorbidity and posttraumatic stress disorder in a Taiwanese aboriginal population. *Social Psychiatry and Psychiatric Epidemiology, 44*(1), 55–62.

Luzzatto, P. (1997). Short-term art therapy on the acute psychiatric ward: The open session as a psychodynamic development of the studio-based approach. *Inscape: Journal of the British Art Therapy Association, 2*(1), 2–10.

Mallow, A., Williams-Gray, B., Kelly, D.C., & Alex, J. (2011). Living beyond the intersection of war theater and home: Protective factors for healthy reintegration. In D.C. Kelly, S. Howe-Barksdale, & D. Gitelson (Eds.), *Treating Young Veterans: Promoting Resilience through Practice and Advocacy* (pp. 13–32). New York: Springer.

Mansfield, A.J., Bender, R.H., Hourani, L.L., & Larson, G.E. (2011). Suicidal or self-harming ideation in military personnel transitioning to civilian life. *Suicide and Life-threatening Behavior, 41*(4), 392–405.

McGraw, M.K. (1995). The Art Studio: A studio-based art therapy program. *Art Therapy: Journal of the American Art Therapy Association, 12*(3), 167–174.

Metraux, S., Clegg, L.X.,, Daigh, J.D., Culhane, D.P., & Kane, V. (2013). Risk factors for becoming homeless among a cohort of veterans who served in the era of the Iraq and Afghanistan conflicts. *American Journal of Public Health, 103*(2), 255-261.

Pietrzak, R.H., Goldstein, M.B., Malley, J.C., Rivers, A.J., Johnson, D.C., & Southwick, S.M. (2010). Risk and protective factors associated with suicidal ideation in veterans of Operations Enduring Freedom and Iraqi Freedom. *Journal of Affective Disorders, 123*(1), 102–107.

Potash, J.S., Ho, R.T.H., Chick, J.K.Y., & Au Yeung, F.S.W. (2013). Viewing and engaging in an art therapy exhibit by people living with mental illness: Implications for empathy and change. *Public Health, 127*(8), 735–744.

Sayer, N.A., Noorbaloochi, S., Fraizer, P., Carlson, K., Gravely, A., & Murdoch, M. (2010). Reintegration problems and treatment interests among Iraq and Afghanistan combat veterans receiving VA medical care. *Psychiatry Services, 61*(6), 589–597.

Seal, K.H., Metzier, T.J., Gima, K.S., Bertenthal, D., Maguen, S., & Marmar, C.R. (2009). Trends and risk factors for mental health diagnoses among Iraq and Afghanistan veterans using Department of Veterans Affairs health care, 2002–2008. *American Journal of Public Health, 99*(9), 1651–1658.

Spaniol, S.E. (1990). Exhibiting art by people with mental illness: Issues, process and principles. *Art Therapy: Journal of the American Art Therapy Association, 7*(2), 70–78.

Tanielian, T., & Jaycox, L.H. (Eds.). (2008). *Invisible Wounds of War: Psychological and Cognitive Injuries, their Consequences, and Services to Assist Recovery*. Santa Monica, CA: RAND Corporation.

Timm-Bottos, J. (2006). Constructing creative community: Reviving health and justice through community arts. *The Canadian Art Therapy Association Journal, 19*(2), 12–27.

Vasterling, J.J., Proctor, S.P., Friedman, M.J., Hoge, C.W., Heeren, T., King, L.A., & King, D. W. (2010). PTSD symptoms increase in Iraq-deployed soldiers: Comparison with non deployed soldiers and associations with baseline symptoms, deployment experiences, and post deployment stress. *Journal of Traumatic Stress, 23*(1), 41–51.

Veterans Prevail. [VetsPrevail]. (2010, June 15). *Veterans and Suicide – We Must Overcome* [Video file]. Retrieved April 5, 2017, from http://youtu.be/6VmUulPab4M.

Watkins, M., & Shulman, H. (2008). *Toward Psychologies of Liberation*. New York: Palgrave Macmillan.

CHAPTER 17

Conclusion
Paula Howie

The revelations of scandal in 2007, which beckoned the public to visualize Walter Reed as a rat-infested facility with dilapidated buildings, were compelling reading. Most people were unaware that what was described was a facility off base which had been rented to house those patients who had mostly recuperated from their injuries because the hospital was overcrowded and caught off guard by the high numbers of vets returning from the Iraq War. It was also averred that funds had been requested prior to 2007 for the renovation of this facility and that this request had been denied due to the reluctance to fund improvements to a facility which was to be shut down due to base realignment and closing (BRAC). I had worked at the hospital on the Walter Reed grounds for over 25 years. Although I had left several years before, something in me protested against this being the last word about the hospital in which many of us had spent our adult lives—a place where the halls were polished, where I was enlightened, frightened, and perturbed daily, and which often appeared larger than life. If I could convey a deeper understanding of this place and the people seen there, it would in some way validate my memories of Walter Reed as more than portrayed on the news, giving permanent record to a larger view of the struggles there. My original intent was to offer the reader another view of Walter Reed and to provide a glimpse of the "internal" living conditions that each soldier and family member confronted daily. The first part of the book chronicles a few of the many soldiers and their families who sacrificed so much for this country and who had paid such a high price physically and emotionally while serving their country.

I was destined to learn more than expected in this endeavor. Along with fascinating art from returning World War II veterans, the Museum of Modern Art held notes from a commission set up in the 1940s to identify why the War Veteran's Art Center (covered in the Introduction) was no longer as successful as it once was. This material contained the discussion of a rather intractable conflict between the occupational therapists and Red Cross workers who were employed in different aspects of the art center. They were at odds as to how much art offered by the Red Cross workers was needed and how much therapy with trained professionals the patients required—what was helpful and what was dangerous. Clinicians and artists were arguing the amount of art and therapy required before our hybrid profession of art therapy even began.

As discussed in the Introduction, I was also impressed by the importance of World War II for the beginnings of art therapy, a finding I did not expect. I have made the case that the term "art therapy" was first used during this war and that it was so useful to those returning in helping to access visual memory, making it an intervention suited to treating the traumatized millions who survived the war and returned to their homes. I think our history will someday include this observation.

The second part of the book was a delight to edit, as I could learn in detail and share with the reader information about programs currently available for military members. In reading through Part II, you will see that the future of art therapy in the Military is in good hands. Those working with the Military helping with trauma, PTSD, sexual abuse, addiction, and self-esteem are adding to our knowledge by working in hospital-based programs, both outpatient and inpatient settings, as well as in trauma treatment centers and community-based programs. With patience and dedication, they continue to hear the tales offered by traumatized individuals, giving them new hope and strategies for dealing with the wounds of war.

Unexpected Learning: Did it Really Take This Long to See?

About six months into this endeavor and after making the acquaintance of my propensity to procrastinate, feel guilty, and then charge on, a paradigm shift occurred in my thinking. A new landscape was revealed to me, a way of observing what my country had been through as a result of two World Wars, Vietnam, and, more currently, the Afghanistan and Iraq wars. I saw connections I had never seen before using a new lens to view the past. It has been a gift that has allowed me to create a whole new perspective of the world and rework my own story and history.

Exploring the background of my employment in the Military, it became most apparent that I, and perhaps many of my baby-boomer generation, are children of war. This was an astounding revelation in itself; however, I did not foresee all the implications this might have for my generation, my parents' generation, and for our children. After reflecting on the aftermath of trauma in my 25 years of working with the Military, coupled with my personal experience of my father's military service in World War II, my life has seemed to make more sense. It only took me into late middle age to accomplish this synthesis of ideas. As my mentor Dr. William Stockton (2005) would say, "now it all makes sense."

It is now clear that many of the vets returning from World War II were suffering from PTSD. What does it do to a culture and population when one million soldiers return from combat to their homes and are supposed to get on with their lives and forget? We now know that PTSD and trauma don't just go away. At the very best these men and women had experienced some trauma, and at the worst they were as hopeless and depressed as some of our returning vets today. How did they ever sleep again, function in their families, continue living with the knowledge of how fragile and how capricious life could be? In order to cope, some of them wrote stories, like my colleague's husband Sergeant Fritz (in the Preface), some of them talked to one another, such as the rap groups after Vietnam, some of them made do as best they could. It is doubtful that any of them ever forgot. My Uncle Richard, assigned to duty on a battleship, never recovered from a blast that threw him down a flight of steps and broke his back. After his back had healed he treated his PTSD with alcohol, which became the source of his ultimate demise. In essence, it was his heart that never healed.

Politically and ethically, this begs the question of how long we will continue to send our soldiers into harm's way denying the aftermath of their living nightmares. Having dismissed this lesson over and over again, we are forever surprised by the cost of war; in World War I demonstrators known as the "bonus marchers," veterans who were demonstrating for their back pay were tear gassed and bayoneted (ushistory.org, 2017); in World War II we thought our soldiers would return, get back into their lives, and forget about the war; in Vietnam we blamed the soldiers for the war and its atrocities; today we continue to be shocked by the high suicide rate and inadequate funding to assist returning vets.

What my generation does not know is that they may also be victims of war. How much do we carry from the past either knowingly or unknowingly? Research on intergenerational transmission of trauma assumed that trauma transmission was mainly caused by the parents' child-rearing behavior. Researchers now believe trauma may have been transferred in other ways. A small study of children (Rosenheck, 1986) whose fathers suffered from post-traumatic stress disorder as a result of combat experience in World War II demonstrated long-term, trans-generational effects from their fathers' combat trauma even though their children had no conscious knowledge of the veterans' combat experience. Although variable, the impact of the veteran on the affective life of his family and on his children showed a continuing legacy of wartime trauma that was apparent in the adult lives of many of these offspring.

Building on the clinical observations of Selma Fraiberg (Fraiberg, Adelson, & Shapiro, 1975) and child trauma researchers such as Inge Bretherton (1990), and Daniel Schechter (Schechter, Moser, McCaw, & Myers, 2014) and Enlow, Egeland, Carlson, Blood, & Wright (2014), the generational transmission of trauma may be more complicated than we ever imagined. These researchers have empirically identified psychological mechanisms that point to intergenerational transmission of trauma, including dissociation in the context of attachment, and communication (non-verbal as well as verbal) of prior traumatic experience as an effect of parental efforts to maintain self-regulatory functioning. Felman and Laub (1992) describe a man who was traumatized as a very young child in WWII and who was united with his traumatized parents after the war. He avowed that the inability to talk about their experiences and to deny the impact of war had a detrimental effect upon the next generation "are we transferring our anxieties, fears, our problems to generations to come?" (Felman & Laub, 1992, p. 47).

Studies of war-torn countries during World War II have shown that those civilians who live through war had poorer health later in life, including more diabetes and depression. Exposure to war (i.e., hunger, persecution by invaders, and loss of property such as a home) showed that those who had dealt with these events of war as adults were less educated, less likely to marry, and were less satisfied with their lives (Rand, 2014). It is estimated that close to six million Jews died in Europe during World War II. The Holocaust was unprecedented in its magnitude. Not only did those who were interned in concentration camps show increased emotional and physical stress, but clinicians also observed that large numbers of children of Holocaust survivors were seeking treatment in clinics in Canada. Further, the grandchildren of Holocaust survivors were overrepresented by 300 percent among the referrals to a child psychiatry clinic in comparison with their representation in the general population (Sigal & Weinfeld, 1989). Bowenian (1993) family therapists have traditionally treated both survivors and immediate witnesses of traumatic events through investigating family history and by discussing their genograms indicating the transmission of family secrets and unconscious behavior through at least three generations.

From the Inside Out: The Baby Boomers and Trauma

Can it be that many of my generation are the product of generational trauma? We are certainly becoming more aware that a parent can vicariously and unintentionally transmit his or her prior experiences of interpersonal violence to a child through behavior and narrative associations by doing or saying something. The parent can also make connections between actions and/or language so the child cannot place this in any familiar context (or by omission) which is frightening or even traumatizing to the child. For example, a parent may react to a sound that is not unusual or frightening to the child by recoiling and moving attention away from the child, inadvertently passing their fear of this sound to the child. This is thought to be the parents' efforts to control their own psychophysiological disregulation and trauma, and may be seen as linked to their post-traumatic psychopathology (Enlow et al., 2014).

Early stress has also been shown to alter DNA methylation of several candidate genes both in the germline of male rats subjected to maternal separation and in the brain; and, for some genes, the germline of the offspring. These findings suggest that early stress persistently alters behavior and modifies the epigenetic profile of genes across generations, providing a behavioral and molecular correlate to complex traits induced by early stress, the epigenetic mechanisms which are turned on (Franklin et al., 2010). In Chapter 7, Newhouse and Albert assert that PTSD is primarily a cognitive disorder that includes a disruption of stress management systems and emotional and non-emotional memory systems. When these protection systems do not turn off, long-term damage and corrosive effects may occur.

The Adverse Childhood Experiences (ACE) study demonstrates that the more trauma one experiences early in life, the more emotional and physical consequences there are, drawing a link between physical illness and early trauma (Feletti, 2002). Parents are often motivated by wishes to spare their children suffering the emotional and often physical pain that the parent had experienced as a child.

Visualizing and symbolizing through an art therapy and other non-verbal interventions can help the client to imagine a better world and a better place. With the help of symbols and work in art therapy, emotionally compromised parents may be able to share trauma and abandonment issues through their art, helping themselves and their children to heal. According to Tinnin and Gantt (2013), when the artist successfully completes the graphic narrative as a complete story with beginning, middle, and end, and avows it as personal history, then any intrusive symptoms that were due to this trauma should cease completely.

The Future

If it makes sense that the baby boomers are touched by trauma passed down from another generation, how would they ever know or be able to address this intergenerational trauma? The following may be symptomatic of familial trauma. If something is missing in your family history or doesn't feel right, there may be gaps in your family narrative, you may not understand why your parent(s) acted the way they did and there was little opportunity for discussion, or there are gaps in your understanding and feeling about your family, these could be secondary symptoms of trauma. Gill, an author who examined the writings of those affected by war from colonial times to the present states "the use of letters or diaries stands as a writer's attempt to fashion a world of meaning … where he or she may find coherence, if only briefly…its articulation allows its narrator to construct an inner universe", p. 274. Trauma and war interfere with self-esteem, self-identity, and one's self-narrative. In other words, war and trauma disrupt our life story. This disrupted story is then handed down to the next generation, which leaves them with a partial and disrupted story, which they then pass to the next generation. As stated above, we are learning that fear and trauma can be passed down through our attitudes, omissions, what we focus upon, and perhaps even in our genes.

Approximately 430 World War II veterans die every day. With them go memories, stories, and opportunities to offer their family a narrative about what happened and how it affected them. The National WWII museum in New Orleans collects tales about the war (The National WWII Museum, New Orleans, n.d.) and is home to thousands of oral histories and hundreds of thousands of photographs. According to the Museum's records, there are approximately 697,000 living service members of World War II. We can lose no time in helping the baby boomers understand the effect of their parents' trauma on their generation and those generations to come. Perhaps one way to heal is to work with vets to tell their stories of their experience before it is too late, not only for their children but for those who follow—Gen Xers, Millennials and Centennials—who have been impacted in as yet unknown ways by their grandparents' or great grandparents' war. If we do not learn from the past, there are cycles which repeat themselves in a similar sequence with similar events through time (Howe & Strauss, 1992).

Let us continue to encourage our current vets returning from the wars in Korea, Vietnam, Iraq, and Afghanistan to discuss and process their trauma. We need to take the time to listen and make sure that those in distress receive the assistance they need and that their names and legacy become part of our conscious dialogue. Art therapists working in military settings can certainly provide therapeutic interventions along with other therapists in the DOD and VA systems. What of those who do not seek treatment: can their spouses, parents, and colleagues help them become unburdened of their sorrows? Not everyone will need treatment but everyone will need to be heard. Why should they have to bear these memories, nightmares, and personal tragedies alone and without support? My dad began to tell war stories to my brother-in-law as he aged. Perhaps time and patience is what is required for our service members to open up. Maybe they have been told they hold classified information and must tell no one. Perhaps they feel those who were not present in the war zone could never understand; or perhaps they suffer the mistaken view that they could spare their families agony by remaining silent. I once worked with a Vietnam-era vet who began having nightmares 15 years after killing a village woman in self-defense. His guilt prevented him from sharing this tragic event with his family or anyone else before meeting with me. At the time, I did not encourage him to tell others close to him, although I would certainly recommend this today. My hope would be that the soldier would eventually see this as an opportunity to give his family a chance to find out what his military service was like, how it had altered his life, and that their shared views of the world would bring them closer together rather than pushing them apart.

Our nation must take these stories into our collective consciousness to begin to heal. Our future depends upon this happening each and every time a soldier is deployed into a dangerous, life-threatening situation. Isn't it better to plan for this rather than being shocked when our soldiers return with symptoms of trauma, sometimes broken and alone? It doesn't have to end this way.

References

Bowen, M. (1993). *Family Therapy in Clinical Practice*. Lanham, MD: Jason Aronson. Retrieved April 5, 2017, from https://www.amazon.com/Family-Therapy-Clinical-Practice-Murray/dp/1568210116

Bretherton, I. (1990). Communication patterns, internal working models, and the intergenerational transmission of attachment relationships. *Infant Mental Health Journal*, 11(3), 237–252. https://doi.org/10.1002/1097-0355(199023)

Enlow, M.B., Egeland, B., Carlson, E., Blood, E., & Wright, R.J. (2014). Mother–infant attachment and the intergenerational transmission of posttraumatic stress disorder. *Development and Psychopathology*, 26(1), 41–65. https://doi.org/10.1017/S0954579413000515.

Feletti, V. (2002). The relation between adverse childhood experiences and adult health: Turning lead into gold. *The Permanente Journal, 6*(1), 44–47.

Felman, S., & Laub, D. (1992). *Testimony: Crisis of witnessing in literature, psychoanalysis, and history*. New York: Routledge.

Fraiberg, S., Adelson, E., & Shapiro, V. (1975). Ghosts in the nursery. A psychoanalytic approach to the probems of impaired infant–mother relationships. *Journal of the American Academy of Child & Adolescent Psychiatry, 14*(3), 387–421.

Franklin, T.B., Russig, H., Weiss, I.C., Gräff, J., Linder, N., Michalon, A., … Mansuy, I.M. (2010). Epigenetic transmission of the impact of early stress across generations. *Biological Psychiatry, 68*(5), 408–415. https://doi.org/10.1016/j.biopsych.2010.05.036.

Gill, D.C. (2010). *How we are changed by war*. New York: Routledge.

Howe, N., & Strauss, W. (1992). *Generations: The History of America's Future, 1584 to 2069* (Reprint edition). New York: Quill.

Rand. (2014). Lasting consequences of World War II means more illness, lower education and fewer chances to marry for survivors. RAND. Retrieved December 31, 2015, from http://www.rand.org/news/press/2014/01/21/index1.html.

Rosenheck, R. (1986). Impact of posttraumatic stress disorder of World War II on the next generation. *The Journal of Nervous and Mental Disease, 174*(6), 319–327.

Schechter, D.S., Moser, D.A., McCaw, J.E., & Myers, M.M. (2014). Autonomic functioning in mothers with interpersonal violence-related posttraumatic stress disorder in response to separation–reunion: Autonomic functioning in mothers With IPV-PTSD. *Developmental Psychobiology, 56*(4), 748–760. https://doi.org/10.1002/dev.21144.

Sigal, J.J., & Weinfeld, M. (1989). *Trauma and Rebirth: Intergenerational Effects of the Holocaust*. New York: Praeger.

Stockton, M.D.W.J. (2005). *Now It All Makes Sense* (1st edition). Charlottesville, VA: Free Will Publishing, L.L.C.

The National WWII Museum, New Orleans: Honor: WWII Veterans Statistics. (n.d.). Retrieved September 1, 2016, from http://www.nationalww2museum.org/honor/wwii-veterans-statistics.html?gclid=CKCj8bzN7s4CFQNkhgody0AGzQ.

Tinnin, L., & Gantt, L. (2013). *The Instinctual Trauma Response and Dual-brain Dynamics: A Guide for Trauma Therapy*. Linda Gantt.

Ushistory.org, The Bonus March, *U.S. History Online Textbook* http://www.ushistory.org/us/48c.asp Thursday, April 20, 2017.

Index

Locators in *italic* refer to figures

Abbreviations used in subheadings
ITR = instinctual trauma response model
PTSD = post-traumatic stress disorder

acceptance, complicated grief 107
acceptance and commitment therapy (ACT) 11–12, 165–6, 168, 173–4; coping strategies 170; group art therapy 166–7; interventions 169–73, *171*, *172*; non-verbal experience of PTSD 167–8; role of art therapy for PTSD 169; Vietnam veterans 166
addiction. *see* substance abuse and co-occurring disorders
Advancing Research in the Arts for Health and Well-being Across the Military Continuum conferences 18
Adverse Childhood Experiences (ACE) study 61, 203–4
Afghanistan war 2, 11, 50, 103, 194
alcohol use in the military 134–5, 138, 139, 142, 143. *see also* substance abuse and co-occurring disorders
alexithymia 154–5, 168
Alice (case study, group art therapy) 67–8

altered states of consciousness 151, 152, 153
ambivalence to treatment: substance abuse 136, 137, 138, 142–5; suicidal ideation 75, 83
American Art Therapy Association 27, 33
American Civil War xiv, 4
American Psychiatric Association (APA): PTSD diagnostic category xvi, 4, 31, 50–1, 87; suicide assessment 76
amygdala 89–92
Ancient Greece, battle trauma 3
anger: complicated grief 99, 100, 102–4, 106, 107; family art therapy 59; group art therapy 65; sexual trauma 180; substance abuse 140, *141*; suicidal ideation 78, 82, 83
anterior cingulate cortex 90, 167
anxiety, neurobiology 88–9, 91–2
APA. *see* American Psychiatric Association

Index

Armed Forces Health Longitudinal Technology Application (AHLTA) 121
arousal levels: military sexual trauma 184–5; neurobiology 87. *see also* fight-and-flight and freeze responses
art as release 79
art gallery, Veterans Outreach Center, New York 194–7, *196*
art therapy: future of 204–5; origins of 2–5, 201; profession of 2–5, 6, 8, 22, 24
Art Versus Illness (Hill) 5
The Arts in Psychotherapy journal 117
assessment: inpatient settings 44–5, *46*; universal trauma treatment 32; Walter Reed Army Medical Center **45**
attachment and trauma xi, 11, 30–3, 37–8, 202; case study 33–7, *35*, *36*; complicated grief 99; family therapy 55, 60–1, *61*
attunement, group art therapy 64, 67
Auden, W. H. 127
Ault, Bob 8, 9
automatic obedience 151, 153–4, 179
avoidance 27; acceptance and commitment therapy 165, 170, 174; attachment and trauma 33; case study 35, 37; grief 99, 100, 103–4; integrative approaches 114; neurobiology 88, 93; sexual trauma 180, 182–3, 184

baby-boomer generation, effects of war on xiv, 201, 203–4
basic assumption groups 65
battle neurosis 4
The Bell Jar (Plath) 75
bereavement 98, 99. *see also* grief
Bethesda Naval Hospital 9
Bion, Wilfred 65
bipolar disorder, case study 80–2, *83*
black and white thinking 138, 185
blame attributions 1, 26, 202
body, re-living trauma in 32
bonus marchers shootings 202
borderline personality disorder, case study 56–61
Bowlby, John 31–2
brain hemispheres: ITR model 149; integration 115, 119; sexual trauma 179, 180

brain system model of emotion regulation 89–90. *see also* neurobiology
Broca's area 115
buddy system, World War II 64–5

Carey, Nessa xv
case studies: attachment and trauma 33–7, *35*, *36*; complicated grief 105–7, *106*; family therapy 56–61, *57*, *59*, *60*, *61*; group art therapy 67–72, *68*, *70*, *72*; substance abuse 143–5, *144*; suicidal ideation 77–82, *81*, *83*
Centre for Applied Research in Mental Health and Addiction (CARMHA) 76
Chapman, L. 179
child abuse 30, 31. *see also* sexual abuse in childhood
Closet of Choices drawing 143–5, *144*
closure. *see* narrative closure
Clothesline Project, 183
cognitive bias, negative information processing 92
cognitive components of PTSD 88–9. *see also* neurobiology
cognitive defusion, acceptance and commitment art therapy *171*, 171–2, *172*
Cognitive Processing Therapy (CPT) 179
combat fatigue 4
combat stress reaction (CSR) 4
command hallucinations 152. *see also* voices, hearing
commemoration box project, complicated grief 107
commitment, behavioral 173
communication, non-verbal 185, 202, 204. *see also* expression of feelings through art; implicit memories; visual encoding of traumatic memories
Complementary Alternative Therapies (CAM) 18
complicated grief 99–100, 107, 107–9; art therapy 104–5; case studies 105–7, *106*; disenfranchised grief 100, 101, 102; involving violent death 100, 101, 105–6; military risk factors for 101–4; *Tree of life* tattoo *108*
confidentiality 136
conflict, inner: complicated grief 106; substance abuse 139, 142, 143, 145

consciousness, bringing to 118. *see also* integration of trauma
containment themes: inpatient settings 46; transition to civilian life 191
co-occurring disorders with substance use. *see* substance abuse and co-occurring disorders
coping strategies: acceptance and commitment art therapy 170; bereavement 99, 103
cortisol release 91–2
Costello-Dubois, J. 158
creative act of recovery 145–6
Creative Arts Therapy (CAT) group, Walter Reed Army Medical Center **45**, 46, *48*, 49
cry for help 75, 77, 78. *see also* suicide/suicidal ideation
CSR (combat stress reaction) 4
cultural dissonance, transition to civilian life 189
culture, military. *see* military customs/culture

De Rerum Natura (Lucretius) 3
The Dead on Culpeper Road poem (Keplinger) xii–xiii
Debby (case study): group art therapy 67–8, *68*; suicide/suicidal ideation 77
declarative memory system. *see* verbal coding of trauma
DeCosta, Joseph 4
deep brain 127. *see also* expression of feelings through art; implicit memories; non-verbal communication
defense mechanisms 37–8
delusions, inpatient groups 46
dependency, basic assumption groups 65
depression 43, 51; case studies 56–61, 79–80; group art therapy 67, 71; memory deficits 89; stress vulnerability model 91; suicide/suicidal ideation 76, 77, 79–80, 83
Desert Storm military action 42, 46
destroyer archetype, Pearson-Marr archetypal inventory 80, 82
Diagnostic and Statistical Manual (DSM): PTSD 5, 31, 43, 174; substance use disorders 135

Diagnostic Drawing Series (DDS) instrument 44
directive art therapy, substance abuse 137–8
disenfranchised grief 100, 101, 102
dissociation of trauma 3, 202, 204; attachment and trauma 32, 33; case studies 34, 35, 37–8, 80; group art therapy 70; ITR model 152
dorsal brain systems 89–90
drafted soldiers 1
drop-in art therapy studio group, Veterans Outreach Center, Rochester, New York 192
dual diagnosis. *see* substance abuse and co-occurring disorders
dual process model, coping with bereavement 99

EBT (evidence-based treatments) 168, 179, 186
ego states, group art therapy 71–2
Eisenhower, President Dwight D. xvii, 20
emotional expression 41, 101, 155. *see also* expression of feelings through art; narrative expression
emotional processing theory 88
emotional regulation: neurobiology 89–90, 92, 93; substance abuse 139–42, *141*
empathy: group art therapy 64, 72; integrative approaches 115
epidemiology: military sexual trauma 177, 178; PTSD 155, 166, 189; suicide 75–6
epigenetics, transgenerational effects of trauma 62, 203
estrogen levels, neurobiology 92, 93
Evans, William R. Jr. 1
evidence-based treatments (EBT) 168, 179, 186
The Evil Hours: A Biography of Post-traumatic Stress Disorder (Morris) 150
evolutionary role of PTSD symptoms 167
explicit memories. *see* verbal coding of trauma
exposure-based therapies 173. *see also* prolonged exposure therapy

expression of feelings through art 3, 25, 26, 33; acceptance and commitment art therapy 173–4; case study: John 79–80; Giant Steps program 127, 128; grief 104; group art therapy 70; ITR model 149, 151, 154–5; integrative approaches 112, 114, 115, 117, 118, 121; military sexual trauma 179, 180, 182, 183–4, 184; substance abuse 137, 139, 142, 143; suicidal ideation 77–9, 77, 79; transition to civilian life 191. *see also* implicit memories; narrative expression; symbolism ; visual encoding of traumatic memories
Expressive Art Therapy group, Walter Reed Army Medical Center **45**, *49*, 49
externalized dialogue technique 72

family art evaluation (FAE) intervention 55–6, 58, 119
family members, deployment of 56
family therapy 11, 61–2; case study 56–61, *57*, *59*, *60*, *61*; historical perspectives 54–5; *Life's Baggage* drawing *59*; military family life 53–4; *Overwhelmed* drawing *60*; tree as symbolic of self drawing *57*
fear extinction systems, neurobiology 92
fear of the unknown, transition to civilian life 189
feelings (soldiers can't feel) 41, 101. *see also* expression of feelings
fight-and-flight and freeze responses 26; acceptance and commitment art therapy 167; group art therapy 65, 67; ITR model 150, 151, 153–4; military sexual trauma 178, 179, 184–5
firearm, suicide by 75–6
flashbacks 26; Giant Steps program 127; ITR model 154–5; integrative approaches 114, 117. *see also* intrusive traumatic memories
Forest Glen, Maryland 4, 21–2
fragmented memories: ITR model 148–9; military sexual trauma 179
Fraiberg, Selma 202
free association 9
freeze responses. *see* fight-and-flight and freeze responses
friendly fire 50

Gantt, Linda 150, 151, 204
garden group, Giant Steps program 131, *132*
gender differences: military sexual trauma 177, 178; neurobiology 91–2
gender roles 54
gene methylation, transgenerational effects of trauma 62, 203
Giant Steps program 11, 17–18, *19*, 124–5, 132–3; art therapy 126–9; clinical approaches 125–6; garden group 131, *132*; historical perspectives 124; special art projects 129–30, *131*; veterans 125
Glass, Albert 64
graphic narrative processing. *see* visual encoding of trauma
grief 11, 98–9. *see also* complicated grief
grim reaper images 80, *81*
group art therapy 11, 64–6, 72–3; acceptance and commitment art therapy 166–7; case studies 67–72, *68*, *70*, *72*; grief 105; ITR model 152–3; integrative approaches 113–15; mask project 46, *48*, 49; outpatient art therapy group 66–7; substance abuse 138–9; transition to civilian life 192–4
group identification, World War II 64–5
guilt 166, 189, 201, 205; and expression of grief 99, 100, 102, 103, 104; military sexual trauma 178, 183; suicidal ideation 70, 76, 82
Gulf wars xvi, 22, 26

hallucinations: attachment and trauma 32; inpatient groups 46; ITR model 152
Harry (case study), group art therapy 68–9
Hayes, Steven 168
Healing Arts Network, National Endowment for the Arts 112
hearing voices. *see* voices, hearing
Hill, Adrian 5
hippocampus 89–90, 91, 92
Hippocrates 3
historical perspectives 11, 27; family therapy 54–5; ITR model 150; lessons learned from recent wars 26–7; military psychiatry 64; Veterans'

Administration, West Haven, Connecticut 17–20, *19*, 124; Walter Reed Army Medical Center 20–5, *21, 23*
holistic treatment approaches 112
Holocaust survivors 203
homelessness, transition to civilian life 190
House, Tree, Person (HTP) assessment instrument 44
Huebner, Angela 53
Huntoon, Mary 9, 79
hypothalamic–pituitary axis (HPA) 91

identification: group art therapy 65; ITR model 153; integrative approaches 114
identity: and bereavement 99; integrative approaches 113, 115; resistance to treatment 143; substance abuse 145; transition to civilian life 192
imagery rehearsal therapy (IRT) 181
implicit memories 2, 36, 127; acceptance and commitment art therapy 167–8; attachment and trauma 32; case study 37, 38; free association 9; inpatient groups 50; ITR model 149, 151–2; military sexual trauma 179–80. *see also* expression of feelings through art; visual encoding of traumatic memories
improvised explosive devices (IEDs) 154
In Remembrance mosaic, 9/11 terrorist attack 129–30
In the Lake of the Woods (O'Brien) 150
Incentive Work Therapy Program, Veterans' Administration, West Haven, Connecticut 131
individual art therapy 57, 117–19, 147
inpatient settings 11, 41, 50–1; art therapy studio *49*; assessment 44–5, 46; group art therapy 66; group mask project *48*; *Love Peace and Harmony* pastel drawing *47*; organizational structure 41–3, **45**; treatment programmes 45–50
instinctual trauma response (ITR) model 11, 147, 151, 155; automatic obedience 151, 153–4; combat trauma group 147, 148; fight-and-flight or freeze responses 150, 151, 153–4; fragmented memories 148–9; graphic narrative scaffolding 148, 151–2, 153; historical perspectives 150; military sexual trauma 179; non-verbal communication 149, 151, 154–5; re-presentation 152–3, 155; time sense/continuity 149–50, 154–5
integrated care. *see* substance abuse and co-occurring disorders
integration of trauma: case study 35, 37, 38; dissociation of trauma 3; Giant Steps program 127. *see also* narrative closure; verbal coding of trauma
integrative approaches to PTSD and traumatic brain injury 11; individual therapy 117–19; mask making 112, 113–15, *116*, 117, 121; montage paintings 119–22, *120*; National Intrepid Center of Excellence 111–13
intergenerational effects. *see* transgenerational effects
internal working models (IWM's) 31, 34
interpersonal relationships. *see* relational perspectives
Intrepid Spirit One (ISO), National Intrepid Center of Excellence satellite, Fort Belvoir 98, 101, 104
intrusive traumatic memories 32; case study 37; grief 100; integrative approaches 114, 117; military sexual trauma 179; neurobiology 87, 88. *see also* flashbacks; nightmares
Iraq war (2003 to 2011) xvi, 2, 11, 50, 103, 154. *see also* Operation Enduring Freedom and Operation Iraqi Freedom
isolation: acceptance and commitment art therapy 167; family therapy 53; grief 103; group therapy 72; ITR model 153; integrative approaches 114; substance abuse 138; suicidal ideation 78; transitions to civilian life 189, 195. *see also* social support
ITR model. *see* instinctual trauma response model
IWM's (internal working models) 31, 34

Janet, Pierre 3
Joe Bonham Project 158
John (case study), suicidal ideation 79–80, *81*
Johnson, David Read 17

Jones, Don 9
June (case study), attachment and trauma 33–7, *35*, *36*

Kathy (case study), family therapy 56–61, *57*, *59*, *60*, *61*; *Life's Baggage* drawing *59*; *Overwhelmed* drawing *60*; tree as symbolic of self drawing *57*
Keplinger, David xii–xiii
kinesthetic memories 3, 26
Kinetic Family Drawing (KFD) assessment instrument 44
Kino, Carol 158
Klein, Melanie 60
Korean War (1950 to 1953) xvi, 10
Kramer, Edith 65–6, 127, 128
Kwiatkowska, Hanna 9, 55

Ladd, Anna Coleman 114
land-mines drawing, family therapy 60, *61*
language of emotion 155. *see also* expression of feelings through art
Lea, Tom 6
lifeline drawing, group art therapy 69
Life's Baggage drawing, family therapy *59*
Lila (case study), group art therapy 71
Lincoln, President Abraham 20
Lisa (case study), suicidal ideation 80–2, *83*
loss-oriented coping 99
Love Peace and Harmony pastel drawing 46, *47*
Lover archetype, Pearson-Marr archetypal inventory 80, 82
Lucretius, *De Rerum Natura* 3

magnetoencephalography (MEG) scans 118
Malchiodi, Cathy 10
Mary Lou (case study): group art therapy 69–70, *70*; suicide/suicidal ideation 77
masks/mask-making: *Closet of Choices* drawing *144*; complicated grief 105; group art therapy 46, *48*, *49*, 66, 71; integrative approaches 112, 113–15, *116*, 117, 121
Medical 203 military classification of mental disorders. 5
memorial box project, complicated grief 107

memories/memory: deficits 89, 90, 91, 93, 94; fragmented 148–9; kinesthetic 3, 26; shrapnel 151–2
Menninger, Karl 5
Menninger Clinic, Topeka, Kansas 5, 9, 45
metaphor: acceptance and commitment art therapy 168, *171*, 172–3, *172*, 174; ITR model 149; military sexual trauma 180; Monsters on a Bus *171*, 171–2, *172*; substance abuse 145, 146
milieu therapy 43, 50, 51
military customs/culture xvii, 41–2; expression of feelings 41, 101; grief 101–3; integrative approaches 115; substance abuses 134, 138, 142, 146; transition to civilian life 189, 190; warrior ethos 53–4
military discipline, automatic obedience 151, 153–4, 179
military family life 53–4. *see also* family therapy
military psychiatry, historical perspectives 64
military sexual trauma (MST) 12, 177–8, 186; arousal levels 184–5; art therapy 178–80; avoidance 180, 182–3, 184; negative emotions 183–4; nightmares 181–2, *182*; recovery 184–5, *185*
military-to-civilian transition. *see* transition to civilian life
mindfulness 169–70, 173, 174
mirroring, group art therapy 64
modeling, group art therapy 65
Monsters on a Bus metaphor *171*, 171–2, *172*
montage paintings, integrative approaches 119–22, *120*
morality, and military discipline 154
Morrison, Toni 149
mourning 99. *see also* grief
MST. *see* military sexual trauma
Museum of Modern Art (MOMA), New York 6, *7*, *8*, 200

naming of emotion 154–5, 168
narrative closure xviii, 3, 36, 37, 118, 204. *see also* integration of trauma
narrative expression 3, 204–5; attachment and trauma 30, 32; case study 36, 37,

38; group art therapy 64; ITR model 150–2. *see also* expression of feelings through art
National Endowment for the Arts (NEA) 112
National Initiative for Arts and Health in the Military 18
National Institute on Alcohol Abuse and Alcoholism (NIAAA) report 134
National Institutes of Health (NIH), family therapy 55
National Intrepid Center of Excellence (NICoE), Walter Reed National Military Medical Center 98, 101, 104, 111–13. *see also* integrative approaches
National Museum of Health and Medicine, Maryland 4
National Veterans' Creative Arts Festival, West Haven, Connecticut 19
Naumburg, Margaret 8–9, 37
negative emotions/thoughts: grief 104; military sexual trauma 183–4; neurobiology 87, 92; transition to civilian life 192
neurobiology 11, 27, 87–8; acceptance and commitment art therapy 167, 174; cognitive aspects 88–9; ITR model 149; integrative approaches 115, 118; military sexual trauma 179; neural correlates 90–1; role of art therapy 93–4; stress vulnerability model 91–2; ventral and dorsal systems 89–90
nightmares 26, 30, 205; integrative approaches 117; military sexual trauma 181–2, *182*
9/11 terrorist attack, World Trade Center 2, 42, 129, 154
Nixon, Richard 20
non-directive art therapy, substance abuse 137–8
non-verbal communication 185, 202, 204. *see also* expression of feelings through art; implicit memories; visual encoding of traumatic memories
numbing, emotional 33

obedience, automatic 151, 153–4, 179
objectivity 26, 36. *see also* evidence-based treatments

O'Brien, Tim 150
occupational therapy (OT) 4
Office of Personnel Management (OPM) 27
Operation Enduring Freedom (OEF) and Operation Iraqi Freedom (OIF xvi; acceptance and commitment art therapy 166; complicated grief 101–2; ITR model 155
out-of-body experiences 152
Overwhelmed drawing, family therapy *60*

'painting out' process 9
pairing, basic assumption 65
PE (prolonged exposure therapy) 25, 151, 165, 179
Pearson-Marr archetypal inventory (PMAI) 80, 82
Pendleton cross 107
People's Art Center, Museum of Modern Art, New York 6
Pershing, General John J. 20
Person Picking an Apple from an Apple Tree (PPAT) assessment instrument 44, 45
Plath, Sylvia 75, 77–8, 83
PMAI (Pearson-Marr archetypal inventory) 80, 82
poly-trauma patients 159–60
portrait sketches of veterans 11, 157–9, 163–4; artists *163*; debriefing 162; therapeutic process 161–2; volunteer recruitment 159–61; waiting periods 161
positive: emotions 32–3; psychology 128
post-traumatic stress disorder (PTSD): diagnostic category xvi, 4, 31, 50–1, 87; Clinical Practice Guidelines 167
The Post-Traumatic Stress Disorder Sourcebook (Schiraldi) 148
power dynamics, military sexual trauma 177–8, 182
PPAT. *see* Person Picking an Apple from an Apple Tree
prayer flags, Giant Steps program 130, *131*
pre-frontal cortex 89, 90, 91
press coverage, Walter Reed Army Medical Center xix, 24–5, 200

Prinzhorn, Hans 3
profession of art therapy 2–5, 6, 8, 22, 24
projective identification 60
prolonged exposure therapy (PE) 25, 151, 165, 179
psycho-education: acceptance and commitment art therapy 167, 169; Giant Steps program 124, 125; ITR model 148; substance abuse 140, 143
psychosis 9; case study 33–7, *35*, *36*; inpatient groups **45**, 46; overlap with trauma 30–1, 32, 33
psychosocial loss, grief 103

rape 50; case study 36, *36*. *see also* military sexual trauma; sexual abuse in childhood
rational frame theory (RFT) 168
Ravenscroft, Patti 22
recovery: creative act of 145–6; Giant Steps program 126; military sexual trauma 184–5, *185*
Recreation and Creative Arts Therapy Section (RCATS), Veterans' Administration, Connecticut 17, 19
relational perspectives: case study 35; family therapy 55; group art therapy 64; mileau approach 43, 50, 51.
religion 34, 106
re-presentation, ITR model 152–3, 155
resilience: attachment and trauma 32; and bereavement 99, 104; case study 34
resistance to treatment 36; substance abuse 135, 136, 142–5
restoration-oriented coping 99
RFT (rational frame theory) 168
rituals: grief 102, 103; transition to civilian life 187, 195
Rubin, Judith 66
rumination 88–9

safety: Giant Steps program 127; integrative approaches 118; military sexual trauma 180, 183–4; transition to civilian life 191, 192–3; universal trauma treatment 32
The Savage God (Alvarez) 75
schemas, mental 88
schizoid personality, case study 79–80

schizophrenia: attachment and trauma 32; case study 33–7, *35*, *36*
self-care, suicidal ideation 83–4
self, component parts (ego states), group art therapy 71–2
self-efficacy, grief involving violent death 100, 105–6
self-esteem 33, 195
self-harm 69–70, 82, 83. *see also* suicide/suicidal ideation
self-reflection, case study 35, 37
self-regulation. *see* emotional regulation
self symbols, tree picture *57*, 57, 66
self-understanding 33, 34, 35, 37
sex differences. *see* gender differences
sexual abuse in childhood 12, 201; attachment and trauma 30, 31, 32; case studies 33, 34, 36, *36*, 38, 56–7, 61
sexual trauma. *see* military sexual trauma
shell-shock 4, 17
Siegel, Daniel 10, 64
sketches of veterans. *see* portrait sketches of veterans
Slaughterhouse-Five (Vonnegut) 149
Sobol, Barbara 55
social support: substance abuse 138–9; transition to civilian life 189, 195
Society for the Study of Traumatic Stress 169
soldier's heart 4
Sophie (case study), suicide/suicidal ideation 78, 79, *79*
stabilization, universal trauma treatment 32
staff: training 44; turnover 42
startle reactions 30; ITR model 151; military sexual trauma 179; neurobiology 88
Stevens, Matthew 102
Stockton, Dr. William 201
storytelling. *see* narrative expression
stress: alcohol use 134; of bereavement 99 (*see also* grief); deployment of family members 56; group art therapy 67; hormones 91–2, 93; military family life 54; neurobiology 87, 89–90, 91, 93, 94; transgenerational effects 202–5; transition to civilian life 192
stress vulnerability model 91–2

substance abuse and co-occurring disorders 11, 134–7; art therapy approaches 137–8; creative act of recovery 145–6; group cohesion/social support 138–9; resistance/ambivalence 142–5, *144*; self-regulation 139–42, *141*
suicide/suicidal ideation xviii, 9, 11, 50, 75, 83–4; artwork indicators/symbols 77–9, *79*; assessment instruments 76–7, 80, 82; case studies 56–7, 61, 77–82, *81*, *83*; epidemiology 75–6; group art therapy 65, 67, 68, 69; inpatient groups **45**, 46; ITR model 153; military sexual trauma 183
Sula (Morrison) 149
Sullivan, Harry Stack 64
survival guilt 103, 189
symbolism 204; integrative approaches 118, 119; mask making 115; military sexual trauma 180, 183, 184; suicidal ideation 77–9, *79*; transformative function 26; veterans' art gallery 195. *see also* expression of feelings through art

tattoo design, complicated grief 107, *108*
TBI. *see* traumatic brain injury
temporal sense/continuity, ITR model 149–50, 154–5
The Arts in Psychotherapy journal 117
The Bell Jar (Plath) 75
The Dead on Culpeper Road poem (Keplinger) xii–xiii
The Evil Hours: A Biography of Post-traumatic Stress Disorder (Morris) 150
The Post-Traumatic Stress Disorder Sourcebook (Schiraldi) 148
The Savage God (Alvarez) 75
themes, group art therapy 66
Themes Art Therapy group, Walter Reed Army Medical Center **45**, 45–6, *47*
therapeutic relationship. *see* relational perspectives
'Three Wishes for Christmas' theme, Walter Reed Army Medical Center 46
time sense/continuity, ITR model 149–50, 154–5
Tinnin, Louis 150, 151, 204

transgenerational effects: abuse 34; trauma xiv–xvi, 60–1, 62, 202–5
transition to civilian life 12, 24, 26, 187–8, 197; art therapy studio group sessions 192–4; consequences of transition difficulty 190; difficult/unhealthy 188–90, 191; family therapy 54; healthy/successful 188; individual therapy 191–2; mixed-media drawing *193*; substance abuse and co-occurring disorders 138; veterans' art gallery 194–7, *196*; Veterans Outreach Center 188, 190–1
Trauma Recovery Scale (TRS) 148
traumatic brain injury (TBI) 51; grief 98, 105; transition to civilian life xviii; treatment goals 112. *see also* integrative approaches
Treatment Planning Conferences (TPCs), inpatient 42, 43
Tree of life tattoo *108*
tree, as self symbol 57, *57*, 66
triggering situations: attachment and trauma 30, 37; Giant Steps Program 127; ITR model 151, 152; military sexual trauma 177, 178, 182; neurobiology 91; substance use 137, 142
TRS (Trauma Recovery Scale) 148
Truman, Harry 20
Twisted artwork 140, *141*
2,000-yard stare (Lea) 6

Ulman, Elinor 50
Ulman Personality Assessment Procedure (UPAP) 44–5
unconscious mind. *see* expression of feelings through art; implicit memories; non-verbal communication
unemployment, transition to civilian life 190
United States army xvii
universal themes 32, 45, 65: acceptance and commitment art therapy 167, 168; ITR model 151; sketch project 160

VA Connecticut Healthcare System (VACT) 17–20
VA/Department of Defense: Clinical Practice Guidelines for PTSD 167

validation: family therapy 56, 57; grief 100; group art therapy 64, 70; ITR model 152; military sexual trauma 184, 185
values, acceptance and commitment art therapy 172–3
van der Kolk, B. 32, 114, 115, 117, 127
ventral brain systems 89–90
verbal coding of trauma 3, 37, 38, 204. *see also* integration of trauma
Veterans' Administration (VA), West Haven, Connecticut 10; historical perspectives 17–20, *19*
Veterans Outreach Center, Inc. (VOC), Rochester, New York 188, 190–1; art therapy studio group sessions 192–4; individual therapy 191–2; veterans' art gallery 194–7, *196*
Vietnam – My Mind's Eye painting 128
Vietnam Experience picture, Giant Steps program 129
Vietnam War (1965 to 1973) xvi, 1, 10, 11–12, 26, 166
violent death, grief involving 100, 101, 105–6
visual encoding of traumatic memories 3, 30, 127, 204; acceptance and commitment art therapy 174; integrative approaches 114, 118, 119; ITR model 148, 151–2, 153; neurobiology 94; nightmares 181; suicidal ideation 77. *see also* expression of feelings through art
voices, hearing: attachment and trauma 30, 34–5, *35*; Giant Steps program 127; group art therapy 72; ITR model 152
volunteer soldiers 2
Vonnegut, Kurt 149
vulnerability to stress: attachment and trauma 31–2, 33; neurobiology 90, 91–2

Wadeson, Harriett 9–10, 78
Walter Reed Army Medical Center (WRAMC) xvii–xx, 10, 20–5, *21*, *23*, 200; inpatient groups/treatment programs 45–50, **45**, *47*, *48*; outpatient art therapy group 66–7; press coverage xix, 24–5, 200. *for later name see below*
Walter Reed National Military Medical Center xix, 25, 33, 45; National Intrepid Center of Excellence 98, 101, 104, 111–13. *see also* integrative approaches
war: cost of 202; impact on baby-boomer generation xiv, 201, 203–4
War Veteran's Art Center, Museum of Modern Art (MOMA), New York 6, *7*, *8*, 200
warrior ethos: group art therapy 71; military family life 53
Washington Post articles, Walter Reed Army Medical Center xix, 24–5, 200
Watts, Anna 4
Wertsch, Mary 53
Williams, Katherine 67
willingness stance, acceptance and commitment art therapy 170–1
Wintemute, Garen J. 75
Winter Veterans' Administration Hospital, Topeka, Kansas 5, 9
witnessing/bearing witness: group art therapy 64, 72; inpatient settings 50; transition to civilian life 194
women veterans, Giant Steps program 125
Wood, Francis 4
World Trade Center: 9/11 terrorist attack 2, 42, 129, 154
World War I 4, 5
World War II xiv–xvi, 2–6, 9, 10, 54, 201, 203

Yalom, Irving 65